# Fast Company

# Jon Bradshaw

---

# Fast Company

---

**High Stakes**

This edition published in 2003 by
High Stakes Publishing
21 Great Ormond St
London WC1N 3JB
T: 020 7430 1021

www.highstakes.co.uk
www.gamblingbooks.co.uk/publishing

ISBN 1 84344 013 X Fast Company

Printed by Cox and Wyman, Reading, Berks

For Anna

Son, you are now going out into the wide, wide world to make your own way, and it is a very good thing to do, as there are no more opportunities for you in this burg. I am only sorry that I am not able to bank-roll you to a very large start, but not having any potatoes to give you, I am now going to stake you to some very valuable advice, which I personally collect in my years of experience around and about, and I hope and trust you will always bear this advice in mind. Son, no matter how far you travel, or how smart you get, always remember this: Some day, somewhere, a guy is going to come to you and show you a nice brand-new deck of cards on which the seal is never broken, and this guy is going to offer to bet you that the jack of spades will jump out of this deck and squirt cider in your ear. But, son, do not bet him, for as sure as you do you are going to get an ear full of cider.

DAMON RUNYON

A man dropped down at the door of White's; he was carried into the Club. Was he dead or not? The odds were immediately given and taken for and against. It was proposed to bleed him. Those who had taken odds that the man was dead protested that the use of the lancet would affect the fairness of the bet; he was therefore left to himself and presently died —to the great satisfaction of those who had bet for that event.

HORACE WALPOLE

There are people who are followed all through their lives by a beggar to whom they have given nothing.

KARL KRAUS

# Contents

# Preface
## Nik Cohn

Jon Bradshaw's subject was adventuring. He was in love with risk and those who dared the fates, and wished devoutly to pass for a swashbuckler himself. He was never entirely convincing at that, but the wish was father to his best writing, which reached its peak in *Fast Company*.

I met him first in London, sometime in the early Seventies. It was a wet wintry lunchtime and I had taken shelter in my agent's office. An urgent step was heard on the stairs, the door flew open, and there stood a big handsome rascal in an open-necked, sky-blue silk shirt, hairy-chested and Caribbean tanned, flashing a lopsided grin. "Where is she?" he demanded, cocking an eye at my agent's desk.

"Out," I said.

"Well, tell her Bradshaw was here." And, just like that, he was gone.

A few years on, we met again. I'd moved to America and was writing for New York magazine, as was Bradshaw. Our desks were adjacent and we became friends.

It was very much an odd-couple affair, for Bradshaw's style and the circles in which he moved were worlds removed from my own. He hung out with the likes of Tom Wolfe and Lord Patrick Litchfield, the gossip columnists Taki and Nigel Dempster, and the record tycoon Chris Blackwell, all of whom adored him. His calling cards were wit and charm, a world-class talent for gossip, and good looks of an almost Hollywood order. A louche, more dissolute version of James Garner, he carried himself with conscious roguery, a Rothman's perpetually dangling from one corner of his mouth and that lopsided shark's grin plastering the other. He sported Turnbull & Asser silk shirts and Gucci loafers, flashed gold lighters and a Piaget watch; slathered himself with vetivert cologne; and tended to speak in mock-abusive italics—"the *awful* Mailer, the *dreadful* Elaine, the *unspeakable* Timothy Leary".

The insults were his style of showing admiration. Awfulness, if married to flair, was golden. Almost anything was permitted, in fact, but tiresomeness. "What can I say? He's *hapless,*" he told me once, when I enquired about someone he'd just interviewed, and his tone made it clear there could be no greater sin.

His devouring passion was for action. He was enthralled by the larger life, by big gestures and tall tales and anything else that helped block out the dull, insistent knocking of age and loss.

Bradshaw's accounts of his childhood and early days varied with each retelling, according to mood and the hour of the night, as well as the number of drinks he'd consumed, but all of them gave the feeling of a man at work on his legend. In the version I heard most often, he'd been born in New York in 1937, the son of an American football player and an Irish fashion writer. Sometimes he said he was illegitimate, at other times his parents divorced when he was seven. Either way, he grew up with his mother, an alcoholic (though glamorous) who packed him off to private tutors and crammers, then to military school. There was a period in County Waterford, another in Pennsylvania. At some point he did a brief spell of college, either at Columbia or Princeton, but was expelled for smuggling a black waitress, "a dusky enchantress," into his dorm. Afterwards, he assembled the CV obligatory for would-be writers of the period—short-order cook, amateur prizefighter, hired hand in a whorehouse, backgammon hustler—before becoming a journalist. Having worked for various small-town papers, he landed a job on *The New York Herald Tribune*, which posted him to Vietnam. A year in Saigon was followed by a longer stint in London, where he reported the Swinging Sixties for glossies like *Queen* and *Tatler*. Somewhere along the way, he married a white Jamaican heiress. The marriage didn't last but his love of Jamaica did. His ultimate fantasy was to buy an estate in Negril and retire there, man of letters turned squire. When I knew him in New York, he was constantly on the look-out for the score—"big bucks"—that would allow him to cash in his chips as a working scribe and head for those far blue hills.

By then, 1975, *Fast Company* was newly published, to modest sales but rave reviews, and Bradshaw was justly celebrated as a magazine journalist.

He specialised in subjects the faint of heart steered clear of and delivered them with an off-hand panache that couldn't disguise the hard work and skill that went into them. Sometimes lumped in with the so-called gonzo writers, notably Hunter Thompson, his approach was actually quite different. The basic trick of gonzo was to turn every story into a stage to strut on, the more outrageously the better. Bradshaw, by contrast, was at heart a purist. All his affectations were reserved for his daily round. The moment he set to writing, they fell away. He had the classic reporter's gifts—innate powers of observation and memory, clean style, an unfailing eye for the telling detail, above all a boundless curiosity—and his best work was as cogent and unfussy as anything by A.J. Liebling or Joseph Mitchell. He wrote about gang wars in the South Bronx, the Baader-Meinhoff trials in Germany, the mercenary Robert Denard in Africa, the bandit Phoolan Devi in India, Rastas in Jamaica: tough subjects and toughly written, but always with elegance.

Many of these pieces were hammered out in my spare bedroom. Like most journalists, Bradshaw could only perform when under the gun. Each assignment was dragged out till his deadline had come and gone. Then he'd go into lock-down mode, surviving on a diet of three packs of Rothman's a day, black coffee and brown alcohol, and a capsule of the latest sports' news slipped under his door every morning like a file in a prisoner's cake.

When at last he emerged, brandishing the finished pages, he'd look like a train wreck. The bathroom door slammed behind him; many hours went by. Next time I saw him, he was again his swagger self, drawling carelessly about *saucy* trollops and *hideous* scoundrels, and spinning stories of sexual conquests—Brigitte Bardot, for one—that would make Baron Munchausen blush.

I was a pretty fair liar myself in those days, but Bradshaw was an artist. His style was built on omission and misdirection, rarely risking a bare-faced whopper unless it couldn't be checked, instead marking out a territory which stood to truth and fiction as "not proven" stands to innocent and guilty. It was his proud claim, for example, that he never took his morning bath without drinking a split of champagne and fresh peach juice. In Bradshaw-speak, this simply meant that he never took a morning bath.

What I recall about him most vividly, though, isn't the flim-flam, but the warmth and vulnerability he tried so hard to paper over. He saw the world and its inmates as hopeless, quite absurd, but loved us anyhow. In fact, he was a born mother-hen, forever tending the bruised and bloodied. The *abysmal* Cohn, he called me, and justifiably so. But he was always on hand when I crashed. Even cooked me chicken soup one time.

When the golden period of New York magazine ended, he moved to Los Angeles. He married again and set up home in Benedict Canyon, where he looked after a baby daughter and two black Labradors. As happens in LA, his writing went off the boil a little and he turned to writing a sub-James Bond thriller that was never completed. His hair was thinning, he'd put on weight, and sometimes when we spoke he sounded death-haunted. But there were other times, hatching some fresh scheme bound—no, guaranteed—to rake in the big bucks at last, when the old Bradshaw resurfaced, as rakish as ever. He'd finally bought his dream house in Negril and was full of plans for it when he dropped dead on the tennis court, aged forty-eight, in 1986.

*Fast Company*, his saga of six big-time gamblers, is his true legacy. It is the one book, I think, in which he expressed himself fully, without compromise.

At one level, its characters—Titanic Thompson and Minnesota Fats, Johnny Moss, Pug Pearson, and the rest—were his surrogates, who lived out in reality the wild adventures and dazzling scams he would have wished for himself. But the book goes far beyond hero worship. If there are passages in his introduction when Bradshaw strikes a pose—"I am not a constant player and gambling does little more than occasionally appease the romantic excesses my gods demand of me. The games I prefer to play emanate a particularly heady form of Angstlust . . ."—once the narratives get rolling, the writing is lean and incisive, the tone pitch-perfect. Bradshaw admires and cares for these men, yes, but also sees them plain. They roister and brag and spin their tales; he hears the words, and also hears what lies below.

Take his evocation of Titanic Thompson, perhaps the greatest of all sports' hustlers, in his prime: "Those had been his dream decades, his fine high-rolling days, when, as a matter of course, he had risen late and read the morning line, practised his propositions, backed a horse or bought a car, killing time till that day's play began."

Now turn to his description of Thompson in old age, living out his last days in poverty and obscurity: "Outside the rain continued to fall, a thin enveloping rain, wrapping itself round the trees in the backyard, the bicycle, the rusty horseshoes, wrapping itself round the house like a winding sheet. A little later when Jeanette came home, she straightened Ty's collar and reminded him to bring his glasses. Looking into the distance Ty ground his teeth. He placed a cheap fedora on his head. Taking his hand Jeanette led him out of the house to the waiting car."

The whole curve of the sporting life is caught in those two passages, and not a word gone to waste. This isn't just lovely writing, it's blood and bone, and embodies the core of Bradshaw's theme: Every bet can be won, every proposition in life finessed, except Time.

Part of his inspiration in *Fast Company* was drawn from a great (and now tragically near-forgotten) book by William Bolitho, *Twelve Against The Gods*, subtitled *The History of Adventure*. A dazzling fireworks display of language and ideas, first published in 1929, it is a meditation on certain figures through the ages who've fallen in love with chance, and have been loved by her in return, only to fly too high, and burn.

Alexander the Great and Napoleon are the most obvious choices. Others include Cagliostro, Maria Montez, and Woodrow Wilson. And the moral that connects their various histories? "It is when the pirates count their booty that they become mere thieves."

Bradshaw uses that line to keynote his chapter on Titanic Thompson, but it applies just as well to almost all his subjects. In his hands, they become the Alexanders and Napoleons of their own worlds, raised up by the same dizzy confidence, brought low by the same hubris, but finally undefeated, in fact invincible. "From the beginning, each of them believed that the force of passion would somehow see him through," Bradshaw writes, "that given time and talent and happy odds all things were possible."

That, not money, was the crux of gambling's attraction. To dare all and not give a damn for the cost. Bradshaw in life could never quite bring himself to make that jump, but *Fast Company* gave him the next best thing. "I consorted with (these) men, not to define myself or them, but to understand that part of myself I believed we had in common," he says in his introduction. Only he could say if he reached his goal. But he wrote an uncommon fine book in trying.

*Nik Cohn*
*Shelter Island, New York, March 2003*

# Introduction

It began, I suppose, with the tales—the tales of gambling for immoderate sums at craps and cards, at pool, at golf and back-gammon. The old gamblers would talk into the night, recalling the days when for a bet of twenty thousand Titanic Thompson pitched a key into its lock or when Nick the Greek, on his final card, filled an inside straight and won a half a million. They cackled softly among themselves and now and then, as if to punctuate their point of view, spun one-hundred-dollar chips into the air. They liked to talk about the past and spoke of it in present tenses. Sitting in hotel lobbies, in clubs and coffee shops in one or another of those Western towns, there would usually come a time toward dawn, when the gamblers frowned and shook their heads, agreeing that those had been fine days and that none of us would see their like again. Despite their age they were hard, shrewd men and put aside my claims that they, perhaps, were merely sentimental. No, the times had changed, they said, the country had aged, become somehow tame and uniform. Gambling was limited to Las Vegas, a town they likened to a zoo. In any case the great high rollers had passed away and few had come along to take their place. America, one of the old men said, was overrun by vulgar tribes of business-men; the high wild players were now extinct or imprisoned in a zoo.

Only the heady tales remained. And for a time, for me, they had been enough. In the course of the next few months, how-ever, I met more than a few of those gamblers to whom the old men had referred. Those first brief encounters were more by accident than aim and only tended to excite my weakened

1

sensibilities. When I came to Las Vegas for the first time and heard the siren sounds of dice and cards on green felt tables, I experienced odd and almost credible sensations of invincibility; given luck and self-control, I, too, might make my fortune here. Clearly it was not a place in which I dared spend much time, lest I linger there forever.

All of which brings me to the point (or nearer the point) of this particular explanation. In the beginning, I had had some indefinite plan to write an account of winners and losers and toward that end had come to Vegas in search of suitable candidates. But it soon became quite clear that while losers flourished everywhere, winners were a rare and reticent breed with preferences for camouflage and anonymity. Having talked to the bookmakers, the pit bosses, the shills, the dealers, the croupiers, all of whom professed intimate and accurate views on the matter, even then, a dark confusion continued to hobble through my mind. How could one be sure? What esoteric qualities actually separated a winner from a loser?

Taught from the start to believe in absolutes, I found myself still half in love with the lie that losers were unlucky, that winners were merely fortunate—privy to none of those sudden catastrophes that snap at the heels of lesser men. But the types are so familiar a part of our mythology, we feel their faces could be picked as easily as twins' from a crowd. One, a cocky fellow with a self-appointed air; the other, drawn and self-defeated, with the look of a man who would pawn his soul if he could somehow ascertain its worth. We have come to see them as little more than trite and quintessential types. As a result, when someone points them out to me, I feel sure he is also trying to convey some flattering evaluation of himself—as if by naming them he had managed in some way to define himself. Nick the Greek, possibly the most notorious of American gamblers, claimed the only difference between winners and losers was one of character, which, he added, was about the only difference one could find between people anyway. But Nick held a rigid view of the world—heads or tails, win or lose, no two ways about it.

He was a gambler and gamblers incline to unconditional views.

Understandably, it was the winner, the successful gambler, who came to intrigue me more and more. Seen in retrospect, there was a certain magic in their lives. They seemed somehow blessed to me, inhabiting some strange and utterly unknowable kingdom. Their casual command of dice and cards, of odds and probabilities, their puzzling immunity to lures of cash or high stacks of multicolored chips astonished me. And yet, when looked at logically—at play, in conversation—they appeared to be such ordinary men.

For more than a year, I consorted with six such men, not to define myself or them, but to understand that part of myself I believed we had in common. I am not a constant player and gambling does little more than occasionally appease the romantic excesses my gods demand of me. The games I prefer to play emanate a particularly heady form of Angstlust, which has enticed me for the usual magnetic reasons. For me, however, gambling is more of a cold than a cancer—incurable, perhaps, but hesitantly held in check. But these men were professionals and I became obsessed with them—their lives, their games, the cold philosophies that seemed to orchestrate their play. In effect, I wished to know what kind of men they were, what it was like to win and win consistently.

To begin with, it would be helpful to explain what a winner is not. It has long been fashionable in psychiatric circles to refer to gamblers as flagrant examples of a particular kind of neurotic behavior. According to the late Dr. Edward Bergler, all gamblers are, in varying degrees, compulsive losers. It is not therefore surprising that such groups as Gamblers Anonymous have used Bergler's texts to reinforce their own contention that gambling is not only morally indefensible, but the outward symptom of a diseased and crippled mind. As a proof of sorts, Dr. Bergler often referred to Freud's essay on the Russian novelist Dostoevski, entitled "Dostoevski and Parricide." In this paper, Freud drew parallels between compulsive gambling and sexual behavior. He believed that the gambling passion was a substitute for the compulsion to masturbate and noted significant similarities in the two activities—the importance placed upon the hands, the fact that both were held to be vices, the irresistible nature of the two acts, which led their devotees to renounce them time and again, only to derive exquisite thrills and subsequent guilt when their resolutions were broken. Dostoevski himself reputedly achieved orgasm while he gambled, but only when he lost. Bergler popularized this theory of Freud's and it has now become generally accepted. Such views, of course, tend to fall in line with the traditional moral attitudes toward gambling, particularly in America. That is, that the gambler is a low jade, remotely romantic perhaps, but intimate with all the usual vices. One remembers that three of the most popular melodramas of the mid-nineteenth century in America were *The Sinner, The Drunkard,* and *The Gambler.* In America, the gambler, at least the serious gambler, has never been held in high esteem.

A more recent example of this cliché occurred in the 1961 film *The Hustler.* In a scene with George C. Scott as the moneyman and Paul Newman as the young pool hustler, the two men discussed why Newman had lost a crucial match to Minnesota Fats. Newman claimed to be a talented player and Scott conceded the point.

"Then, what beat me?" Newman asked.

"Character," Scott replied. "You're a born loser. You have no trouble losing when you have a good excuse. It's one of the best indoor sports, feeling sorry for yourself. A sport enjoyed by all, especially the born loser."

Thus, a classic description of the gambler has come to be defined not only as that of a born loser, but a compulsive loser as well. And although we feel rather superior to the insolent upstart and not a little compassionate, since he is seriously disturbed after all, we cannot help expressing an instinctive romantic interest in his flamboyant life style. I have few doubts that Dr. Bergler and his followers are reasonably accurate about the vast majority of gamblers. But I am not concerned with them. I am more interested in a different species altogether —a small minority of men who are, if anything, compulsive winners. "Winning is my business," one of them said to me, but each of them might well have claimed that slogan as his own.

So much for what these men are not. In the strictest sense, they are not even gamblers. The Penguin dictionary of English defines a gamble as "a risky venture, that which depends on chance." This alone would disqualify any of these six men as gamblers, since none of them believe in risky ventures or would be prepared to gamble on anything solely dependent on chance. Rather, they have devoted their efforts to games in which there is a direct relation between success and skill—tennis, golf, pool, backgammon, bowling, bridge, and poker. They are, in the best sense, gamesmen—experts at specific games.

Gambling, however, invariably involves a certain risk and the success or failure of that risk is rewarded or punished in terms of money. It is the greed and hence the fear of money that intoxicates most gamblers. With professionals, however, money is considered in another light and so acquires a different value. Most professionals would agree with Nick the Greek, who said that the majority of people share a common goal and a common failing: "They believe that money is something more than a handy scorekeeping device." By which he meant that the majority of gamblers develop a kind of love affair with the cash.

In those high-rolling circles of which I speak, money is a means of keeping score, nothing more. There is a case in point in the tale of the gambler who arrived at one of the larger Eastern tracks some years ago with five dollars in his pocket. He was a familiar figure in his rumpled suit and scuffed shoes, a punter down on his luck of late. In the first race of the afternoon he bet the five dollars on the second favorite and the horse came in paying $30. In the second race he bet the $30 on a long shot going off at 12–to–1. The horse won easily and the gambler collected $390. For the remainder of that afternoon, in each successive race, the gambler bet his total winnings on some previously selected choice. By the sixth race, he had amassed

$4,000 and he placed it all on the nose of a 3–to–1 shot. The horse, a tip from one of his friends in the paddock, spurted from behind to beat the favorite in a photo finish. The gambler now had $16,000 in his pocket. In the final race of the day he bet the lot on the heavy favorite. The race began and the favorite, taking an early lead, held it into the top of the stretch. At this point, the horse was more than a length in the lead but, tiring, she was nipped at the wire by a head. The gambler was broke. Buttoning his rumpled suit, he shuffled slowly from the track. At the main entrance he was hailed by an old acquaintance, who asked how he had fared that afternoon. Lighting a cigarette, the gambler shrugged and said, "Not bad, not bad. I lost five dollars." And that, though it is not often so badly managed, is what money means to professional gamblers—a handy means of keeping score.

In America, as short a time ago as the Thirties, there existed an energetic society of professional players, road gamblers who hustled round the country in search of high action in the great Midwestern pool palaces, the small-town poker halls, the plush coast casinos, the Southern country clubs. But because of innumerable economic factors and a burgeoning sense of bourgeois civic pride, most of these gathering places were forced to shut their doors. At one time or another, the gamblers depicted in the following pages worked what used to be the great American gambling towns—Hot Springs, Saratoga, New Orleans, Norfolk, French Lick, Miami, Chicago, San Francisco, New York, and of course Las Vegas. Today, all but one are gone and in these tame times Las Vegas itself is a kind of museum, a place in which the tourist can bet his weekly salary and sense that he has somehow set himself in the company of Nick the Greek and Bet-a-Million Gates.

Three of the gamblers in this book—Titanic Thompson, Johnny Moss and Pug Pearson—were raised in Southern shantytowns. Gambling for them represented a means of exit, a way out, the golden road to Avalon. The other three were city boys. Tim Holland and Minnesota Fats were born in New York,

Holland in comparative luxury, Fats in squalor. Bobby Riggs was born in a drab suburb of Los Angeles. Their games were city games and so not only more generally acceptable, but in a social sense, even fashionable. Billiards, backgammon, and tennis are not games one learns in Appalachia.

With the exception of Titanic Thompson and Minnesota Fats, both of whom remained freebooters, the others became national champions at their particular games—Riggs at tennis, Holland at backgammon, and Moss and Pearson at poker. Excluding Fats, they were excellent athletes at a wide variety of games. There is a difference of nearly forty years in their ages, and it is interesting to note, given the radical changes in gambling mores and attitudes in America, that the oldest of them, Titanic Thompson, gambled at everything. Winning or losing was unimportant; he played for the game itself, for the sake of the gamble, whereas Tim Holland, the youngest, devoted himself to games involving some loose social status—golf and backgammon—in the end acquiring more than a few of the sober attributes of the respectable businessman. Some seventy years ago Ambrose Bierce wrote: "The gambling known as business looks with austere disfavor upon the business known as gambling." That is more true today than ever and in the case of Holland, at least, the appropriate compromise has been achieved.

Concerning that, the old gamblers were right—the country has been domesticated, been put to sleep by the fire. The true professional gambler was an outlaw, a truant traveling along back roads, but because so much has been softened, cleansed, or simply swept away, because so much has been homogenized in the land, the paths along which those men passed have disappeared, and such men will come no more.

In one sense that is of little consequence, since even the most successful gamblers will secretly explain that the risks are great, the rewards are few, that gambling is in the end, perhaps, an exercise in impotence. Still, they were, or seemed to me to be, splendid freebooters. They wished no more to conserve than they wished to acquire. And it is beyond the imagination of a true conservative to comprehend a man who feels no special allegiance to money, a man who will risk all for the risk itself. Such men are confined to a special solitude of their own making. They are not prepared to pay the moral-social tax that society attempts to extract from the rest of us. They have no desire to do well, to get ahead, to set a good example and they remained, for the most part, undefeated. There was about them a superb and enviable insouciance. When they have gone, something important, some last fine flamboyant gesture will have vanished with them.

These men shared that passion which someone once called the joyful acceptance of risk. Beyond that there was little they had in common. It was only in the pursuit of their passion that they could be said to have been alike. That pursuit was more important to them than God or love or money, even. They were excessive men and now and then they overreached themselves; but these were trifling retrogressions. From the beginning, each of them believed that the force of passion would somehow see him through. Much later, when I first encountered them, these six men, the separate sons of a telephone repairman, a bootlegger, a gambler, an oil executive, an evangelist, and a soldier of fortune, continued to believe with some queer unquenchable conviction that given time and talent and happy odds all things were possible.

# Pug Pearson

---

He was a salesman.
And for a salesman, there is no
rock bottom to the life. . . .
He's a man way out there in the blue,
riding on a smile and a shoeshine. . . .
A salesman is got to dream, boy.
It comes with the territory.

ARTHUR MILLER

---

## I

His name was Walter Clyde Pearson, but few of his friends or
acquaintances knew it. For as long as he could remember, he
had been called Pug—because of his nose, irrevocably flattened
from a boyhood fall. Everyone called him Pug with what
amounted to an implied familiarity—the doormen and carhops
at the Strip hotels, the shills, the showgirls, the dealers and
grifters, and all the hapless players who came to sit with him
at poker. Only his mother, in keeping with the Southern custom, called him Walter Clyde. He must have liked the nickname or had grown accustomed to it; when telling me comic
tales of his early gambling days, he sometimes referred to *himself* as Pug—as though he were talking about someone else, a
pigeon, some extravagant friend perhaps, whom, he implied, it
might have amused me to know.

But that would have been unlike him; it would not have been
in keeping with his homespun, Southern style. He had a candid

sense of humor, brusque and down-to-earth. He would not have noticed irony nor appreciated it if he had. He wasn't that kind of man, nor did he have that kind of circumambulatory mind. He saw things simply and then brought an inspired logic to bear. He once, for example, explained to me why there were so few good poker players in the country. "Poker," he said, "has a language all its own, but you don't expect most folks to understand it, any more than you expect 'em to understand Egyptian." His sense of humor was like that—shrewd and folksy and rooted in fact, since it was always related to the two subjects he knew best, himself and gambling. And blunt as he was, he was never offensive. Pug seemed to know that what one said was somehow unimportant, so long as one knew how to say it. I make a point of it, because it was his persuasive talents that I remember best about him.

Pug was good with people in the way some men are good with dogs. People responded to some quality of self-belief in him, which gave them an illusion of potential warmth and safety. It was the quality usually described as charm. Pug used it, as charming men do, to exert an influence in order to control. His voice, filled with unchallengeable assurance, simply extended and completed the illusion. But these were things I learned much later. In the beginning, when we first met in Tennessee, I remember thinking that I had come a long way to see a man whom, but for his name and heady tales of his prowess at cards, I knew nothing about at all.

I had been told I would have no difficulty recognizing him. "You'll know him," Jimmy the Greek had said. "Ain't but one nose like it in the world." Pug waited for me in the airport lounge, a tall, heavily built man in his early forties. He was almost completely bald. He had the round mischievous face of an elderly troll, a troll with a fondness for Cuban cigars. He had come to Nashville to compete in a golf tournament and to that end, I suppose, wore multicolored striped trousers, a lime-green shirt, green shoes and a wide-brimmed plastic straw hat. There was an air of jauntiness about him and of inexhaustible good spirits, the air of a man who had had his share of passing pleasure.

"Good God," he said, when I had introduced myself. "I was lookin' out for a man of fifty. You sounded like that on the telephone. You've got the voice of an old man, son. Comes from wicked ways." He grinned, continuing to puff at his cigar. "That all you got? That little bag? Well, come on, let's go. I've got some golf to get to. And them old boys ain't much on waitin' around. You play golf? I'd rather play golf than breathe." He picked up my bag. "But there ain't no money in it."

Despite the way Pug immediately took one into his confidence, his accessibility, he had been a difficult man to meet, implying that it would detract from his anonymity. Nick the Greek had liked to say that in gambling "fame is usually followed by a jail sentence" and Pug, at least temporarily, had held some similar belief. "Son, you can't be too careful," he explained in the car. "The government is like the gestapo on gamblers. Like they was some kind of outlaws. But I'll tell you. Gamblers are the most broadminded people in the world. If more folks were like 'em, there would be fewer laws. That's on the square. You've got to be sharp in this world, no matter what your business is, or the world is gonna gobble you up. That's what it's all about, son. That's what they call life."

Parking his Cadillac in the parking lot and taking his clubs and a handful of Cuban cigars, Pug hurried out to the course. Despite the early hour, the grassy area sloping down from the clubhouse to the first tee was crowded with nearly a hundred golfers. It was, Pug explained, the last day of a three-day tournament, held annually in memory of Teddy Rhodes, the first black to break the color barrier in professional golf. Because Pug had helped to arrange the first of these tournaments, he was one of the few white golfers invited to play. During the rest of the year, this was just another municipal golf course in the black neighborhood of West Nashville. But Pug always used it when he was in town. He avoided the fashionable country clubs, which had better courses, because there was more action here than anywhere else in Nashville. Today, the players had come from all over the country. There were a few black professional golfers such as Lee Elder and a few black celebrities such as Don Newcombe in the tournament, but the majority were prominent black businessmen from the South or the Midwest and most of them, confided Pug, were connected in one way or another with the business of gambling. There, for example, in the purple blazer was the man who ran the numbers racket in Kansas City, and there in matching red was the most successful bookmaker in Detroit. All in all, it was *the* black golf tournament of the year.

Although Pug was officially competing, the tournament was of little consequence to him. He had, he knew, no hope of winning and besides, he did not play for trophies. No, Pug had come for the side action and to that end he had matched himself with three other players for sizable stakes. As golfers go, Pug was little better than average. He had taken up the game fifteen years before and only then because he had won a set of clubs in a poker game and had not known what else to do with them. Pug had a handicap of about nine, though it fluctuated according to whom he was playing against and the stakes involved. He employed what politely might be described as an eccentric swing—a looping, half-jerked swing which would have repelled a novice. It was a swing which appeared to compensate for some physical deficiency—an arthritic shoulder, a withered arm—but, as Pug explained, it was merely the way he had learned to play, practicing day in and day out without professional advice, until he could drive a ball two hundred and fifty yards with surprising accuracy. Pug also knew that his swing added a few strokes to his handicap, since it was improbable that anyone could hit the ball with such a motion, much less control its direction. But the swing was deceptive and Pug had worked hard at his game. "Hell," he said, as I watched him practice, "when I first won these here clubs, I went to a course to see how they played and I thought, hell, they put their britches on same as me. If they can play, I can play. It's a question of application."

The tournament had begun at eight o'clock that morning and just before nine Pug's foursome was summoned to the first tee. Before setting out, Pug and his three black opponents sorted out their various wagers. This involved long and intricate negotiation—pained talk of handicaps, of colds and bad backs, off days, a lack of practice, and the difficulties of playing on a strange course. But the four men knew one another well and after some minutes satisfactory and not altogether unexpected compromises were reached. Pug drove his first ball straight down the middle of the fairway; then riding out in the golf cart he attempted to explain the delicate art of negotiation to me. "Now, what does a politician do?" he said. "He projects himself in such a way as to capture the people's train of thought and turn 'em to his way of thinking, don't he? He's got to talk 'em into the bottom line. Well, in gambling, it's the same way. The con and the bullshit is very important. And in golf, which ain't the same as poker, you can't bluff. In golf, the bullshit has got to be backed up. Otherwise, you're a loser, son. A dead man."

Approaching the first green, Pug suggested that I bet a moderate amount on him for the eighteen holes. "Well," I hesitated, "what do you usually shoot, Pug?"

"Oh, about a seventy-seven, seventy-eight."

"And the others? What do they shoot?"

"Oh, them old boys'll shoot anywhere between seventy-two and seventy-five. Depending on the day."

Pug looked surprised when I expressed what seemed a reasonable doubt that the odds against him appeared to be unfavorable. "Son," he said, "I don't think you understand the game. We bet by the hole, not on the total number of strokes." Even so, the mathematics seemed clear to me. Whether they bet by the hole or not, at the end of the match, Pug's opponents were going to be anywhere from two to six strokes ahead. Pug laughed loudly. "The percentages are all right," he said, "as far as they go. But I don't think you're takin' into account your human element. Hell, I know them old boys. I know 'em real well. And I know their chokin' points."

"Their choking points?"

"Their chokin' points," said Pug. "The point where they begin to cut their own throats." He looked at me out of the corner of his eye. "Where you been, boy? You don't know nothin'. I was only tryin' to help you, being a newcomer and all. And I'm tellin' you, a bet on me is a sure thing. Can't fail."

As I have said, it was Pug's persuasive talents that most impressed me and by the time we had reached the first green I had bet three hundred on him at even money. Pug merely laughed and by way of assurance pointed out that two of his opponents had driven into the bunker.

The rest of the morning was spent in the golf cart in pursuit of Pug's eccentric drives. At the end of the first nine, Pug had somehow managed to remain even with one of his opponents and two holes up on each of the others. Chortling to himself, his cigar swiveling back and forth in his mouth, Pug scuttled off to the tenth tee. Within three holes, however, his good humor had been replaced with puzzled frowns and a garbled progression of low oaths. On the fourteenth tee they were all even and during the next three holes Pug, in spite of singularly consistent drives into the rough, the water, or the sand traps, managed to produce those few, apparently lucky, last-minute shots that kept him out of serious trouble. When they reached the eighteenth tee, Pug was two holes up on one man, one hole up on another, and even with the last—a bad-tempered, burly man called Joe Louis.

On the eighteenth fairway, at the edge of the rough on the left-hand side, there was a tall linden tree. Pug teed off first and his drive, one of his longest that day, was traveling at great speed, when it hit a branch of the linden tree and bounced some forty or fifty yards back toward where we were standing. Staring in disbelief, Pug grabbed the cigar from his mouth, then swore and struck his club on the ground. Joe Louis, standing to one side, smiled broadly, but expressed his sympathies. Pug turned angrily round and seeing Louis's smile he seemed to lose his temper. He continued to strike his club on the ground while Louis waited patiently. At last Pug announced that he wished to press all bets. Louis and one of the other players promptly agreed. Pug stalked to his cart cursing all the way and when he slid in next to me, winked and then relit his cigar. As Louis lined up to take his final drive of the day, Pug neglected even to turn around and watch him, continuing rather to light his already lighted cigar.

An extraordinary thing happened then. Joe Louis did something he hadn't done all day; he sliced his ball deep into the dense rough some hundred and fifty yards away. And the next player drove his ball very nearly into the same spot. Neither of them could believe it. They looked incredulously into the distance, as though they were seeing something they had never seen before. Pug accelerated his cart down the fairway and tried not to smile. As Pug's drive lay closest to the tee, he played first. It lay in the middle of the fairway, and using his driver Pug drove it to within fifty yards of the green. Getting back into the cart, he rode into the rough and stopped behind Joe Louis. His ball lay in six-inch-high grass just behind a small tree. It was practically unplayable. Pug studied it for a moment and said, "Now that's what I call real unlucky, Joe." He examined the ball again. "Damn, do you think you'll be able to play it from there? It's a bad break, Joe, real bad. Just ain't no justice in this world. None at all." Joe Louis looked over his shoulder at Pug. "You're a lucky son of a bitch," he said.

Riding up the fairway in the cart, Pug chuckled to himself. "Now, that's what I mean about a chokin' point, son," he said. "Old Joe couldn't keep his mind off the money." Despite his early error Pug parred the hole. It took Joe Louis three strokes just to get out of the rough. Pulling a wad of one-hundred-dollar bills from his pocket he paid Pug on the green. Pug took the money, a big smile on his face. Joe Louis scowled. "You're a lucky son of a bitch, Pug," he said. "Real lucky."

Later, in the clubhouse, Pug said, "I'll tell you what luck is, son. It's a line which on one side is wrong and on the other side is right. Now, most folks try to keep as close to that line as they can. To be on that line always would be perfect and that's impossible. You keep on sliding back and forth across it. That line is what most people define as luck. And that's on the square. I know, 'cuz I've been tucked in next to that line all my life."

Taking a roll of one-hundred-dollar bills from his pocket Pug gave me my share of the winnings. Then, holding his roll in his hand, he said quite firmly, but as though he were trying to reassure himself of something, "I'll tell you one thing. Gambling isn't the money, you know. I've been broke lots of times. That don't mean nothin'. It's the competition. It's laying your ability on the line and invitin' challenge. That's all I can do. I do it for myself. That's what I take pride in—being a winner. That's what life's all about, ain't it? It's the satisfaction of performing well." He spread his hands about two feet apart. "You live from here to here, you understand? And, in between, that's all you ever get if you're smart. Just a little self-satisfaction and enjoyment. And that's enough. Why hell, there ain't a breeze in the sky floats freer than I do."

Pug liked to remind me that he knew more about life than he pretended, that he was free, and that money had nothing to do with it. Yet, despite his disregard of being broke, Pug was one of those men who believed in money, as in a talisman. Money was the mainspring of his life. Given his obvious air of opulence, emphasized by the roll of one-hundred-dollar bills he carried in his pocket, I tended to forget that his life had not always been so prosperous—that once prosperity had seemed not only improbable but beyond the ken of any experience he or his family had ever had.

The odds are less than probable that a man can choose with any accuracy a given moment in his life, selecting it from all that has gone before in order to say: *this* was the decisive moment, it was at this point that the tide turned. Given the

million false starts we make along the way, it would seem a
random designation, one of those particularly futile shots in the
dark. But Pug claimed to know precisely when his turning point
had come. He could narrow it down, if not to the day, then to
a series of days, which, because they were endlessly poor and
endlessly repeated, were fixed in his memory like one long
impoverished afternoon. Pug, however, rarely referred to his
past nor seemed particularly interested in it. The past lacked
definition; it lacked the order that appealed to him. And because it had also been impoverished, he preferred not to speak
of it. But like many realists Pug was inordinately sentimental
and one afternoon he agreed to take me back to his childhood
home in the hollows of northern Tennessee—so that I might
understand, if not the turning point of his life, then at least the
place where he had encountered it.

Traveling north from Nashville in Pug's Cadillac, we crossed
into Jackson County, dropping down through the delapidated
towns of Reese Hollow, Farn's Branch, and Caney Fork River
—towns not recorded on the state map nor on any of the local
signposts. The towns themselves were little more than crossroads and appeared to be uninhabited. At one point, having lost
our way, we stopped in a general store to ask directions. The
only people in the store, four men, sat in the back on potato
crates playing dominoes. Pug introduced himself and asked
directions. "Pearson, eh?" said one of the men in a low, sing-
song voice. "Wouldn't be old Bill Pearson's boy?" Pug wasn't
entirely certain, but allowed that Old Bill was probably a distant cousin. Further pleasantries were exchanged, directions
were given, though the men held little hope that we would find
our way through the tangled countryside. We left. I was surprised that Pug, who had not been here in years, should be even
dimly remembered. "It's the family name," he said. "I probably
got so many kinfolk back in these hills and hollows, I could
swing an election if I could get hold of 'em all."

Away from the main road the countryside is still and ominous. The dusty tracks wind down and farther down through

the barren hollows—precipitous hills on either side. There is a
growing sense of isolation, of having been shut off from the
outside world. Everywhere—calm and secrecy. There are no
people. Here and there, the clapboard shacks of the poor, an
outside lavatory at the edge of the yard with its door off the
hinge, a bony mongrel staked to the ground—nothing more.
Round a narrow bend in the road a wooden church is suddenly
visible on a distant hill. A funeral is in progress; gathered round
an open grave, the local population, some twenty people, are
silhouetted against the sky. They do not look up as we drive by.
There is no wind and the heat hangs thick in the hollows. Only
with effort can I imagine anyone spending more than an hour
here. Yet here is Pug in summer silk and wide straw hat, still
speaking in the off-key drawl of the region. Beneath his air of
ease and affability I imagine a hard streak of resentment running like a fuse back, far back to his Appalachian upbringing.
Which is why, I think, he feigned disinterest in the past. He
preferred to think that it had somehow been cast off, that he,
as he liked to put it, had "evolved," that he had escaped against
insuperable odds. Only the memory remained. Pug would never
forget the dirt tracks, the flimsy shacks, the barren hollows cut
out of the land like a series of unmarked graves.

Pug was born in nearby Kentucky in early 1929. It was not
an auspicious time, he recalled, and he was not referring to the
Depression. Reports of imminent depression would not have
meant much to his family. There had been no joy in Appalachia
for a generation or more. "My folks were what we used to call
'God-fearin' people,' Church of Christ," he said. His father was
a sharecropper, tilling other people's land, though he worked
at any job that came his way, including a stint at building roads
for the WPA. When times were lean, as they often were, he ran
bootleg whiskey, till a competitor's gun removed his little
finger. Pug shows me the spot where as a boy of six he had taken
his father's finger and buried it. There is a portrait of the old
man in Pug's mother's parlor in Nashville. Posed in his rough
Sunday best, he looks as many men of that period did in their

photographs—stern and upright, with a look of moral condescension. Whatever else the photograph implied, it reminded
Pug that his father was often sullen and usually unemployed.
In 1934, the family drifted south into Jackson County, Tennessee, following rumors of work from one hollow town to another. Before Pug was ten he had lived in nearly twenty of those
towns. They always moved for the same reason—slipping away
in the dead of night because the rent was due at dawn. They
moved from Reese Hollow to Farn's Branch by covered wagon
and Pug can still recall the blackened pots and pans swinging
from the wagon as he walked behind it in the dusty road. There
was never any money. They lived in the clapboard and log
houses of the region, using coal for light, wood stoves for heat
and cooking. The potatoes and whiskey were buried in the
ground, the perishables were stored in the well-house, the meat
in the small smokehouse, and when there was fruit it was dried
and hung inside from the rafters. Times were hard and the nine
children often went for days with nothing to eat but beans. Pug
never saw a loaf of bread until he was ten. Even after they had
moved to Nashville at the beginning of the war the family's
main diet consisted of cornbread, molasses and biscuits. "We
never had meat," Pug remembers. "When I ate lunch at school,
I was always conscious of the little our family had to eat. The
other kids had good food—peanut butter and crackers and jam,
but we ate biscuits and molasses. The other kids used to rib me
a lot and believe me, kids on kids is tougher than anything."

Once they had moved to Nashville, much else could be over-
looked. They were in a city and they settled down. Back in the
hollows the Pearsons had never settled—they had never cleared
the land, or plowed, or built, or created for themselves a single
place of permanence. They *had* created an identity of a kind,
that is, they were remembered, since to this day the up-hollows
are filled with Pearsons, but they were remembered as tran-
sients, as people who had passed through. But that was all
behind Pug now; he had gone. Standing now and watching the
mourners move down the hill from the church in their old

sedans, Pug said, "I don't know how I ever got out. A miracle, I guess. Evolution on the move." And that was what he had meant by his turning point. These empty rundown towns, the scarred hills and hollows, which loomed so large in his sentimental recollections remained for Pug the prison of his early youth. "Did you ever see that movie about that space odyssey thing?" he suddenly asked. "You know. *2001?* It was about evolution. About things endin' and beginnin'. And that's what life's all about. Everything that ends begins again. I've always thought that. Things are beginnin' and endin' and beginnin' again all the time. And that's what I like about life. You're always in there with a chance."

Wheeling his dusty Cadillac like a jeep through an obstacle course, Pug headed back to Nashville. It was suddenly late, or seemed to be. It was only four o'clock, but the long afternoon shadows already blanketed the deep hollows, creating an eerie artificial twilight—while far above, the narrow ribbon of visible sky was still translucent and incredibly blue.

Nashville. Pug still has great affection for the city, though it lacks the rush and color of his youth. There was much to do in the city then, particularly for a boy accustomed to an absence of temptation. At fourteen Pug left school. He had already discovered where his real talents lay. "I started hustlin' real young," he recalled, "at ten or eleven. I just started playin' cards and pool with the other paperboys. In those days, there was a pool hall on every corner and Eddie Taylor and New York Fats were our heroes. They came through Nashville all the time. The first time I ever faced Fats was at seven-card rummy. I never fooled with him at pool. He was awful tough as a matchmaker. Wouldn't play less'n he could fix the odds in his pocket." At thirteen Pug had hitchhiked to Tampa with three dollars in his pocket. In two weeks he made over a thousand dollars, more money than he thought existed, playing pool. "But I was burglared," he said, "so I had to go home." At fifteen he drove forty miles a day to a small town north of

Nashville to pitch half dollars to the line. He traveled a lot in his early teens and soon began to feel he had exhausted Nashville's possibilities. His appetite for action had become insatiable, though he expressed it in different terms. It was just that Nashville seemed somehow smaller and more confined than Farn's Branch or Reese Hollow had ever been. In 1945, at the age of sixteen, Pug joined the Navy to get what the Navy assured him would be an education.

"I didn't really start to play poker till I got in the Navy," he said. "I learned the game real good there. While everyone else was throwin' their money on drink and women, I was organizin' poker games and playin'. When I got out, I'd saved about twenty thousand dollars." He returned to Nashville. He opened a couple of bars, but they soon bored him. He had an itch to play cards and Nashville was no place to play poker. In those years after the Navy, Pug traveled all over the country, learning the ways of the grifter—how to use false names when registering in cheap hotels, how to deal with the police and generally how to scuffle.

"Between 1951 and 1957," Pug recalled, "I had this poker route, you see. Used to make that trip at least twice a year. I'd get in that old car and drive up to Salina and Hopkinsville, to Bowling Green, to Louisville, Atlanta, and Chicago and sometimes down as far as Miami. But mostly those towns were tiny with only a gas station and a drugstore which doubled up as the grocery store. Nothin' else. A poker game every night. Them old boys could always count on me droppin' in on their little games. Knew I was comin'—same as Santa Claus. I played most everything. I played a lot of git-you-one and coon-can, an awful lot. But I loved poker. I got so good at that game I could play with folks that used marked cards and signals and God knows what and beat 'em every time. Them old boys used to call me 'Catfish Jones, swimmin' up a muddy stream,' because they never saw me comin.' I came in right on their blind spots. The poker rooms, where we played, were usually one-room shacks, the sort of place where you'd spit on the floor. And in places like that, you always had to worry 'bout bein' heisted. I was hijacked three or four times. It doesn't happen as much as it used to. Gamblers used to get heisted all the time, particularly in the South. That's why most of 'em carried guns and let it be known, so that the heisters would stay away. I carried a gun in them days, but mainly I was careful. I'd only take as much money as I needed into the game and hide my main bankroll. My favorite trick was to lay my bankroll on the ground, then drive my car on top of it, so that it was buried under the tire. And I played and played. The thing of it is that when you're a kid, you've got no sense of time. And time passes the quickest during a poker game. Why, I got up from a game once, turned around a couple of times, and five or six years had gone by. That was in 1957. For years on that poker route I played one game after another. That's all I did."

Pug had an excellent memory. The story of the poker route was the only one he told me twice. I assumed it disturbed him, that somewhere along the way he had nurtured other dreams, which he had not had time to follow. But his dreams had been conventional enough. He had never had what are called "illusions"—no sense of the elusive ideal. It would have contravened his sense of order. "When I first started gamblin'," he remembered, "I suppose all I wanted was a big Cadillac, my own cue and cue case and a pocketful of money. What would you expect a poor kid from down yonder to want? Now, I sometimes feel I haven't accomplished a damn thing. I gambled out of necessity to start. Now it's too late for anything else."

## II

The Aladdin is no gaudier than any other hotel on the Las Vegas Strip. Given the ambiance, the names of the hotel's main rooms make as much sense as its mock-Byzantine façade—the Sabre Room, the Sinbad Lounge, the Gold Room, and the Baghdad Theatre. The card room is in the Sinbad Lounge, the large main room on the ground floor, where nightly some of the biggest poker games in the world are played. It is here that Pug Pearson holds court in a way Neil Diamond must have had in mind when he sang of "a high-rolling man in a high-rolling neighborhood." At first, it seems more than a little preposterous to find Pug, "a poor country boy from down yonder," in such an opulent environment, until one understands that here the American ideal has been carried to its most practical conclusion: a place where regardless of differences in background, taste, or intelligence, money makes everyone equal, or momentarily creates that illusion. On the wall above the card tables is a sign that reads: POKER—24 HOURS EVERY DAY. Above the sign is a spread royal heart flush. The card room is not a room at all, since it occupies a side of the Sinbad Lounge and is open to traffic between the slot machines in the lobby and the stage, from which pours the amplified noise of resident talent. Round about the card tables is the crowd of tourists and hopeful high rollers, as ridiculously dressed as jesters, the shills and stickmen, the security men and bad-credit boys acting as a kind of palace guard, and here and there an itinerant hooker. The people come and go like refugees, the places of the departed so quickly taken by new arrivals that there is little impression of real movement—just a kind of tense restlessness, and the garbled sounds of the machines and the music and the mob lifted in endless crescendo. It is here that Pug, who had never been as innocent as any of them, makes his daily bread.

Pug has lived in Vegas for ten years. Once before that he had come here but the local players broke him and sent him home. Now, however, he and his wife, Andrea, his son and daughter occupied a rambling house on the suburban edge of the city. His wife was also from Nashville and Pug claimed they still missed the hills and streams of Tennessee. But Vegas was where the action was and his wife accepted his way of life, because, as Pug explained, "There ain't no changin' it." Now, action does not mean easy money, though there is that, too. But some of the best poker players in the country live in Vegas. Almost to a man they are Southerners—from Texas, Oklahoma, and Kentucky, and, like Pug, poor boys become well-to-do because of a talent at cards. It is a curious fact that, like the American military (eighty percent of whom above the rank of major are Southerners), the majority of professional cardplayers (and cardsharps) are from the South. Thus, in one sense, by playing cards with his peers, Pug maintains a loose hold on his roots. Eliminate the slot machines and the vulgar Western crowds, listen to the players in the Aladdin Hotel and one might easily be in Abilene or Tulsa or Bowling Green.

The night I walked into the Aladdin Hotel, I was told I could find Pug at the poker table, where he had been for the past twenty-four hours. He was dressed as he always was—the striped trousers, the short-sleeved shirt, the colored shoes, and the wide straw hat. He looked no more outlandish than anyone else in the room; he looked perfectly at home. There was an air of permanence about him, the slightly bored authority of a teacher who has taught the same course for twenty years. He was in the middle of a hand and looked, as Nick the Greek had once been described, "like a guy sitting with an icicle up his ass." Looking round the crowded, noisy room, I remembered that this was the place that Pug had called his office, a place of business to which he came each night; his opponents, seated now round the green felt table in various attitudes of peevish dejection, he had referred to as his clientele. They were all there —Johnny Moss, Alabama Blackie, Treetop Jack Strauss, Nigger Nate Raymond, Texas Dolly Doyle, and a group of lesser players, all of whom looked like they had ridden in that night from the ranch.

In Las Vegas Pug was deferred to, as parents defer to favorite sons. Everyone seemed to know him. Waitresses assured themselves his glass was always filled with water or tea or Seven-Up; passers-by stopped to chat or to whisper urgent messages in his ear; and players, en route to other games, paused to discuss old times or future plans. All of which Pug accepted as his due. "Of course, they know me," he said. "If you were the principal of the school, wouldn't all the kids know you? Folks know me real well out here. I could sit down in the middle of the freeway and get a game going, because people like to play with me. They like my action. They know I'm gonna give 'em a square gamble. That's what it's all about. I can beat 'em and beat 'em and they'll always come back. But fuck 'em out of a quarter and they'll leave forever. It gives 'em an excuse for losing."

Pug thought of himself as a winner; it was something he knew about. As a winner he also figured he knew more about loss than losers did. "Losing," he told me, "is like smoking. It's habit-forming, believe me. Some of the players at this here table couldn't beat Tom Thumb at nothin'. But loss is inevitable. The question is how much you control it. A winner is first and foremost a controller. That's why in life, I'm just a little better than even—and an odds-on favorite to stay that way.

"You've got to remember that in poker there are more winners than losers. At least at the higher levels. I'd say there was a ratio of twenty-to-one. But losers are great suppliers. One loser supplies a lot of winners. And the better the player, the bigger the cut. That's what they call the great pyramid of gamblin'. Sharks at the top, then the rounders, the minnows, and at the bottom the fish—the suckers, the suppliers. Scavengers and suppliers, just like in life.

"It's a funny thing—gamblin'. It's like running a grocery store. You buy and you sell. You pay the going rate for cards and you try and sell 'em for more than you paid. A gambler's ace is his ability to think clearly under stress. That's very important, because, you see, fear is the basis of all mankind. In cards, you psych 'em out, you shark 'em, you put the fear of God in 'em. That's life. Everything's mental in life. The butt was made to lug the mind around. The most important thing in gamblin' is knowing the sixty–forty end of the proposition and knowing the human element. Some folks may know one of 'em, but ain't many know 'em both. I believe in logics. Cut and dried. Two and two ain't nothin' in this world but four. But them suckers always think it's somethin' different. Makes you think, don't it?

I play percentages in everything. Now, knowing the percentages perfectly, the kind of numbers you read in them books, is all right, but the hidden percentages are more important. The real thing to know is that folks will stand to lose more than they will to win. That's the most important percentage there is. I mean, if they lose, they're willin' to lose everything. If they win, they're usually satisfied to win enough to pay for dinner and a show. The best gamblers know that."

Pug continued to play poker till ten in the morning. I sat next to him or just behind like a stowaway, and between hands or when he folded early, we talked. There were usually five or six players sitting round the table with piles of one-hundred-dollar bills and various stacks of colored chips in front of them. Occasionally a player went broke, or another would leave and someone would take his place. There were no introductions. They all knew one another and Pug referred to them as "environment." They played limit poker—usually five- or seven-card stud— which Pug believed was the best kind of poker, because there was less jeopardy and the best player always won. Once, in the middle of a hand, Pug suddenly turned as though he had forgotten something and said, "Always remember, the first thing a gambler has to do is make friends with himself. A lot of people go through this world thinking they're someone else. There are a lot of players sitting at this table with mistaken identities. You wouldn't believe it."

The hands continued throughout the night. At midnight Pug's wife phoned to say good night. She had accustomed herself to his hours long ago. "Sometimes, I'll phone him up," she said, "and say, 'Hon, you're tired, it's time to come home,' and he'll say, 'I'll be home in a few minutes.' And I might not see him for days." As she talked Pug continued to play, the telephone cupped on his shoulder. At one point he was almost ten thousand dollars ahead, but by four in the morning he had lost most of it. He was tired. He had been up too long. "When you get to slidin' in gamblin'," he said, "you better have enough strength to quit. When you get beat on and beat on, you bet when you should check and you check when you should bet. Folks get so they can read your mail." Pug, however, began winning again and his game was soon interspersed with running comment and criticism. Toward the end of one hand he turned up his cards and said: "This will beat your two queens, pally."

"Christ, Pug, how'd you know I had queens?" said his opponent. "You see through my cards?"

"Hell, no," laughed Pug. "I'm a gambler, not a mind reader."

Another player, a Texan, decided to leave, taking nearly eight thousand dollars with him. As he left, Pug said, "He'll be back. He's a great poker player, but like most gamblers he's got a lot of bad habits—craps, roulette, and the football." Beating another player for a small pot, Pug said to him, "Son, if I'd had your hand, I'd of won." He laughed. "That's the thing of poker," he said. "Ideally, you want the winning hands to pay and the losing hands to win. And the only way to do that is to control the game. You know how an actor is on the stage? He acts in such a way as to keep every eye in that audience on *him*. Right? Now, a poker player's the same way. I want all them players' eyes on *me*. I want them to sweat out what I'm doing. I want them all involved with me. And I'll do anything to get their attention. Otherwise I wouldn't be there. If you don't act the way you should, you ain't there. Most players will sit at a table right through the night and they might as well have been home in bed. They just don't act right. And they don't learn nothin'. Everyone's got habits and you've got to recognize them. You know how cows always take the same path to the watering hole, one behind the other? Well, we're the same way. People, I mean. Hell, even the beasts of the jungle, them elephants, take the exact same path when they go away to die. Poker players are just the same."

At ten in the morning Pug was about twenty-five hundred dollars ahead. He decided to play a final hand. The calls and raises went back and forth until there was some four thousand dollars in the pot. Only Pug and one other player had stayed in. Pug was very quiet. The seventh card was dealt. It was his call. He hesitated for a moment, then looked up and, pushing a pile of one-hundred-dollar bills into the pot, said: "I'm gonna raise you, son, cause you ain't got nothin' in your hand but dreams." Pug didn't wait for an answer. Turning over his hand he pulled in the pot. The other player put down his cards and, shaking his head in disbelief, said, "Puggie, you're the goddamnedest lucky player. You really are."

Pug grinned, lighting up a fresh cigar. He put his money in his pocket and we left. "They all think I'm the luckiest son of a bitch that ever lived," he said. "I like that. It brings 'em back. Hell, ain't no one can fill an inside straight quicker'n me. I'll tell you 'bout luck. I believe in it, sure, even though I know there ain't no such thing. But other folks believe in it and sometimes it's downright polite to go along with their beliefs. One thing's certain, though. Luck ain't never paid the bills."

That morning Pug told me the story of the biggest hand he had ever won. "I was playin' Johnny Moss," he said, "at deuce-to-the-seven lowball. Kansas City lowball, they call it. Straights and flushes count against you. The perfect hand is two–three–four–five–seven. Now, I'm dealt a two–three–four–seven–jack. There were six or seven players in the game, a two-hundred-dollar ante. After the first round, there ain't but three of us left in the pot—Johnny, me, and another guy, who was sitting on my right. This guy opens with a thousand. I raise twenty-eight hundred, Johnny calls and raises five thousand and then this guy only calls. Well, I know this guy, see, and he's a tight player, and when he calls, I figure either he's got a perfect hand, what they call a bicycle, or he's gonna draw, and it's a hundred-to-one he's gonna draw. So, I push all my checks into the pot —about twenty-five thousand—hoping to pick it up right there. Well, there's about forty-seven thousand in that pot now. Johnny sits there and stalls and stalls and does a lot of whispering with his confederate. I know he's got a real tough hand, possibly a two–three–four–seven and a ten or a jack. And I'm worried. Well, I know what Johnny's thinkin' and he's a good

enough player to know that I know what he's thinkin', just like
he knows what I'm thinkin'. Hell, we're environment, we know
each other like hills and streams. Finally, Johnny calls for what
he's got left, which is fifteen thousand. By calling, you understand, he thought he was getting two-to-one on his money.
Which is what I thought. But, what happens, the guy on my
right throws in his cards. He folds. Now Johnny knows he ain't
but getting about six-to-five on his money and that just ain't the
same investment. That's the main secret in cards—getting the
right price on your money. Now, had the other guy drawn, I'm
gonna get rid of that jack, but he drops, so I stand pat, figuring
to make Johnny come off his hand. Hoping he'll dog it. Johnny
is in last position. And he's uncertain. He knows I play kinda
wild. Now, he stalls and stalls. I can see the BB's goin' round
and round in his head, just like he sees mine, though not so
clearly—Johnny's gettin' on. No more bets can be made, so he
knows I'm not stealin'. He also knows I'm not bluffin'. I'm not.
I'm playin' a fine line, son. I was reading my people real good
and I knew it. I was like one of those guys with a baton in front
of an orchestra. I was playin' it like Liberace. And Johnny,
Johnny knows I got a hand. But what kind of hand do I have?
He probably figures I've got a slick nine or an eight, so what
does he do? He pooches it and draws. Now, once he hits that
deck, I'm an eight-and-a-half-to-five or maybe an eight-to-five
favorite to win. As he draws I flop over my hand and say,
'Johnny, you made a mistake, now beat that jack.' He had
discarded a ten and drawn a king. 'Oh, my God,' he says, 'I
dumped the winning hand.' And I raked in the pot of sixty-two
thousand. Now that's what I mean about knowin' your human
element."

It was nearly noon. Pug took me round his garden, which he
had reclaimed from the desert at the back of his house. "It's a
long way from Jackson County, ain't it?" he said with a grin.
Even here, in Las Vegas, Appalachia wasn't far away, it
seemed, and it reminded me that for all his practicalities Pug
would have to play and keep on playing in order to push it

farther from his mind. But it was always there; it was responsible for the dream in which he had become marooned. It was why he talked so intimately of loss and why, suddenly, as if in answer to a question I had asked some time ago, he began to talk of it again.

"Losers," he said, "have an overwhelming ambition to win. They con themselves that they can win and that's why they keep on coming back. They make regular appearances. They *have* to, you understand, 'cause they'd hold a bad opinion of themselves otherwise. But, without 'em, there would be no winners. No me." He paused, then added: "And that would be contrary to the laws of nature. Wouldn't be right."

Pug believed in what he liked to think were the laws of nature, one of them being that he would always be a winner. Although he had been broke before, he believed the odds had set things right and that they had also promised something more. And perhaps they had—though it continued to evade him. Like his father before him, chasing rumors of work from one hollow town to another, Pug still pursued that dream of high elusive action. And in his darker moments he must have wondered why it had not materialized before. No matter. He was a patient suitor. Tomorrow it would come. Tomorrow . . . or the day after. It was in the cards.

# Bobby Riggs

The word "charade"
is derived from the Spanish *charrada*—
the chatter of clowns.

## I

Currently I am less than ten miles beyond the small town of Ramona, temporarily detained in the lunar wastes of the Southern California desert. It is not the best place to begin, nor even the most convenient, but since this absurd charade has ended here, it will give a neat and cyclical turn to the tale. And besides, the place could do with a bit of form.

Today began as spring days do in this particular desert. The wind broke and fell away before first light, the skies are gray and drawn with underlying fog—the kind of fog that gums the windshield of the car with odd curlicues of oil. Earlier in the day, when I asked a gas station attendant about it, he laughed and said, "That's not oil, it's Southern California." That kind of fog, trite and commonplace. In the desert beyond Ramona one merely senses the presence of the sun; it is impossible to see. Already the heat is thick and motionless in the canyons: and down on the canyon floor, among the spiraling piles of awkwardly balanced stone, the silence is immense, indomitable. Should those three-hundred-foot-high stone totems collapse, the silence would muffle the sound of their fall—as in some early film. In such a place one's sense of reality is dulled and disconnected.

Only the road, twisting high above along the canyon's rim, indicated the presence of some separate and recognizable reality. And by ten in the morning it was glutted with hundreds of cars, buses, and limousines pushing down from Ramona, Escondido, San Luis Obispo, and from as far north as Carmel. Ramona had not been so perturbed since the summer of '72, when the temperature soared to 117 degrees and all of the chickens died. Ramona is not accustomed to a tourist trade, which helped explain why signs to the town were so haphazardly marked. Today, however, May 13, very little had been left to chance. Every thousand yards along the road, beginning on the outskirts of the town, on linden trees in the Cuyamaca Mountains, on telephone poles on the Barona Ranch Indian Reservation, or on overhanging rocks down through Wildcat Canyon, large colored posters proclaimed that the Riggs–Court Tennis Match was at hand and immediately ahead.

Their destination was a still incomplete desert development called the San Diego Country Estates—a man-made oasis some thirty miles north of San Diego. At first glance the resort appeared to be a failed promoter's final fling at a money-making proposition. True, there was a golf course out there among the craters, three tennis courts, and a swimming pool, but the heat and the eerie lunar spaces prevailed. Nonetheless, it was here, on what might have been the moon, that this large crowd had gathered. Having heard the shrill, relentless prophecies of an old, forgotten athlete, and traveling, in some cases, for thousands of miles, they had trooped into the desert to see if the prophet would eat his words.

Down on the sidelines of what would become the center court, the CBS electricians and carpenters scuttled to and fro, tampering with wires, adjusting dollies and microphones. A high platform had been raised at the rear of the court, on top of which the four cameras would rest. A scoreboard had been erected opposite. Workers hung colored banners around the stands while others set the wind barriers in place. Out on the red and green cement court Bobby Riggs plodded through his morning practice with Lornie Kuhle, a Las Vegas tennis pro. Moving lethargically about the court, bandy-legged, bespectacled and partially deaf, Riggs looked like an account executive who had been advised by his doctor to take some exercise once in a while. Rather than hitting out, he tried to intimidate the younger Kuhle with an assortment of junk shots—chips and dinks, slices and spins, and high topspin cross-court lobs—but most of them were off the mark. Between shots Riggs muttered to himself or complained out loud, reciting the grim list of his deficiencies: his overhead lacked power, his serve lacked speed, his lobs lacked depth and accuracy, his ground strokes had no pace, his volleys were forced, the balls were too heavy, his legs too old and his elbow, he feared, would never loosen in time for the match. All of which the reporters in the stands recorded faithfully and would, that afternoon, transmit to every major newspaper in the land. Unquestionably Riggs looked like a man past his prime, flat, dispirited. Serving again, he drove the ball into the net and adjusting his glasses and shaking his head, he shuffled to the sidelines. "Hey, how do I look?" he said to no one in particular.

"Terrible."

"Terrible, huh?"

"Clapped out."

"As bad as that?"

"Worse."

Riggs toweled his face and grinned. "Heck, I'm fifty-five years old. I've got one foot in the grave."

"Which one, Bobby?"

He looked around. "The one I'm not going to need," he said. He grinned again and walked away.

Bobby Riggs had the face of a man who sold encyclopedias from door to door; one was suspicious, but never offended. There was always a sense of sincerity in his pronouncements. And so, at first, there was no way of knowing just how serious he was or how seriously he meant his inquisitors to take him.

He was what is known in the trade as a conniver—the sort of man who ostentatiously juggles a kind of charming conceit with sharp self-deprecation, in order, it happens, to keep his options open. He had, in fact, only one straightforward role to play— that of the evasive innocent. "Do you think you will win, Bobby?" was the question reporters asked most often, expecting, I suppose, some simple positive or negative reply, or, at worst, some modest avowal of affirmation. But his reply was always a variant of the same equivocal theme: "Well," he would say, looking perfectly confounded, "she's the best woman player in the world, y'know, and gosh, I'm an old has-been with one foot in the grave, but if I can get a few breaks here and there, I think I'm in with an even chance." His lackluster practices on court, however, indicated that his chances were less than that. Next day, in the tennis writers' private pool, eighteen out of twenty-four experts picked Margaret Court to win and most of them in straight sets.

When news of their verdict reached Riggs, he said, "You don't say?" and smiled with a barely perceptible shrug. He had the air of a small-town mayor seeking re-election. Polls? What did polls have to do with him? Full of impulsive promises and braggadocio, he reminded me . . . well, if a film had been made of this charade, Mickey Rooney would have played the part of Bobby Riggs—the artful, buoyant, cocky underdog. His euphoric chatter and adolescent exaggerations were reminiscent of *Boys' Town* and *A Yank at Eton*. He had that habit of referring to himself in the third person, as if he were talking of his fondest invention. Garrulous and completely self-possessed, his head or his hands orchestrated his every word. He talked endlessly and brokenly, a sentence often left unfinished as he rushed into the next one. It was as though the manic flood of his words swelled, only to crash against some invisible reef in his mind, before gathering speed again.

"You don't say?" he said, and smiled with a barely perceptible shrug. "What experts? Those reporters out there? Those guys? Those guys from papers I never heard of? Those experts?

Let me tell ya. I'll tell ya about experts. They've been saying that all my life. Right from the start. All the way back. Riggs is gonna lose, he's gonna lose. The loudmouth's gonna get what he deserves. They take one look at me out there, those guys, and whatta they see? I'll tell ya what they see. See what I want 'em to see. A tired old man, who's past it, dead'n gone, always moaning and groaning, they see an old guy living in the past, who can't serve, can't volley, can't even see the ball without glasses, much less get it across the net. And what does he do? He keeps on talking and boasting and bragging, he keeps on . . . Sure. They wanna see me get my brains beat in, served up like a pig with a tennis ball in his mouth. That's what they want. Heck, I *am* old, I'm practically a grandfather, maybe several times over, and sometimes the flesh won't do what the mind tells it to. And maybe it won't. Who knows? Experts. What can I tell ya? It's even money. You can cut it both ways. What a beautiful deal. Beautiful. You can see for yourself, day after tomorrow, right here. You watch. You'll see. Sure, the old skippiness is gone, the old zing. The way of all flesh, right? But I always rise for the big occasion. I get right up there for it. Heck, you know that, you know that. You know that much."

His tennis match with Margaret Court had become his chief obsession. And yet, for all his talk, he seemed like a man who had gone too far, as though, by accident, he had unleashed a monster he could neither explain, control, nor comprehend. For the moment, however, the attendant publicity seemed to appease the majority of his fears.

In the beginning Riggs had issued a light-hearted challenge to Billie Jean King. He had offered to bet five thousand dollars of his own money (added to a five-thousand-dollar offer from San Diego Country Estates) for a best-of-three-set challenge match. Ms. King, whom Riggs called "the real sex leader of the revolutionary pack," had long insisted that because the women players provided a kind of tennis comparable to men's and because they drew an equal percentage of the crowd, they should also receive an equal share of the rewards. It was a just complaint, but, as in other areas of the women's movement, the men saw sexual rather than economic threats lurking in the tide. In his challenge Riggs claimed not only that she could not beat a top male player, but that she could not even beat him— "an old man of fifty-five." For reasons best known to herself, Ms. King declined and, following a flurry of negotiations, Mrs. Court accepted.

Now, two days before the match, it had become, next to Watergate, the most fascinating affair in the land. The press boys in the back room called it "a very important phenomenon" and nearly a hundred tennis writers and women's lib columnists had flocked to Southern California to be on hand. Riggs had not had so much notoriety since he had thrashed Don Budge for the world professional championship in 1949. Or, as he had said to me on the drive down to Ramona from his home in Newport Beach, the large Lincoln Continental (license plate: R. RIGGS) cruising confidently at seventy-five: "Heck, I haven't had any attention for twenty-five years. And I love the limelight, an old ham like me, I really love it." Little wonder then that he continually referred to the confrontation as "the match of the century between the battle of the sexes." Little wonder that he put himself forward as the man who could throw back the advancing female hordes. As Graham Greene said: "Fame is a powerful aphrodisiac."

## II

Robert Larimore Riggs was born in Los Angeles on February 25, 1918. His parents had come to California from Riggs Crossroads in Tennessee, the site of a large, though now demolished, homestead owned by his Scotch-Irish forebears. Bobby's older brother Dave, who takes pride in such matters, is quick to point out that the Riggses always owned their own property, that they were never tenants; nor, as certain critics have implied, did they come from the wrong side of the tracks. Riggs Crossroads

today, however, is little more than an occasional bus stop on the
Nashville run and is rarely indicated on the state maps of
Tennessee.

Bobby's father, Gideon, attended Bible school in Nashville,
became an evangelist and traveled round the South and Southwest of the 1880s and '90s, spreading the word of the Lord. His
church, the Disciples of Christ, was a fundamentalist sect of the
fire-and-brimstone school and Gideon's particular labors were
to preach and convert and to create permanant places of worship. To that end he moved his family to the Lincoln Heights
section of Los Angeles in 1904. When Bobby, the youngest, was
born at the end of the First World War, he already had five
older brothers and a sister; a framed family portrait taken two
or three years later still sits on a table by Bobby's bed.

They were a religious family; they said grace at meals and
Bobby's father could quote the Bible from memory. Bobby
dimly remembers all-day revival meetings conducted in
cramped tents, and that his father regularly denounced smoking, drinking, gambling, dancing, and organ music as utterly
evil. His older brothers remember that they were all modest,
honest, God-fearing, hard-working, middle-class people.

There was nothing modest about the family's athletic ambitions, however, at least insofar as they concerned Bobby. "I was
born into a billion-in-one environment," he recalled. "A perfect
climate and a family crazed with dreams of winning. Particularly my older brothers. I was actually programmed to be a
champion. I had to beat all the kids in the neighborhood at
anything they played—at marbles, top spinning, jacks, pitching
to the line, and when my brothers weren't looking, at blackjack
and penny-ante poker." Mickey Rooney was one of that game's
regular participants and throughout his adolescence Bobby
hustled Rooney at table tennis. "Sometimes I think I was born
in a contest. My earliest memory was being goaded into a
footrace when I was four. My brothers arranged it, they threw
me into everything, and the deal was always the same. If I won
I got to go to the movies and if I lost I was kicked in the ass.

What a house. You'd think with all that religion I'd've ended up in the school choir. But I don't remember being raised to believe in God. I grew up believing I was going to be a world champion. A world champion at something. I didn't know what."

What is politely known as "the competitive spirit" was instilled in Bobby before he was seven. At that age he remembers fleecing a playmate in a marbles match. "Afterwards," he recalled, "I traded him a hundred marbles and two aggies for the tennis racket his sister got for Christmas." That accomplished, Bobby got down on his knees, not, as his father might have preferred, to give thanksgiving, but to win back the hundred marbles and the two aggies.

He began to play tennis when he was twelve. "In those days," he said, "all the kids I knew thought tennis was a sissy's game. We looked down on it. But I played anyway. The so-called experts always said I was too small, that I couldn't hit the ball hard enough. If I'd been anybody else, they might have been right. But what they didn't know was my environment, how I was programmed, and how much I believed in myself. Believe me, environment is the most important thing there is. To them it was the mystery factor. They didn't know I'd solved it long ago."

Ironically, Bobby learned to play tennis from a woman— Esther Bartosh, then the third-ranking woman player in the Los Angeles area. By the end of that year he was spending most of his spare time on the tennis courts. At thirteen his penchant for hustling had been firmly established. Waiting for courts at the public park, he played penny-ante poker on the sidelines. As he rarely had any money he played the other boys for new balls and picked his opponents carefully. In 1930 he was runner-up in the thirteen-and-under championships of Southern California. The following year he won it. In 1932 he went to the state championships in Berkeley. He and his brother John hitchhiked to San Francisco and stayed with a friend of their father's, another preacher, who, when Bobby had won, rewarded him with a baptism. Later that year he went to the fifteen-and-under championships in Culver, Indiana, where he lost in the semi-finals. The following year, 1933, he lost his state title to Bob Harman and lost again to Harman in the finals of the nationals, but he won the doubles with him—the first of forty national championships.

"Nobody gets to the top in tennis," said Bobby, "who hasn't played at least ten years, three hundred days a year, six hours a day. It's a rule of thumb." It was an axiom that rarely left his mind and he remembers that most of the hard work in his life was performed between the ages of twelve and seventeen. In 1934, when Bobby was sixteen, he beat Frank Shields, the number-one ranked national men's champion, in the Los Angeles County Championships. His father, now blind, would sit on the sidelines and listen to the umpire call the score. The following year he won his first national singles title for the eighteen-year-olds-and-under and also won the doubles. In 1936 he was asked to defend his national junior title but refused. He wanted to play with the men. As a result the Southern California Tennis Association withdrew their support and *Liberty* magazine referred to him as "Peck's Bad Boy of Tennis." Unperturbed, Bobby blithely described to amused reporters his five-year plan to become the world's amateur tennis champion. "I guess," Bobby conceded, "I was what you might call a fresh kid." But his was no ordinary fantasy. It haunted all his waking hours and at night he dreamed of it. The dream was always the same—playing at Wimbledon on center court before a packed gallery of sixteen thousand people with the King and Queen in the Royal Box, playing against someone like Bill Tilden or Don Budge, running in that final game to his right to hit a looping forehand, which brought up a puff of white chalk as it caught the sideline for a winner, then a deep, perfectly placed lob, which caught the baseline for match point, then jumping the net and shaking hands with Tilden–Budge and, as Champion of the World, bowing, with just a little condescension, to the King and Queen. Bobby loved that dream.

In 1936 the national clay court championships were held in Chicago. As Bobby had no financial support, a friend agreed to drive him there. Before the tournament began, he and his enterprising friend took all available bets that Bobby would win. Obtaining overwhelming odds, Bobby breezed into the final, where he beat the then "boy wonder of American tennis," Frankie Parker, in three straight sets. "I had all the money I could use after I won the juniors," he said. "I was always subsidized after that." He played the national circuit that year and in September he went to Forest Hills.

Forest Hills was meant to be the first of his giant kills, the final riposte to those staid authorities who had sneered and withdrawn their support. But the night before his first match he became involved in a crap game at the Waldorf Towers in New York. "It was my first experience in really big action," he recalled. "Every high roller in New York was there and I didn't get back to my hotel till eight the next morning." That afternoon he lost to Johnny Van Ryn in the second round. Later in the year, when the national rankings were published, Riggs was number four. He reckoned his loss at Forest Hills had cost him the number-two ranking behind Don Budge. "Still, it wasn't bad for a junior," he said. "I was only seventeen."

Even so, he knew excuses of an all-night crap game would have had scant appeal to his brothers. Rather than returning home to face them, he accepted an athletic scholarship to the University of Miami, arranged by Gardnar Mulloy. He was not much interested in school; he had only just managed to graduate from Franklin High School in Los Angeles earlier that year, so he looked on college as an unexpected and altogether undeserved reward. But his pleasure was short-lived. Looking back on what he now calls "that comic interlude," he remembers taking comic books to class, or, when his professors rebuked him for not appearing at all, retorting: "What do I want to go to class for? That's not going to help me win Wimbledon." Some three months later, he decided that he was unfit for "student activities" and, in January of 1937, returned to California.

During the Twenties Big Bill Tilden had dominated American tennis, winning seven national titles. By 1937 the two best players in the world were Don Budge and Fred Perry. Perry had won Wimbledon and Forest Hills three times each and Budge won them both in 1937 and 1938, the year he also became the first man to win tennis's "Grand Slam"—the Australian, French, British, and American championships. Bobby hungered for similar recognition—though he was three years younger than Budge and Perry's junior by seven—but his wayward behavior was frowned upon by the sober heads of the American Lawn Tennis Association. In 1937 they excluded him from the Davis Cup team on grounds that he had broken training repeatedly that year. Bobby had not done well on the national circuit and though he vehemently denied the rumors at the time, when pressed today he admits to a fondness for craps and cards during that period. But he insists that it had not affected his tennis and that barring Budge he was still the best player in the country.

"The good part of my game," he explained without a trace of humor, "was that there weren't any weaknesses in it. I was good at covering the court. I was a great defensive player. The press called me 'The Retriever.' I climbed the fence for balls. I was quick and fast and agile. I was renowned for my wonderful touch, my mobility, my tenacity. I was a great counterpuncher. You make a good shot and I'd make a better one. I forced players into being overly offensive. And forcing errors. I was a total mystery to the tennis experts. But, none of them knew how competitive I was, that I never gave up and that I was always ice cold under pressure. I was also a great change of pace man, which is always based on a knowledge of your opponent's strengths and weaknesses. I always played percentages."

Those apparently invincible attributes, however, were not to be of much assistance to him at Forest Hills in 1937 and 1938. He was knocked out in the semi-finals on both occasions. But there was hope. Fred Perry had turned pro, and after winning Forest Hills in 1938, Don Budge followed suit. The twenty-year-old Bobby Riggs looked forward to 1939 with the confidence of a man who knew his time had come.

Hollywood, formerly a place of elegant façades and papier-mâché mansions, is the most seedy section of Los Angeles today. Seedy and, despite its bustle, somehow forsaken, yet, here and there, it has contrived an air of respectability. Beyond the gaudy boulevards are cute suburban streets and straggling palms and unkempt lawns and the drab stucco homes of the bourgeoisie. One of these was the home of Mr. Rheo Blair. Blair, a muscular man of indeterminate years, whose hair was teased up into a kind of permanent Fifties pompadour, described himself as a "nutritional scientist." Bobby Riggs, a blunter man, referred to him as his "bloodpusher." For a fee of five thousand dollars, Blair had persuaded Bobby that if he followed his program to the letter, adhered to the diet and imbibed the pills, he would not only get back into shape, but would actually feel some ten years younger. Blair called it his "rejuvenation program." The match was still some weeks away, but Bobby had rarely used a tennis racket in twenty years. A few days before, while looking at his flaccid body in the bathroom mirror, he said, "Gosh, I won't last a set with that Amazon."

It was to Blair's white stucco home that I had gone to observe the more delicate side of Bobby's training program. On entering the house, Blair instructed me to take off my shoes, a custom I assumed he had acquired in the Orient, but no, it was only to protect his lush, white carpets, over which he had laid sheets as an extra precaution. The main room, in which Bobby was being massaged, was kept in semi-darkness "to promote complete euphoria." The walls were cluttered with photographs— before and after poses of previous patients, whom he had cured of diseases ranging from flat feet to malnutrition. Blair, a peevish man, complained that Bobby had not given him time in which to effect maximum rejuvenation, but that he was quite prepared to draw on all his powers.

Blair's methods required Bobby to take four hundred and fifteen pills a day. The pills, in assorted shapes and colors, included all the vitamins and their extracts, wheat germ concentrate, liver extracts, calcium, amino acids, and predigested protein. In much the way that acupuncture changes the body's energy flow, the pills were meant to alter the chemistry of Bobby's body and make him younger. Hardly a day passed without the guru mentioning in as much of an astonished aside as possible: "Gosh, Bobby, you're responding well, *really* well. You look so much *younger,* you really do." Blair's program was designed to last for ninety days, but as Bobby had only five weeks, he was given a concentrated crammer course. Despite this adversity, Blair was optimistic. But Bobby, during the two-hour period each day devoted to swallowing the pills, wondered again and again whether it was he, for once, who was being hustled. It struck him most forcibly when he looked into the mirror to see if his double chin had disappeared. Still, Bobby had a kind of built-in guile and when the guru asked him for a down payment, Bobby gave him twenty-five hundred dollars and said, "You'll get the rest, Rheo, *if* I win the match." The guru's face fell and then reformed into what I can only describe as his oracular expression. "We'll see, dear," he said quietly, "we'll see."

During my visits to Rheo Blair's dark laboratory, while Bobby was being massaged or rejuvenated in his whirlpool bath, I would sit and listen to long accounts of his surprisingly untroubled past. His life, if it had not run straightforwardly, ran smoothly nonetheless, with little error or interference. As he recounted it, it seemed to have floated down some long, protected corridor, waywardly perhaps but always aloft, like one of those eccentric planes made of spit and notebook paper. There had been no setbacks or reversals, no messy contretemps, no rumblings of distant drums. A surface life devoted to a single success.

Throughout most of 1939 he played excellent tennis on the national circuit and that summer at Wimbledon he entered, he believed, the periphery of his desires. The local line, however, considered him to be something of a dark horse. His starting price was 3–to–1. Before the tournament began he went to a bookmaker and asked what the odds would be on Riggs to win the singles, the doubles, and the mixed doubles on a parlay. At first the bookmaker refused to consider the proposition, but Riggs persuaded him and, getting odds of 3–to–1, 6–to–1, and 10–to–1, he bet £100 on himself. A fortnight later, he beat Elwood Cooke in five sets for the singles championship and went on to win the doubles and the mixed doubles. Later in the week his bookmaker sent him a check for £20,100—a great deal of money in 1939. Two months later he won the American championships at Forest Hills and was recognized as the number-one amateur tennis player in the world. That December he married his first wife, Kay Fischer, in Chicago. They spent their wedding night in the Palmer House and next day Bobby was back playing tennis. But it was not an auspicious time either for him or for tennis. Because of the London blitz Wimbledon was discontinued. The following year, blowing a two-set lead, he lost to Don McNeill in the finals at Forest Hills. But, just before entering the Navy in 1941, he won Forest Hills again, beating Frankie Kovacs in four sets. The next day the Associated Press account of the match said: "Riggs came back to win the title he held in 1939 by beating a player who would have been a 2–to–1 favorite if there had been a bookmaker within the sacred precincts of the West Side Tennis Club." "For once," said Bobby, "the newspapers weren't entirely wrong. Two-to-one was what I got." It was his last amateur tennis match; shortly afterward he turned professional.

During the war Bobby traveled throughout the Pacific and Australia giving exhibition matches. He didn't like it very much. Tennis was his obsession and anything, even a world war, that interfered with it was a waste of time. As a result those years remain something of a blur for him, a time in which very little of importance actually happened. One incident he does remember happened in Pearl Harbor in 1944. A young man challenged Bobby to play some tennis for money. The stranger did not know who Riggs was and when he suggested they play for high stakes, Bobby thought it indiscreet to tell him. At the end of two hours, Bobby had relieved the man of most of his savings. Doubling the bets, he proceeded to win the young man's car and finally his bungalow outside Honolulu. Distraught, the young man slunk from the court. Bobby summoned him back. He told him who he was, returned his money, and said to him: "Let this be a lesson to you. Never play strangers for money. At any game." Much later, when his largesse was more closely questioned, Bobby conceded that he had retained five hundred dollars for the advice.

The war ended none too soon for Riggs and he returned eagerly to his tennis. In December of 1945 the first world's professional championships were held in Los Angeles. The finalists were Don Budge and Bobby Riggs. Bobby had played Budge five times during the war, winning three of the exhibition matches. "They were close matches," he said, "but it showed me that Budge wasn't invincible. He wasn't in much shape at the time though, he was dogging it, so I knew this would be a greater test." But, again, Budge seemed not to be in prime condition. "He claimed he had a bad arm," said Bobby. "I won two of the first three sets and Budge retired to the dressing room to have his arm massaged. In the fourth set he started grasping his arm on court. He was a terrible ham. And then he did a complete El Collapso. I won the last set 6–0 and the match."

A month later, in January of 1946, a rematch was staged at the Pan-Pacific Auditorium in Los Angeles. It was the biggest promotion in tennis up to that time and attracted a capacity audience of some seventy-five hundred people. The match was highly publicized and several thousand people were turned away at the gate. All the tennis experts agreed that Don Budge would win this time. "No one could believe that a little runt like me had a chance against the great Don Budge," said Bobby. "The time before had been a fluke, the master had been wounded and out of condition. There wasn't a tennis expert in the country who would make it even money. Which was fine with me, since I got terrific odds. That night in the dressing room before the match, Errol Flynn came in with some friends and they bet me twenty-five hundred dollars each at odds of two-to-one that I would lose. It was terrible. Even my supporters were worried. I got all the pre-game bets I could handle."

There was a large clock in the Pan-Pacific Auditorium suspended some thirty-five feet above the center court. In the very first game Riggs began to lob Budge. Now, to get just the right depth, the ball had to be lofted about three inches beneath the bottom of the clock. Anything lower, and Budge would use his powerful overhead to make unreturnable smashes. Anything higher would hit the clock and Bobby would lose the point. The clock and Don Budge's racket were to become the two most crucial factors in the match. Budge used the heaviest racket then available in tennis and was openly proud of it. With that racket and his awesome power Budge was famous for his overheads. "Budge was a straightaway smasher," said Bobby. "He killed the ball, never to the right or to the left, but directly down the middle. When he was fresh they were almost impossible to return. But how fresh will a man remain, when he has to rely on his overhead for ninety percent of the game? Just about a set, I figured."

Budge was very impressive that night. He took the first set 6–4 and jumped to a 5–2 lead in the second set. His fans were screaming wildly and waving pennants in the air. While toweling off at the end of the seventh game, Bobby remembers Errol Flynn smiling broadly at him from his sideline box and making dollar signs. "But it was obvious to me," said Bobby, "that Budge was getting tired. That racket of his was beginning to feel as though it weighed twenty pounds. But I'd figured that much out before the match."

Between the first and second sets, while Budge toweled off on the sidelines, Bobby had gone into the box seats, which were only about twenty feet from the court, in order to obtain further bets. The odds had skyrocketed by then and Bobby and his brother, who was taking bets on the other side of the court, were getting odds as high as 10–to–1 against.

"Gosh, it was an amazing performance," said Bobby. "I must have lobbed him about seventy times during that match. Only three of them actually hit the clock. Every time I lobbed I could hear the crowd holding its breath to see where that ball would go. Most of them fell within six inches of the baseline." Eventually Bobby saved two set points and took the second set 9–7.

"By the middle of the third set," said Bobby, "Budge was getting sick of those lobs. He was deathly ill. At one point in the third game of that set I gave him seven straight lobs, all of which missed that clock by a hair. He smashed them all back, except the last one, and after that it was all downhill. I took the last two sets 6–4, 8–6, and Budge retired to the dressing room with a steel elbow."

The following day the newspapers talked of "luck" and "cheap tricks." But Riggs had won and was grudgingly acknowledged to be the best tennis player in the world. Accordingly he grinned and collected all his bets.

As a professional tennis player, his other memorable match was on December 27, 1947, at New York's Madison Square Garden. The match was almost a disaster, since twenty-seven inches of snow fell on the city that night. Nonetheless sixteen thousand fans turned up. According to Bobby, his fans would have braved a tidal wave to see him play. That night his opponent was Jack Kramer, who was making his professional debut. At that time Kramer was the hottest player in tennis. He had won Forest Hills in 1946 and Forest Hills and Wimbledon in 1947. "I think Kramer had lost only one match in 1946," said Bobby. "He hadn't lost any in 1947."

Jack Kramer, at twenty-six, was three years younger than Bobby and an advocate of what was becoming known as The Big Game—the powerful serve and volley game. Although Bobby had beaten Kramer nine out of ten times as an amateur, he had not played him since 1941, six years before. Again the experts predicted that Kramer would be too strong for the fading Riggs and tipped him to win. Unconvinced, Bobby bet twenty-five thousand dollars on himself.

"I was counting on Kramer figuring me for a baseliner," said Bobby, "a backcourt player who would be extremely reluctant to take the net. So I made up my mind to lob him and go to the net every time. He also had a faulty backhand and so, unless I had an open court, every shot would go to his backhand. Not most of them, all of them. He was also, of course, under extreme pressure. The amateur officials and the newspapers had built up the match in Kramer's mind as a great chance for him to prove what a magnificent champion he was, that they were right and that Riggs, the loudmouth, had bitten off more than he could chew. The pressure was enormous. But, heck, I'd been through it all before—the strangeness, the crowds, the lights. It wasn't strange to me at all. It was also to my advantage that we hadn't played in years. I could be fairly sure of what kind of tennis he would play. He couldn't know what I would do. Well, except when we were serving, I spent my time at the net, just cruising back and forth like a shark. I won comfortably in four sets. And the next day, the press put up the usual squawk."

Following that match Riggs and Kramer went on tour. After a month Kramer was ahead 13–12. "But after that," said Bobby, "I hated it and fell apart. I'm not a grind-out man. That Garden match was a clutch match, a natural for me. I'm always up for those kind of matches. I'm only really good when we play for all the marbles. Who's got the nerve? That's my game. I can't play a grind-out, a match a day for two months. I'm no good at that. I'm a now-or-never guy. Always have been."

After the Kramer tour Bobby promoted tours with Kramer, with Pancho Gonzalez, Pancho Segura, and Gussie Moran, but the heart had dropped out of his game. In 1949 he published his autobiography, *Tennis Is My Racket,* and in 1951 retired from tennis altogether. He still felt that he was the greatest tennis player in the world, and more, that he had been that game's greatest entertainer. Or that is how he sometimes spoke of his reputation. His brother Dave, however, refers to it as "that deplorable image"—namely that of tennis's foremost hustler. Not that Bobby had not always hustled in one way or another, but over the years he had turned that underhand art into an extravagant charade. It was during his early days at the Los Angeles Tennis Club that he devised his more notorious hustles—putting four chairs on his side of the court, playing with a poodle lashed to his leg, or, if that were not handicap enough, playing with poodles lashed to both legs. He once played in a raincoat and galoshes while carrying an open umbrella in his left hand, and sometimes he would give his mark the alleys while limiting himself to the singles. "At Easthampton," he said, "I once played four people. Four is much easier than, say, two because they keep on getting in each other's way." They were, of course, all money matches and in each case his opponent believed he had been given favorable odds.

"The Thirties were the Golden Age of tennis hustling," he said. "Money was tighter and the professional game was not taken seriously anywhere. The basic hustle in tennis is the handicap. Thirty points a game or a 5–0 lead in the set. You'd be amazed how many people think a lead like that is insurmountable. It's only when the score is 5–5 that that crazed look comes across their faces, when they realize they're never going to win." While still in his teens Bobby knew that whatever edge he gave it was not going to be enough to beat him.

"I always rise to the occasion for that big bet," he said. "Pressure makes me produce. Kills most guys. Mortifies 'em. I love a contest, a game, a challenge. To be a winner, you've got to be an appraiser. You've got to be able to play at your best under pressure. And more money creates more pressure. Money is the finest fuel in the world."

Those were the heydays of Bobby Riggs, and listening to him talk of it is like listening to men who refer to their times in the Army or at college as "the good old days"—when friendship flowered, when love, however brief or misbegotten, bloomed, times when all the prospects pleased. Although he was to play in other important matches, the Kramer match was what

Bobby liked to call his last sure thing, the last of the really big tennis action; and now, some twenty-five years later, he talked of it as though it had happened yesterday. His whole life seemed capsuled for him now, miraculously foreshortened, so that this current match with Margaret Court seemed to follow in some kind of consecutive sequence, as though it were still 1947.

But twenty-five years *had* passed. He had gone straight, more or less, he had divorced and remarried, he had gone into business, he had played the other guy's game and observed the rules, he had been a good boy, a kind husband, an indulgent father—and what did he have to show for it? One day, he had gone to a party or walked into a bar—he couldn't quite remember—and no one, not one of them, remembered his name. "Heck," he thought, "gosh, you mean? Gosh, I'm Bobby Riggs, goddamn it," and they had given him those infinitely polite, but quizzical looks, as though he had said something they had not quite understood. Like all men, particularly athletes, who reach the peak of their lives at thirty, the rest was anticlimactic, a dull addendum to what had gone before. But that was no longer true. Bobby had been given one further game to play; the crowds would come, there would be apposite applause and his name would be in the headlines again. And this time it would be even better, since nearly sixty million people would watch his act on television. Sixty million converts. Gosh. Bobby couldn't wait. He believed in an immediate immortality.

# III

On Friday, May 11, two days before the match, a practice session had been arranged with Don Budge, who had flown in from his home in Acapulco. The practice was held on the courts of Park Newport, Bobby's residence in Newport Beach, an hour's drive south of Los Angeles. In his small townhouse, which he shared with his brother Dave, the press wandered in and out discussing the pros and cons of the match with Budge and Riggs. Their puzzled inquiries were always the same: could Riggs win? Did he have the legs, the wind, the stroking ability, the concentration, the incentive, and the confidence to beat a woman at the top of her game? Or, as the Los Angeles *Times* reporter put it next day: "Much depends on whether Riggs can keep Mrs. Court, who plays a man-type game, away from the net with his return of serve and his assortment of junk shots, including his once-famous lob." But Don Budge predicted that Bobby would win 6–3, 6–3. He pointed out that he had beaten Mo Connolly after she had won Wimbledon in 1953. "I was past my prime then," he said, "and she only got a couple of games off me."

But the reporters were dubious and Bobby said little to change their minds. "When I run for the ball," he said, "the legs feel like they're going to cave in. It's like running in quicksand. The old skippiness, that's what I'm missing. I don't know why I'm hoping on the day of the match I'll wake up and have this feeling of lightness and spring in my legs. A guy doesn't feel himself growing old, y'know. You just look into the mirror one day and say, where did the last forty fucking years go to anyway?" He shrugged. "But they're gone."

Bobby was still taking his daily quota of vitamin pills. "At the rate you're taking pills, Bobby, you'll be four years old by Sunday," said Lornie Kuhle. Nonetheless, after five weeks Bobby remained skeptical. Every so often he would ring Rheo Blair and scream abuse down the telephone. He felt more tired than he had ever been. "Gosh," he said, "if this keeps up, I'll have to take some pep pills on Sunday morning. For extra zip. Do you think that bloodpushing fag knows what he's doing?" He adjusted his glasses and looked befuddled. "And where the hell is Margaret Court? Do you think she'll stand me up?"

At that moment Mrs. Court was in San Francisco. Earlier in the year she had won her eleventh Australian championship and was again prepared for a run at the Grand Slam. The week before she had completed a grueling thirteen-week tour on the Virginia Slims circuit, competing day after day against the best women players in the world; she had won 89 out of 92 matches and 10 of the 12 tournaments. Now, in San Francisco, she practiced with Dennis Vandermeer, a tennis pro who professed an intimacy with Bobby's game. "Yeah, I think he saw me play once," said Bobby. Practicing that week, Margaret Court was tired and more than a little bored. She was looking ahead to the French championships and to Wimbledon. She could have rested but decided to practice. She was also concerned. During her last match of the tour, she had acquired mysterious cramps in her legs and had had to default. She practiced. Why take a chance? Why risk anything? Even with a ridiculous old Yank.

Meanwhile, in Newport Beach, a minor contretemps had flared. For the match itself Bobby insisted on using the lighter, faster Spalding balls. Tony Trabert, the tennis director of San Diego Country Estates, had promised him they would be used, but now, at the eleventh hour, Mrs. Court declared that she wouldn't play unless the heavy-duty Wilson balls were used and Trabert backed down. A hurried compromise was reached. The argument would be settled, Trabert decided, by the flip of a coin. Mrs. Court sent Vandermeer to Newport Beach as her representative. A small amused crowd watched as the coin was tossed. An old hand in these matters, Bobby called tails—and lost. He appeared to be disconsolate and that night at dinner, surrounded by friends and journalists, he referred to it in mournful tones as "the flip of the century."

The odds against him, he insisted, were even greater now. "I play like a woman, she plays like a man," he said. "She's younger and faster and bigger and stronger. She's absolutely ferocious. She's got a bigger serve, a better volley and a stronger overhead. She's got me beat in every department, except maybe thinking, strategy and experience. She has a fast court and now she's got advantageous balls. Also, because it's Mother's Day, the crowd will be in sympathy with her. And all those screaming women-libbers. It's not fair."

Bobby had seen Margaret Court play only once. Earlier in the year he had traveled to Richmond to check her out. When reporters asked him what he had learned, he said: "I'll tell ya. I learned that as a player she doesn't have any weaknesses at all. But as a woman she's a bit short on balls. You could use her as an example of tennis perfection. She's as perfect a player as you can get, probably the best of all time. She's much better than I am." While in Richmond he discussed his prospects with Julie Heldman, who played on the women's tour and whose mother, Gladys Heldman, was the woman behind women's lob and the editor and publisher of *World Tennis* magazine. Among the girls she is known as "The Great Liberator." Her daughter informed Bobby that he had only an outside chance of beating Margaret Court.

"Come on, Julie," insisted Bobby. "What do you mean by an outside chance? Would you say three-to-one?"

"No way, Bobby," she said. "I said an outside chance. Maybe ten-to-one."

"Imagine," said Bobby, "ten-to-one. I've never been ten-to-one–against in my life. It's a great bet. Grab it."

In 1952 Bobby divorced his first wife and married his second —a marriage that would last for twenty years. This was his "straight and safe" period, by which he meant that he gave up gambling, more or less, gave up tennis altogether and took what is called a steady job. He was thirty-four years old. He and Priscilla moved into a large house in Manhasset on Long Island and Bobby went to work as the executive vice-president of the American Photograph Corporation, a company owned by his father-in-law. His efforts earned him a salary of eighty thousand dollars a year.

Today, in a leather-bound family photograph album, which Bobby displays in his home in Newport Beach, it is possible to refer to that "straight" period. The pictures speak of peace and plenty, of a life gone fat with pleasure—the family mansion, the tree-shaded tennis court in the garden, the cars, the kids, the dogs, the brash display of the *bourgeois gentilhomme*. Given Bobby Riggs, *enfant terrible* and master hustler, these seemed the drab reminders of some older, more conservative man. Even the photographs of Bobby himself seemed those of an older, portlier, grayer, and altogether duller man. He stands there stiffly, almost against his will, his wife at his side, the children gathered round, the gray hair brushed back from the forehead, neatly dressed in suit and tie—the model image of the right-minded family man, an example to all, a credit to the community. Yet despite references to his life as "a bundle of laughs" and to his wife as "a swell gal" and "a really beautiful doll," he found that image impossible to sustain.

He had given up tennis, however, and within months of his marriage he began to cast about for other outlets. "You've got to stay in action," he maintained. "It's good for the arteries." In 1952 he had played golf only six or seven times. "I was told when I began," he said, "that it didn't matter how well you shot, it was how you managed yourself that mattered. I was a one-hundred-shooter when I began and my handicap was eighteen or nineteen. But I practiced and it wasn't too long before I was breaking ninety. I learned all the angles, I mean *all* the angles. I learned everything I knew from Mike McClaney, who was the best angler in the business. Now, it's the winter of 1952, early '52. I stayed in Florida till June. With my handicap I was killing everybody. I just out-competed them. Fuck the tennis tour, I thought. Golf is easier."

In the early Fifties Bobby played at those clubs where the big action was—the Seminole and La Gorce in Miami Beach. La Gorce, also known as Hustler's Haven, had more than a hundred millionaires as members. "It was like an open-air poolroom," said Bobby. "La Gorce was a den of thieves. All the ringers, hustlers and smart guys were there. If you didn't know what was happening you wouldn't see an elephant if it jumped up on the table. But if you didn't let yourself get outmatched, you won. You've got to get into the right match-ups, know your own levels, and the other guy's, whether you're playing tennis or golf. They're both games of planes and levels.

"At that time there were some terrific players there. Tim

Holland could've made the pro tour, but he preferred cards and backgammon. Al Besselink was hustling just prior to joining the tour. They called him The Viking. There was John Montague. He was beautiful. He once beat Bing Crosby for a wad of money using a rake, a hoe, and a baseball bat, while Crosby was allowed to use his regular clubs. There was Bill Gould, The Rubber Man, who became so well known in Florida that he couldn't get a game. So he changed his name and went to California. A lot of hustlers were there. George Lowe, the greatest putter I ever saw, Hawthorne Fats and Danny Miller and then Marty Stanovich, who was called The Fat Man. That Fat Man had the most ludicrous swing in the world, but he always seemed to hit the ball a little farther and a little more accurately than anyone else. The Fat Man always gave you what you thought was a fair game. Trouble was, you were usually wrong. He was treacherous, and I learned a lot from him. I got caught in the middle too often not to learn something."

Bobby made a great deal of money in his golfing days, but his biggest coup occurred in 1953. Early that year a golf match had been set up at the Greenbrier Country Club, Sam Snead's home course in White Sulphur Springs, West Virginia. The match was played among Bobby, Dan Topping, and a certain Count Dorelis "who wore a monocle." The mark was Ray Ryan, a rich oilman from Evansville, Indiana. Ryan, a mediocre golfer, loved to bet high. Normally Ryan was coached by George Lowe, but Lowe wasn't available at the time and Ryan decided to chance it on his own. The match lasted for the better part of a week. Bobby gave Ryan a stroke a hole, two on the par fives, and sometimes two on the long par fours. "I started out playing for what I could afford to lose," said Bobby. "Now Ryan, he thought he could win. He thought he had a license to steal, a real bargain, but that week he went completely crazy and shot above his game. He was hitting the ball sideways he was so bad. He was pressing bets with both hands and by the time he got to the eighteenth tee the first day he was deep in the hole. I'll never forget. He pressed again on that hole and by three-putting he lost one hundred thousand right there. Boy, they were big times. At the end of that week he owed something like five hundred thousand dollars. Now, you bleed a lot of rich guys and you oughta hear 'em squawk, like they'd been stabbed for crissakes. But not Ryan. The next day he asked us boys to stop by his suite. We arrived and he was sitting behind a card table with a suitcase full of thousand-dollar bills. We lined up and he paid us off without flinching. With a smile. He was a great high roller. None better. All he said was: 'Boys, if I win tomorrow, I want to get paid in the same way.' Course, the following week, he got most of it back in gin.

"Let me tell ya. Listen. I love millionaires. I really do. Give me a millionaire every time. There were a lot of them around then. Beautiful, the salt of the earth. Wherever I went, they were lining up waiting for me. They loved playing with me. It was a challenge. They liked being taken by the best.

"But they worried too much about their money. You see, if you're betting all the time, everything is just another bet. You don't even think about the money after you've made the arrangements. You're used to it. And you're usually playing with people who have more money than you do. Now that's an advantage, because they're thinking about the money and they play six strokes worse than they usually do. I play better under pressure. I remember the bookies used to jump and cough and talk when I was teeing off, but it never bothered me. It's a question of confidence and concentration. When I'm playing for the money, the bottom line is that I'm practically deaf. I'm practically deaf anyway. And I was always a good manager. I knew how to make action and how to keep it going."

During those years Bobby rarely played a game on which there was not something riding. He still offered eccentric propositions to the innocents at the Tennis Center in New York and believed that he could still take on any pro, "if he was limited to one serve and I could use his alleys. That's the handicap. It's an even bet then . . . uh . . . plus two games a set." But tennis did not preoccupy him much. And despite the lamentations of his brother Dave, who continually referred to tales of Bobby's derring-do as "cheap mythology," Bobby tended to promote that image of himself. "Hustler is a term of endearment," he liked to say. "It's like being called an old pro. But I'm not some cheap nickel-'n-dime hustler. I got a million in the bank. A million, see, drawing interest."

Bobby insisted, however, that he was not making any bets on his current match, a fact that Dave, with mawkish pride, repeated endlessly. But his hustling image was so widespread that more than a few interested parties wanted to know which way he was going, so that they could put their money on the right side. "I'm not a tank man," Bobby yelled. "I don't take dives. And I'm no Joe Namath either. I can't give you any guarantees. If you want to bet, you bet at your own risk. I'm not going to bet on myself. There's enough at stake without it. If I lose, I'll feel bad enough. If I win, that's all I'll need. I'll either experience maximum satisfaction or maximum depression. The eyes and the ears of the world are on me. This match is unbelievable. I am the greatest money player in history. Margaret Court is the greatest women's tennis player of all time. It's a mystery match, the battle of the sexes, the match of the century. Gosh, wouldn't you go for that? It's beautiful. What a deal."

## IV

On Saturday, May 12, the day before the match, San Diego Country Estates seemed on the verge of some gigantic party. Throngs of reporters, photographers, agents and producers milled about the grounds. Electricians and carpenters made final adjustments to the stands, the center court and the public-address system. The cement court had been painted red and green the week before, making it slower. A bulldozer had leveled out a parking lot not far away and the single road of entry had only just been given its final coat of macadam. The country club had sponsored sporting events before and the bartender recalled how the two golf matches and the rodeo had been rained out. In the dining room the waitresses wore large paper emblems on their uniforms with the Virginia Slims slogan, YOU'VE COME A LONG WAY, BABY, in modish type. The emblem was printed under the likeness of a closely cropped, darkhaired flapper, who dangled a cigarette holder in one hand, while hitting a tennis ball behind her back with the other. And Bobby Riggs continued to give a kind of nonstop interview. Lounging in his room or eating in the dining room, he was besieged by endless interrogations. Often, while he was talking to the man from Boston, Milwaukee or Birmingham on the lobby telephone, other reporters would cluster round and copy down his monologues. And Bobby, anxious not to offend, raised his raspy voice another octave.

His monologues were always performances, routines—potted versions of which he would read next day in the daily papers. A simple question elicited floods of flashy answers, rhetorical replies. When interrupted, his raspy voice would rise in opposition or slide away into noisier non sequiturs. Despite his hysterical pronouncements he rarely uttered an outright lie; rather, they were a stream of brash exaggerations. His was the art of hyperbole; by exaggerating, he deceived. In Bobby's company one's sense of honesty and fair play became curiously elastic. He implied that directness, "the simple honest truth," was for dupes and dummies. The truth was an admission of defeat, something you said in the dark or when you were caught with your hand in the till. No, everything was "great" or "terrific" or, most elusive of all, everything was "beautiful." This happened most blatantly when Bobby spoke with reporters. On those occasions, he talked and talked, as though the sheer volume of words would somehow pin posterity to the floor—assuring him of not just a momentary win but an eternal victory that would be remembered, as he sometimes said, "for always and always."

"The reason why so many people are interested in this

match," he said, "is because it's an entertainment, it's a laugh. And that's what we need. The tennis players of both sexes today are boring. A yawn. The Seguras, the Gonzaleses, and, yeah, the Riggses—that's right—are gone. Tennis has been taken over by the serve and volley gang. The blockbusters. The mashers. Who wants to watch that sort of tennis? Not me. Everybody's forgotten that you can win and still entertain the crowd. They've forgotten what tennis used to be like. How terrific it was. I could tell you stories you wouldn't believe. Beautiful. Really beautiful."

Cast from the beginning in the role of arch male chauvinist pig, Bobby wisely decided to feed the fires. He had no real feelings on the matter, but the bandwagon was moving in the right direction and he went along for the ride. Anticipating his outbursts, Rosemary Casals and Billie Jean King had given Margaret Court a pair of earplugs to wear during the match.

"Women's tennis?" ranted Bobby. "Sure, I think it stinks. Sure, they hit the ball back and forth. They have a lot of nice volleys, I guess, and you can see some pretty legs. Sometimes. But it's night and day compared to men's tennis. Women play about twenty-five percent as good as men, so they should get about twenty-five percent of the money men get. I've been told there are about three billion people in the world, that's what I'm told, and fifty-two percent of them are women. Now that's an awful lot of women looking to Margaret to salvage their honor. Gosh, I wouldn't want that kind of heat on me. It's like I told Billie Jean, who's their real sex leader, incidentally, the real screamer. I told her women players are overrated and overpaid. Margaret will have to answer questions all over the country. How come she couldn't beat that horrible old man, they'll ask. And they'll want to know. She's the best of 'em, she's carrying the banner. And if I lose, so what? I played all my best tennis twenty-five years ago. The pressure on Margaret will be tremendous. She'll have that snarling pack of women-libbers at her heels saying, 'Please, please, don't let that cocky old pig beat you.' But she has a history of blowing the big ones and I'm at my best under stress and strain. Heck, at fifty-five, I'm a senior citizen. I can't see, I can't hear, I can hardly walk. She's the slugger, but I'm still the knockout artist. Gosh, I'm the Jane L. Sullivan of women's tennis."

That morning Margaret Court made her first appearance on the tennis court. She had arrived the night before with her husband Barry, and their fourteen-month-old son Daniel, who wore a large button on his shirt which said: "BOBBY RIGGS— *Bleah.*" Mrs. Court smiled as scattered applause broke out from the women in the press corps. She walked onto the court with Tony Trabert and began to warm up. For most of the session Trabert hit lobs and soft angled returns, attempting, as much as possible, to imitate Bobby's style of play. "Who's side are you on anyway?" shouted Bobby, who was watching from the stands.

Margaret Court was bigger than I had imagined her to be. At just under 5'10", she was more than two inches taller than Bobby and at about 140 pounds they weighed much the same. She possessed physical endowments not ordinarily associated with her sex. Besides those essential to tennis—swift reflexes, balance, speed, bounce and coordination—she had unusual strength and reach. According to the London Biomechanics Laboratory, which tested her, she exerts a force of one hundred twenty-one and one quarter pounds in her right hand, which equalled or exceeded that of most men taking part in the experiment. Her arms are about four inches longer than those of the average woman. The girls on the women's tour call her "the arm." She was a sprinter of Olympic caliber, but gave it up for tennis. The differences between the two players were amusingly ironic: Bobby played like a woman, Margaret like a man. Bobby, the male chauvinist manqué, Margaret, the unintended feminist, Bobby, physically soft and delicate, Margaret, manly, strong and silent, or, as a Chinese medical student once said of her at Wimbledon: "Look at those legs. The lady is a man."

After only a few minutes on court it was obvious that her ground strokes were strong and accurate and her fierce serve often sent Trabert lurching sideways to retrieve it. Bobby sat in the stands and watched. He appeared to be overwhelmed, claiming she had not looked that good in Richmond. "Did you see that forehand? Gosh. Look again. Gosh, I didn't know she could serve that strong. Look, can you believe that overhead? Boy."

"Come on, you hit them that hard, Bobby," said Lornie Kuhle.

"Yeah, but I can't bounce them into the stands. Maybe she's having an unusual day, huh? Look, look at that reach on her. Did you ever see anything like it? I won't have a prayer if she plays like this tomorrow. She's making Tony look like my father."

"Quit complaining, Bobby," a reporter said. "You're not going to get any bets here. Our money is down already."

An hour later she completed her practice and sat in the stands while Bobby played with Lornie Kuhle. She talked to her friends and seemed to pay scant attention to the court. But once, when Bobby served, she laughed pointedly at the weakness of the shot and at the comical way he scuttled about the court. Between shots Bobby continued to talk to anyone within earshot. At one point, when Tony Trabert walked into the stands, Margaret said to him, "Can't you do anything about the loudmouth?"

Trabert smiled. "Not unless I can make you deaf," he said.

Margaret laughed. She seemed relaxed and confident and if Bobby's pathetic play continued, she had every reason for remaining so. "Bobby doesn't worry me too much," she said. "There is no way to psych me out. I've been through all this before. He can't get up to too much mischief. He can't make a fool out of me without making a fool of himself. But maybe that's the idea."

In spite of her outward calm, the idea caused Mrs. Court a certain discomfort. She knew she had been thrown up like a gladiator to Riggs and the crowd. In the beginning, she had agreed to play three sets of tennis, but found herself, she now discovered, in a game of musical chairs. It offended her. Looking at her was like watching a novelist taking part in a quiz show on television. It was Bobby, of course, who had manufactured the charade. It suited his style, it was his métier. Watching him practice or listening to his bubbling asides, there was no escaping the underlying boyishness of his behavior. At fifty-five, he was still Peck's Bad Boy of tennis and, apparently, preferred to be—the perennial schoolboy with all of the schoolboy's ebullient jargon. Life was "cute" or "neat" or "really fun" and his reactions to it were best expressed in terms of "gee" and "gosh" and "wow." Such exclamations were so much a part of his delivery that when he occasionally and unexpectedly went beyond the use of "heck" and "darn" and swore, he made the word sound obscene, as though he were putting it on with the boys behind the barn. Whenever Bobby talked of girls I thought of panty raids. His name (he is even listed in the telephone book as Bobby) only emphasized the point, smacking as it did of chumminess and schoolboy bonhomie. (America must be the only country in which grown men are called Buddy and Butch and Chuck and Bobby.) Thus all his boys-will-be-boys bravado seemed perfectly in character. The adolescent "I dare you" and "double-dare you" had merely been transformed into "I bet you." Bobby had grown older, that is to say he had aged (despite the tinted auburn hair falling boyishly over the brow), but his sentiments were much the same: "Bet you. I'll bet you a hundred. What a deal. Wow. I'll lay you odds of three-to-one. What'll the traffic bear? Gee, come on. You afraid? Bet you, bet you, bet you a hundred."

When the practice session was over, Margaret Court was asked if she would change her game plan should Riggs begin to make passing shots. She shrugged and said, "Lots of women have passed me and it didn't make me change."

"You mean you wouldn't change a losing game?" said Bobby, who had walked up behind her.

"I'll let you know when we play our match tomorrow," she replied.

"Listen, Margaret," said Bobby, becoming chummy and confidential, "why don't we just stay back on the baseline and have nice long rallies? We can have a lot of fun. We don't want to finish the match too fast."

Margaret smiled.

"Come on, Margaret. Just think of how many women are counting on you."

"Get off it, love," she said, and smiled again.

"Do you think Mother's Day is a definite advantage for you?" Bobby asked. Again she smiled. "It's not fair," shouted Bobby. "You only have one child and I'm the mother of six."

"You would agree that this is an important match," he said.

"No," she said. "I think Wimbledon is more important."

"Gosh, Margaret. I don't understand that. I really don't. This is the most important tennis match in a hundred and fifty years. It's the match of the century."

Bobby spent a few more minutes trying to seduce her game plan from her, trying to reverse the decision about the heavy balls and being generally light-hearted. Margaret remained aloof, poised, demure. And in the middle of one of Bobby's monologues she walked quietly away.

That night, over dinner, changing his glasses to read the day's late press reports and quibbling over the reporters' choice of adjectives or their predictions, he talked on. Interrupting, one of the reporters turned to him and asked if he believed in God. The rest of the company fell quiet. It was an important moment. Bobby, his mouth full of avocado, gulped, changed his glasses and looked thoughtfully into the middle distance. "I don't know," he finally said. "I don't know if there is Someone Up There, All-Seeing and All-Wise. I don't know if there is. I don't think we're supposed to know. But if there is, then He's gotta go for the dedicated guy, the guy that don't screw around or party with the girls or drink on the job. The guy in the know. It figures. Those are the odds. That's the way I see it, anyway.

"It may be a mismatch. I don't know. But if the first set is pretty close, say 3–3 or 4–4, and she isn't overpowering me, then I think I'll have the edge. The closer the match, the better chance I'll have. That's where the tension factor comes in." He smiled. "Whatever happens, boys, this match is good for tennis. The two greatest boons to modern tennis were Open Tennis in 1968 and now, in 1973, Sex Tennis. We're making history."

Walking back to his room after dinner, Bobby said he would have an early night. He wanted to think, he said, to go over his game plan for the next day. At his door he paused and looked out into the dark. "Whatever happens tomorrow," he said quietly, "I've loved the build-up to this, the fun, the publicity. I really had a swell time. It's been so much fun, I wish the match could be postponed, so we could go on like this for another six weeks. Heck, I really wish we could."

## V

The next day, Sunday, Mother's Day, was damp and muggy; it looked as though it would rain within the hour. And yet, on a day when the San Diego area was covered with fog and low cloud, when six miles away in Ramona motorists were turning on their headlights and windshield wipers, a few minutes before noon the sun eased through the clouds over San Diego Country Estates.

That morning Lornie Kuhle told Bobby he had had a dream in which he had seen Bobby win 6–2, 6–1. "It was very clear," he said.

"That *is* a dream," said Bobby. Nonetheless, Kuhle doubled his bets on the match and Bobby could not resist the omen either. "So I called this guy in New York and lay down a grand," he said. Privately, beyond the earshot of his brother, he admitted to having "a few more customers stashed away."

Bobby practiced twice that morning. Rheo Blair had traveled down the night before to prepare arcane solutions and a breakfast consisting of half an avocado with sour cream, a little blue cheese dressing, half a baked potato with two teaspoons of margarine and a handful of liver extract pills. By eleven o'clock the parking lot was nearly full. The stands, built to seat four thousand people, were crowded. Up at the clubhouse, the press scurried desultorily between the court and the pressroom bar, talking constantly of odds, percentages and fluctuating Vegas prices. The calls had gone out to Chicago, New York and points east for the morning line, but few bets were being taken. "There isn't a dime of Court money in town," lamented a local punter. "Never bet against Riggs in anything," advised Pancho Segura.

Practicing on the main court Margaret continued to look powerful, her serves and ground strokes booming across the net. On a lower court Bobby took his second practice with Lornie Kuhle. And continued to talk. "This is what she'll do, see. She won't go for the lob much, she'll go for the power. And the angles maybe. She'll try to run me down. Or run me over." While serving he would mutter, "I've got to give it the American twist. I don't care about depth. And it doesn't matter if she makes some good shots. I can make some good returns. This match is all about me. It's got nothing to do with her. I won't even have to practice my junk shots. They're on the tip of my tongue."

"I got a lot of money on you, fella," shouted a spectator. "You'd better win." Bobby paid no attention and continued to curse the heavy Wilson balls. "Christ, this ball feels like a shot-put." After a particularly bad serve he said, "My elbow's acting up again. I don't know what I'm going to do." Lornie Kuhle's fears were that Bobby would not be able to run. "Remember," he shouted, as Bobby tried to reverse direction, "you can't change direction while you're running. You gotta stop first." Sweating heavily, Bobby suddenly announced that he had had enough.

Walking back to his room, members of the passing crowd who recognized him offered their good wishes. Many of them wore buttons, all of them anti-Riggs. "We should have made up buttons going both ways and sold them at the gate," said Bobby. Teddy Tinling sashayed by in modish gear. "Are you gonna win, Bobby?" he asked, stroking his conical bald head. "I flew in from Tokyo for this match."

"It's a mortal lock," said Bobby, without enthusiasm.

"Crazy boy," said Tinling, putting a hand on Bobby's shoulder, "you crazy boy."

Now that it was nearly time to play Bobby appeared confident, though uneasily nervous. Like a little boy about to attend his first party he pleaded for final suggestions on what he should or should not do. It was difficult to tell whether this was part of his elaborate game; there was still no real way of knowing whether he was hustling, he was so insouciant about it. Essentially his game had not changed in forty years—all chat and strategy. "Let them make the mistakes," he said. "I'm nothing but a wall. The ball just bounces back and stays in play." Bobby was expected to employ guile and gamesmanship in the match —such as taking extra time between serves, tossing up the ball to serve and missing it, tying and retying his shoelaces or chattering to Margaret between court breaks. It had even occurred to me that he would appear on court in white baggy flannels, as he had done at Wimbledon in 1939. But he didn't want to talk about it. Whatever he thought moments before the match began, he had rehearsed it a thousand times. Only the game was important now. The game and the action—to be on center court again, shooting for the moon with both hands.

The crowd hummed with excitement in the heavy heat, waiting impatiently for the players to arrive. Finally they appeared from separate directions at the top of the stands—Margaret in bright yellow and green and Bobby in a light-blue jump suit, a bouquet of red roses in his hand. They descended slowly to the court to the wild applause of the crowd. At the net Bobby presented the roses to Margaret in honor of Mother's Day. Surprisingly poised, she curtsied. More applause. "Do you think these flowers will soften up Margaret a little?" he asked a television announcer. "Gee, I don't think so," he replied.

They began to warm up. For the first two minutes they felt one another out with long powerful ground strokes and powdery returns, Court wondering, perhaps, how easy it would be, Riggs how difficult. Midway through the brief three-minute warm-up, Court hit a solid winner and the crowd applauded enthusiastically. Bobby, walking cross-court to pick up a ball, seemed wholly self-absorbed. Because they were so intent, so serious, there was something ridiculous and rather obscene about the spindly old man and the lithe young woman confronting each other across a net—more of a stunt than a competition.

Practicing her serve, Court judged that she was hitting the ball only tolerably well. She anticipated trouble. Practice had been an effort and she felt she was pushing herself unnaturally. I've got to get up, she thought, I've got to get up. She was keenly aware that Bobby had built up the tension to a fantastic, almost lunatic pitch, so that later she would remember little more than the loud carnival atmosphere of the event, its cheap circus quality. Early that morning her son Daniel had thrown her favorite tennis shoes down the toilet and that, she thought, as she walked to the sidelines, had not helped much either.

Waiting for the spin of the racket, Bobby thought: She's a front-runner. She likes to break into the lead, so she can hit out and just keep rolling. I've got to come out with a real fast start. Shake her. He looked round at the crowd. I wonder if I've opened my big mouth once too often?

Margaret spun the racket. Bobby called smooth, the racket spun to the ground and was smooth. Bobby paused, then elected to serve. As the two players walked to their respective positions one felt the excitement rising like sap in the crowd. The tiny court seemed supercharged. Hunched over, at almost a forty-five-degree angle, about a foot outside the baseline, her left hand lightly holding the neck of her racket, Margaret waited for the serve. She had not liked being rushed through the warm-up, three minutes, God, and she had wanted to serve first. To make an impact and to make it now. Balancing on the balls of her feet, she wondered what the bloody man would do. He would try things, try all his tricks. She wished he would quit dallying and get on with his serve. Get on with it, man.

A slow starter, today of all days Bobby wanted to be loose.
The warm-up, he knew, could not have done her much good.
Thank God, I had two practices. At first he had considered
letting her have the serve, thinking it may have been a psycho-
logical advantage just to let her have her way. But if she were
nervous it would be better for him to serve first, then break her
before she could recover, hold his own serve again for a 3–0 lead
and, quite possibly, the first set. But I've got to get my goddamn
serve in first. He adjusted his glasses and clamped his white,
visored cap to his head.

Tossing the yellow ball lightly into the air Bobby waited
fractionally, his body already moving in, and, using the American twist, sliced it into her forehand. Margaret moved tentatively, almost awkwardly, into the alley and drove the ball
feebly into the net. 15–love. Bobby had expected more strength,
more assurance. Again he sliced wide, this time into her backhand, her good shot, and again she put it into the net. 30–love.
There was a low muttering in the crowd. Margaret moved back
to the baseline and waited, her crouch, this time, even lower and
more determined. Bobby served and the ball floated up across
the net, a watermelon ball. Taking two long strides in, Margaret
smashed the ball deep into the opposite corner for a clean
winner. 30–15. The crowd broke into relieved applause. Moving
back to serve, Bobby thought, where did that come from? I
haven't used that in twenty years. Again he sliced to her forehand, the ball bouncing crazily into the alley. She returned it
to his forehand. Bobby looped his return to her backhand and
moved into the net. The ball hit close to the baseline and lazily,
almost absentmindedly, she backhanded it into the net. 40–15.
The next point was much the same and Bobby had held his
opening serve. Riggs: 1–0.

Toweling off on the sidelines Bobby said, "A cheap first
game, Lornie. She wasn't ready. Gosh, she's more nervous than
I am. She's really tight." Margaret was bothered by the slow-
ness of the court. The balls didn't seem to bounce. It was
supposed to be cement and fast. Why was it only painted last

week? She walked out to the baseline to serve. Now. But her first serve did not go in. A good second serve and Bobby lobbed it into the sun. Moving back, her right arm pumping, she leaned back and smashed the ball into the net. Love–15. Again she served. Again Bobby lobbed. Not deep enough, however. Smashing again, she drove the ball into the net. Love–30. On the next point she hit out and the ball missed the baseline by a foot or two. She could not settle down. Again she missed her first service and the second was wide. Riggs: 2–0. Bobby walked back to serve. She's really nervous. I wonder why she won't lob with me, play pattycake until she loses her butterflies? Dumb. Just plain dumb.

At the end of that game Margaret wondered what would have happened if she had put that first, easy lob away. Things might have been different, more relaxed. But she knew she should not think that way. Loser's thoughts. At 15–love in the third game Bobby angled the ball toward the alley. Taking it on the volley after a good run she pushed it beyond him. The crowd cheered and Bobby saluted the shot by hitting his racket with the palm of his hand. 15–15. But she got only one more point in the game and Bobby went ahead 3–0. In the first three games he had lost only four points. How long has this been going on, he wondered. This isn't the world's champion, this is a park player and a nervous one at that. This lady is up in outer space. It's duck soup.

Between the third and fourth games Margaret felt that everything was going too quickly. She could not remember much about the first three games. On the sidelines Dennis Vandermeer urged her to serve, get to the net and volley—to use her power. Her husband smiled at her from the stands and she came out to serve, feeling more relaxed. Serving powerfully, she lost only a single point and held her serve to thunderous applause. Riggs: 3–1. The crowd was solidly behind her now. Now was the moment to get back into the match, she thought.

What the hell, thought Bobby, she's got to win her serve sometimes. I just got out of the pattern a little, that's all. As

though moved by some deep atavistic urge he drew the disap-
proval of the crowd around him like a blanket; he felt positively
inspired. He served. Margaret returned down the line and
Bobby angled a dink just over the net. Moving quickly cross-
court, Margaret angled a dink to the other side, but somehow
Bobby was there, and chipping into the corner out of Margaret's reach he won the point. 15–love. He had outmaneuvered
her. That was something he wasn't supposed to be able to do.
She grimaced and returned to the baseline. He'll have a heart
attack if he keeps this up much longer. But Bobby held his serve
to love. Riggs: 4–1. Margaret's confidence began to seep away.

On the sideline, Bobby appeared to be pleased and waved to
someone in the crowd. He was playing his air-tight game. She
would have to force him into error. He was not going to give
away anything. Or, at any rate, not for nothing. As Margaret
moved out into the sun to serve a spectator complained,
"Christ, he's forcing her into a game of patball."

Margaret looked hot and moody. To a certain extent she
always does, a deep look of sullenness on her handsome face.
So far there had been no loss of reflex or stamina in Bobby's
volley and it perplexed her. He barely seemed to move, somehow anticipating her returns. She was playing, she knew, his
game. Stepping into her shots he looped them back or teased
them delicately over the net. He was in complete control. In the
sixth game, a dazzling drop shot, Margaret's second double
fault, and a cross-court lob into the sun, which she only just got
her racket to, put Riggs ahead 5–1. He had won a love game
on Margaret's serve. She stood there, staring into the sky, then
repeatedly tapped her head with her racket, as though to clear
it of confusion.

In the seventh game, an attempted slice died on Bobby's
racket and fell to his feet. He looked down at the ball and
grinning kicked it away; the crowd laughed. He then served his
first double fault. "He's trying not to make it look so good,"
said a man next to me. Preparing to serve at deuce, Bobby
thought, if she serves first in the next set, she might gain a little

momentum. I can't afford it. He began to play what he would later call "a loose game," playing against the score. Tennis runs in streaks. She might as well win two or even three games in a row, but now, not in the next set. He eased up. It's a giveaway game, he thought, it doesn't count. Nonetheless it was a hard-fought game, which went to deuce twice. At advantage in, Bobby turned to the scoreboard, as though to make sure he was still that far ahead. But apparently he had lost his rhythm. Employing a good smash and two delicate drop volleys, Margaret broke serve for the first time to reach 5–2.

At the changeover she looked at her husband with a stolid, almost baffled expression. The game had not done much for her; she seemed somehow resigned. Barry shook his fist in encouragement. Up until now Margaret had remained in the back-court, imprisoned on the baseline by Bobby's deep lobs and long looping returns. In the eighth game he continued to keep her there and at 15–30 a weak backhand gave him two set points. A fine smash retrieved one of them. 30–40. But another accurate lob of Bobby's was driven into the net and Bobby took the first set 6–2. Margaret walked grimly off the court. Her handsome face showed strain, exasperation and the beginnings of defeat. Toweling off, she shook her head in disgust, then walked purposefully back on court. But Bobby stopped her, explaining that they had a minute-and-a-half break for a television commercial. "I feel really good now, Lornie," he said. "I'm really in stroke. I think it's all over." "Just watch it," said Lornie. "She's famous for coming from behind. If she beats her nerves, she's dangerous. Watch her carefully." In the crowd the odds changed from 7-to-5 to 2-to-1, but there were no takers now. The betting press was disconsolate, embarrassed by its own expertise.

Bobby opened the second set confidently and held serve. Riggs: 1–0. Margaret pounded the gut of her racket in an attempt to raise the level of her game. Serving powerfully, she held serve with ease. 1–1. "Do you think he'll throw the set and make a match of it?" someone said behind me. In the third game Bobby executed two great drop volleys, forcing Margaret to run from alley to alley in futile attempts to retrieve them. A beautiful lob made it 2–1. Serving again Margaret wavered. I'm not confident enough to go for the big point, she thought. My overheads are missing, not by inches, by yards. She tried to sweep such thoughts from her mind, but found it difficult. At love–15 in the fourth game she knew her serve was off and tried again to control it. She remembered that not long ago, in Boston, she had aced Billie Jean six times. But here everything slipped away so quickly. When one thing goes, everything goes. At 30–40 an excellent passing shot down the line on her first serve cost her the game. Riggs: 3–1.

Till now Bobby had rarely missed a shot, letting Margaret make the errors. He taunted her with sliced serves and high twists to her backhand, cunning volleys and always those eccentric, off-speed ground strokes. In the fifth game, leading 30–15, Bobby suddenly aced her twice in a row. Previously he had gone for the percentages on his first serve, keeping it soft and controlled. But now he decided to try a hard flat one. It was so clean and beautiful, he thought, that he tried another one, a cannonball to the back corner, which Margaret did not even move for. Both serves surprised her and cost her the game. Again this was something the book said he couldn't do. But Bobby was confident now and capable of anything. Riggs: 4–1.

On the sideline, sitting down, her racket held between her knees, Margaret realized those silly soft shots were ruining her rhythm. Even the girls on the tour hit harder than that, she thought. She found the chips and the high shots difficult, as well as the angled spins and chops. He keeps hitting the ball back soft and high or soft and low. I'm not used to the pace. Once or twice Margaret appeared to have slugged the ball, hoping it would come back harder, but each time, using careful chops and slices, he had managed to reduce its speed. He appeared to caress the ball, as though he were unwilling to hurt it in any way.

Returning to the court to serve, Margaret seemed hypnotized, at the mercy of Bobby's bidding. But there was also courage in her face; at least she had accepted the challenge and seen the damn thing through. She shrugged. Now, behind on her serve again, she found she could not concentrate. She began to hear noises from the crowd and the television booths. It was like a circus, she thought, a bloody carnival. She shook her head. He plays like this every day, betting on himself, showing off, talking to people in the stands. It's not serious. It's not real tennis. Blowing another easy overhead, she relinquished the game. Riggs led 5–1.

When the house falls in, Margaret tends to bite her nether lip and stands, arms akimbo, staring at the object of her displeasure. She did so now, waiting for Bobby to serve. Slowly she went into her crouch, determined to make the best of it. Bobby made seven errors in the seventh game. It was the hardest fought of the match, going to deuce five times. "I couldn't *give* her the game," Bobby said later. "She didn't want it." But she did. She tried hard in that last game, "hoping to extend it, just to show the people that I could play better, to have a chance to get another game or a couple of games." But she knew it was lost. On the second deuce one of Bobby's volleys hovered briefly on the net, and then, as the crowd held its breath, fell back on his side. He threw his hands in the air and the crowd tittered nervously. A Court error, however, brought it back to deuce and another gave him match point. Bobby adjusted his hat, bounced the ball several times and served, but a good return and his error brought it back to deuce. A Court drop volley gave her the advantage and for a moment it seemed as if she would rally and break his serve. But on the next serve, she hit the ball beyond the baseline to make it deuce again. A soft second serve was netted and it was match point for the second time. Now Bobby served, Margaret returned, Bobby looped the ball toward the baseline, as he had done all afternoon, and Margaret obstinately drove it out to end the match. The crowd clapped tentatively. Bobby, pushing the net down with one hand, hurdled over, and raising his hat, gently shook her by the hand.

The battle of the century had taken just fifty-seven minutes.

Margaret had made forty-two errors, twenty-one in each set; Bobby made only seventeen, seven of them in the final game. Margaret double faulted three times to Bobby's once, but only eighteen of her thirty-seven first serves had actually gone in. Against his soft serve alone, she had committed ten errors. That, more than anything else, she felt, had cost her the match. She had felt the loss of her big serve much more than Bobby's soft, slow pace and repertoire of lollipops. A few minutes after the game, John Wayne presented Bobby with two checks for $5,000 each.

At the press conference Bobby sat and drank ice water from a Wilson's tennis ball tin. "Six weeks of vitamin pills put me over the hump, see," he proclaimed. "I was ready and she was all in knots. I usually take four hundred and fifteen pills a day, but this morning I only had time to take two hundred and seven. Otherwise it might have ended sooner. I may even bring out a Bobby Riggs vitamin pill. Look what they've done for me. Taken ten years off my life. I may look fifty-five, but don't let that fool you.

"The question was not whether she was a better player, or whether she could beat me if she was in better shape, or if I was in better shape and younger, or whether she could beat me yesterday or last week or the day after tomorrow. The question was could she beat me today, this afternoon, on this court on Mother's Day. And she couldn't. I could see the pressure on her. She was trying to beat herself just as fast as she could. But it was really a false score. It wouldn't happen again. She didn't play well at all. If we kept playing she'd win half the time, maybe more. Gee, I don't know what her coach told her to do. She tried to make me run, to tire me out. Heck, that's no way to treat an old man. I can play fourteen sets a day.

"I know they advised her to come into the net more often, but she couldn't come in. Too many shots were dropping on the baseline. I was playing at about forty percent. At half-speed, nothing maximum. Heck, I was looking around for friendly faces in the crowd. That's how much I was concentrating. I didn't have to make a shot. Just place the ball. No sense using a dagger and fire till you see what you're up against. Today she couldn't hit her backside. Everyone makes the mistake of slugging it out with her. The girls see that big serve and volley game and they go out and try it themselves. Dumb. Why run when you can walk? I never show them any more than I have to. I've never tried to beat anyone bad. I try and win and usually not by very much. But I took no chances here. Has anyone said how good I was? No. Of course not. They say how bad Margaret was. Why is it that great tennis players keep on having bad days against me? It's happened all my life.

"I don't think Margaret had any practice for my kind of game. I played my bread-and-butter game. I played my usual municipal park tennis. All those women think they're men. Some of them might be smarter if they played like women—like I do. Another thing. She psyched herself out of the lighter balls. She heard that I wanted to use the lighter ball, so she opts for the heavy one. I wanted the heavier one all along. With the heavy ball she was hardly breaking an egg out there. And I can't break an egg anyhow. I turned her every which way but loose. I psyched her out of her socks. But I played according to the Queensberry rules. I didn't talk to her, I never even looked at her except when she was on court. I mean, the book on her said she had a tendency to choke. That's what it said in the book and that's what happened. She said the match didn't mean nothing. Why did the greatest woman player in the world choke over a little match like this? Slit her throat in front of a crowd? It was a classic case of El Choko."

## VI

The following day, claiming the match gave a poor impression of the difference between men's and women's tennis, Billie

Jean King issued her challenge to Bobby, though she had begun
to refer to him as Roberta. She stipulated that they play according to international men's rules, that is, three sets out of five.
"I feel I owe it to women's tennis," she said.

"I want to play her," shouted Bobby. "Serve her up. Heck,
she's the real sex leader, isn't she? She calls herself the old
lady. All right, the old lady can play the old man. I'll play
any of them—on cement, on marble, on grass or clay or
on roller skates, I don't care. But they've got to put up their
own dough this time. I'm not giving them any more free
shots.

"Let's keep this sex thing alive. I'm going to specialize in
women's tennis from now on. After all, I'm the women's
champion now. They should have a Bobby Riggs knockout
competition to find the logical representative to play me. I
want to join the Virginia Slims women's tour. I'm going to
send in my application right away. Everybody knows there's
no sex after fifty-five. So there's no reason why I shouldn't
be eligible. I'll claim sex discrimination if I'm turned
down."

The offers kept on pouring in, long after the press, the publi-
cists, the television crews and the crowds had dispersed—leaving San Diego Country Estates to the desert. Willie Mosconi
offered to play Bobby pool left-handed for ten thousand dollars;
a promoter offered substantial sums if Bobby would wrestle a
beauty queen on television and Amarillo Slim suggested a little
head-to-head no-limit poker. All of which Bobby declined. "I
don't play the other guy's game. That's dumb. I mean, that's
dumb. But I'll play any of them tennis. I'll play them all at once
and give them some very serious handicaps. Listen, all life's a
leverage play, a matter of position. If one guy has more
strength, more power, more savvy, he's gonna make his own
rules, 'cause he's got the leverage. That's right. It's as simple
as that." Bobby grinned. There  as no containing him now.
"I'm the tops," he said. "I sho  ed them I wasn't just some

cheap loudmouth. I showed them what an old man can do. Didn't I? Shut up or put up. And I put up. And that's why people like me."

And perhaps he was right. Bobby Riggs had risen from the dark side of the American dream. In a world of doubt and ambiguity, he had leaped from the dark and had somehow found the light. He was the hustler, the go-getter, the poor boy made good, a modern if somewhat tainted Horatio Alger. And he had performed his little miracles not in the back room behind closed doors—he was no fly-by-night performer, no thimblerigger—no, he had played out his hand before our very eyes, out there in the bright American sun. He had done it with a laugh and a line and a skippy step: a native son dealing for fame and fortune on native soil. It was the oldest hustle of them all, it was Walter Mitty all over again—brave words, heroic deeds, the *beau geste*. (George Plimpton has milked the same syndrome, though his humor is based on failure, whereas Bobby, if he is to continue to amuse, *must* succeed.) Fallen stars no longer amuse, as Bobby knew too well. Lose, just once, and he would be back in the dark again.

The last time I saw Bobby Riggs we walked out into the desert, those huge stone totems throwing grotesque shadows into the late afternoon, and he continued to talk. He couldn't stop now, that high rough voice of his rushing on and on, preaching, as his father must have preached, not of fire and brimstone, but of leverage plays and angles, of odds and deals and bottom lines, of percentages and propositions. There was more than a little of the evangelic zeal in him. He talked with the same concentrated passion, the same desire to convince and convert, trying desperately to describe that outer edge of reality where he had seen the golden fleece.

When it was dark he suddenly stopped. He looked utterly exhausted. He worked up a grin. And then, with the brusque modesty of a boy who has saved the day by scoring the winning goal, he said, "Oh heck, it was nothing, it doesn't really matter.

Let's go back to the bar and have a beer and some fun. I've been a good boy too long."

(NOTE: *On September 20, 1973, in a best-of-five-set challenge match for $100,000 each, Bobby Riggs was defeated by Billie Jean King in straight sets—6–4, 6–3, 6–3.*)

# Minnesota Fats

---

I myself have
accomplished nothing of excellence
except a remarkable and,
to some of my friends,
unaccountable expertness
in hitting empty ginger ale bottles
with small rocks at a distance
of thirty paces.

JAMES THURBER

---

## I

It was now nearly one in the morning and the old man, his cue clasped between his knees, sat by himself in the back room pretending that nothing had happened.

"Hey, Daddy," said the younger of the two men at the table, "change your mind and have another game. I'll spot you a ball and give you the break. A sawbuck a game. Whatta ya say? It's a steal." He looked at the other man and smiled.

The old man shook his broad bald head. Unscrewing his stick, he slid the two halves into their alligator case. He shook his head again.

Aiming, almost casually, the young man hit the cue ball; banking off two sides of the table, it returned to its original position driving the three ball into the corner pocket. He looked up, a grin on his face, and said, "Come on, Daddy. Tell ya what I'll do. I'll spot ya two." He held up two fingers. "Two balls.

79

How's that? It's a good price. You might even get some of your money back."

The old man stood up and tucked his cue case under his arm. He was 6′2″ and weighed about 200 pounds; there was something gentle, but ominous in his size. He looked at the young man. He had a way of looking at you as though he had never seen you before. "I ain't never played for favors nor for peanuts neither, boy," he said. "Not in sixty years. And I sure as hell ain't gonna start with you." He began to leave, but turned round. "And quit callin' me Daddy, y'hear? The name's Cokes, boy, *Mr.* Cokes."

Outside in the darkened main room, the old man said, "I shouldn't pay attention. It's not his fault. But there comes a time when you don't shoot as good as you did. Not even close. It hits you sudden like, you know? It's a hell of a thing." He looked into the darkened room—crowded with spectators watching the semi-finals of the one-pocket competition. A dry staccato clack of ivory balls filled the air. "Five years ago," he said, "I'd've robbed that boy blind."

Grandstands had been erected from floor to ceiling on three sides of the main room. The old man sat down on a seat nearest the floor. Opposite, in the center of the room, there were four pool tables. Over each table a large light was suspended; surrounded by rectangular sections of black cheesecloth, the light was directed to the green tables, throwing the rest of the room into heavy shadow. All the tables were in use and the players moved from light to shadow and back into the light again like insistent apparitions. "Look at 'em," he said, indicating the players with his cue case, "not one of 'em was alive when I started hustlin' pool."

His full name was Hubert Cokes; but in keeping with poolroom custom he tolerated the nickname of Daddy Warbucks—the character in "Little Orphan Annie," whom it was said he resembled. At seventy-six he no longer played as much pool as he used to, but he liked to come to the tournaments, particularly to this one at the Stardust Hotel in Las Vegas, to play and to back the occasional dark horse. Unlike most of the other players he did not have to play for a living. He had struck oil in Evansville in '39 and the wells had not yet run dry. Paulie Jansco, who ran the tournament, referred to Mr. Cokes as his "class entry."

On one side of the room a huge blackboard covered the wall, listing the names of the players and the latest results of the nearly completed competition. Running from floor to ceiling, the incongruous names might have been the bastard branch of some entangled family tree—Coslosky, Staton, Di Liberto, Spaeth, Murphy, Butera, Allen, Marino, Balsas, Evarlino, Cokes, Jones, and Florence. These, in fact, were the names of some of the best pool hustlers in the country. But only some of the best, since several of the more notorious players had failed to appear: Wimpy Lassiter was in Alaska at the home of a millionaire, where, for a fee of five hundred dollars a day and unlimited expenses, he had agreed to instruct the gentleman in some of the game's finer points. Irving Crane's eyes were no longer reliable. Eddie ("The Knoxville Bear") Taylor was just plain old and Minnesota Fats had declined to play, he said, "for fun and trophies with a bunch of third-rate Boy Scouts."

Daddy Warbucks sat in the bleachers and chuckled to himself. "That fat man," he said. "You couldn't give Fats enough morphine to get into the same poolroom with me until I got sick back in 1970. Course, my game fell down a rabbit hole then. And when it did Fats beat a path to my door. The reason he don't come to these tournaments anymore is that he don't know the caliber of the play, particularly among the younger players. A good hustler always wants to know your pedigree before he goes to bat."

In the center of the room the hustlers went about their chores. They chalked, leaned, aimed, shot, rose and moved round the tables with brash élan. Most of them had the misbegotten look of unsuccessful stick-up men—in the manner of the young Peter Lorre. Given the pomaded hair, the sleek and dated clothes, it was difficult to know whether they had made concerted efforts to appear well dressed or had simply grown disillusioned with fashion around 1955. There was a striking sameness in the seedy gathering, as though they had all come to audition for the same part.

Between matches, in the shadow of the sidelines, the hustlers stood round arguing, bragging and telling jokes or made side bets, criticisms and stubborn predictions. Cornbread Red would hamstring Handsome Danny; unless he were drunk, Fast Eddie would steal the tournament; Daddy Warbucks had been unlucky and was out of stroke; The Butcher would carve up The Kid and Weenie Beanie could break a leg and still beat Tuscaloosa Squirrelly. Round them gathered a rabble of girl-friends and hangers-on, backers, handicappers and buxom waitresses in black tights and frosted hair serving potato chips and beer. Low Down Dirty Red, a tall Negro in a shiny suit, took photographs with an old camera and attempted unsuccessfully to sell a small box, from which, if one inserted a dime, a hand sprang out, snatched the coin and vanished into the innards of the contraption.

On his way to a card game farther up the Strip, Pug Pearson stopped in to get up a game in the back room. A poker player, he had started life by hustling pool and harbored a certain nostalgia for the game. But he could not get the right match-ups. He stood on the sidelines, a straw hat tilted toward the back of his head, and bit at the end of his cigar.

"You gonna play some, Pug?" said Daddy Warbucks.

Pug laughed. "Hubert, these boys want too much," he said. "They want to play even with a part-time player like me. They want a free ride. Pool players don't have no class." Like many professional gamblers Pug looked down on pool hustlers. "We're a different class of people," he said. "Pool players are a bit short on brains and they don't have no management. No offense, Hubert. You ain't a common thief. But these guys. It's an economic thing. Look at 'em. They ain't never evolved from them nickel-a-game pool halls they came from. No class."

"Oh, I dunno, Pug," said Daddy Warbucks. "A pool player with any intelligence can make a world of money before he's well-known. Even today. When I was a kid, I used to average twenty dollars a day above expenses and that was better than fifty years ago. I remember I used to hustle a bunch of mutes in one town in Ohio around about 1915. I could speak that deaf 'n dumb lingo pretty good and at half-dollar nine ball, I could make thirty, forty dollars a day."

"No class," said Pug.

Behind Pug, Paulie Jansco stood at the large blackboard listing the latest scores. A large and sullen man, he had the look of an elderly heavyweight who had lost too many fights in his time. With his late brother George, Paulie had been responsible for the revival of pool in 1961 with his annual Hustler's Jamboree in Johnston City, Illinois. Today, however, Paulie feared that pool had fallen on evil days. His last tournament in Johnston City had been raided by federal police and more than a few of the boys had been temporarily detained on charges of illegal gambling. His contract with the Stardust had expired and Paulie was uncertain as to whether it was worth his while to renew it. He considered himself the patron of pool and tended to treat the hustlers as likable but wayward boys. In turn, the hustlers required his patronage. The finances of the average hustler were perilously close to the pawning of cues and overcoats and his forwarding address was usually that of his hometown poolroom. In spite of their brashness, they were the sort of men who instinctively gave assumed names and covered their faces when cameras were produced.

Although Paulie Jansco awarded trophies and cash prizes to the winners of the three classes of competition—nine ball, eight ball, and one pocket—the hustlers had not come to Vegas for trophies. It was the unofficial late afternoon and early morning action which had drawn most of them here. In pool there is one absolute—the cash. Everything else is a con. Hence the elaborate negotiations to lure opponents into what appear to be certainties. Hence the self-deprecation, the lush avowals of humility, the assertions of illness, the claims of age and over-work, of being out of stroke—hence all the Byzantine dodges that create what is called "the soft con." It is an old art, this conniver's art, the art of diplomacy and politics. In pool, the art lies in the hustler's ability to ease his opponent into some kind of conversational cul-de-sac, where, in accordance with the jargon, he will be "shot down."

Beyond the noise of the competition, outside in the lobby, the hustlers gathered to talk and to negotiate the terms of that evening's games. "Hustlers don't gamble, boy," said Daddy Warbucks. "Only suckers gamble. The odds have to be in the hustler's favor. Or he's got to think they are. Otherwise, he don't play."

"No class," said Pug.

When one hustler meets another, the conversation is meek and delicate and the meeting is always accidental. Thus, toward one o'clock in the morning, a short man in elevated shoes had just left the lobby lavatory when the elevator doors slid back to reveal a pallid man with a high red pompadour. They both carried cue cases under their arms.

"Well, look who's here. How you do, Red?"

"Oh, bearin' up, Shorty, bearin' up. All things considerin'. You?"

"Not too good. I lost myself fifteen hundred on them slot machines downstairs."

"You're just crazy, boy," said Daddy Warbucks, who was standing nearby. "My daddy, he always told me—'Anything that stands with its ass backed up against the wall and challenges the world, well, son, you just leave it be.' "

The other men laughed.

"That's nothin'," said Red. "I dropped eight thousand at craps last night."

"Yeah? I heard you won a bundle."

"I did. At roulette. But I blew that and more at craps."

"No kiddin'? Well, I'm glad to hear it ain't affectin' your pool none. I hear you're shootin' the eyes outta them balls."

"What? In these conditions? Not me. Man, these tables are like tombstones, got pockets like sewers. Can't play *marbles* in these conditions."

"That's funny," said Shorty. "They tell me you was lookin' for a little eight ball."

"Me?" Red shook his head. He took out a comb and ran it through his hair. "Not me. Ain't you heard? I've been sick. Real sick. A man-eatin' flu. Haven't played in a week. And even if I had, ain't no match for you. Not playin' even, anyhow."

"That's what I'm tryin' to tell ya, Red. I'm dead on my feet. I'm practically a zombie. I haven't been to bed in a week. I can't even remember where I'm stayin'."

"You shoot good with your eyes closed, Shorty."

"What about you? You took me to the cleaners last year when you had double pneumonia and were fit to die."

"I was lucky, Shorty, that's all. I had this fabulous doctor. In constant attendance. The little bald geezer. Remember? In that seersucker suit."

"I thought he was your backer."

"Nah. He just stood behind me in case I fell. I guess he's outta town this year. Man, I really need him too."

Shorty shook his head sympathetically. "Well, seein' how you're outta stroke 'n all," he said, "I'll give you the break. Hundred a game."

"Don't see how I can," said Red. "What with the flu and all. Runs right down my arm. Right along here. Can't even shake hands."

"And, uh, I'll spot you a ball."

Red shook his head. "You're tryin' to stick up a sick man, Shorty."

"Christ, you're a tight one, Red." Shorty turned to Daddy Warbucks. "Where's Fats?" he said. "Pity Fats ain't here. Fats could start up a conversation in an empty room."

Red laughed. "I wish he were here too. I sure do. I'd beat that fat man's ass from here to kingdom come."

"I thought you was sick?"

"I *am,*" said Red. "But just thinkin' of old Fatty warms my blood. Makes me feel one hundred percent real quick." He ran the comb through his hair again. "You say one ball *and* the break?"

"Fuck you," said Shorty.

"No class," said Pug.

Minnesota Fats was the favorite target of every hustler in the room. During the course of the tournament, mention of his name was guaranteed to produce jeers, snorts of derision and raucous laughter. The late Danny McGoorty, one of the best billiards players in the country, when he wasn't drinking, called Fats "a promotion man" and few hustlers would have disagreed. "When he gets on television," said McGoorty, "and says that he was the best, that everybody was afraid to play him, dozens of guys around the country jump out of their chairs and try to get to the toilet before they ruin the rug."

"Fatty wouldn't know the truth if it looked like a dragon," said Red.

"Maybe so," said Paulie Jansco, "but Fats is still the king of hustlers, no question. Him and that fat mouth of his have done more for pool than anything. And don't let these hustlers con you. A few of them can take Fats, sure, maybe more than a few, I dunno, but you've got to reckon him. Fatty is still a good pool player, but he's an even better talker."

Just before two o'clock in the morning, a small group of youths swaggered through the door. They were all dressed in a kind of West Coast Mod—flared trousers with cuffs, loose, balloon-sleeved shirts with long collars, knit sleeveless sweaters, Superstar shoes and two of them wore large floppy caps. Their leader, a man of about thirty, carried a cue case under his arm and looked round the room as if he expected an ovation.

"That's Ronnie Allen," said Daddy Warbucks, "or Fast Eddie as he calls himself. The man behind him is his stake horse. You won't ever see one without the other. Like Mutt and Jeff."

Fast Eddie had a glass of beer in his hand. He laughed a lot.

He treated the other hustlers with a kind of affectionate condescension. He had been eliminated from the nine-ball competition but still contested one pocket, his speciality. Around him
his friends negotiated terms and side bets with the handicappers. Fast Eddie stood there sipping beer, looking cocky and
disinterested. He was scheduled to play Weenie Beanie the
following day and one of the punters in the crowd wanted odds
of 8–to–5 on Weenie Beanie. Brushing aside his backer, Fast
Eddie intervened. He seemed angry and shouted at the man.
"You want eight-to-five? You crazy? That guy's a champ. He
damned near invented the game and you want odds? You're on
at even money, baby. That's the price."

The man shook his head. "I want eight-to-five," he said.

"Man, you crazy," said Fast Eddie. He walked away. To one
of his confederates he snapped, "Grab the dummy's money."
He laughed and, walking across to the bar, blew a kiss to a
blonde in the bleachers.

Fast Eddie ordered another beer. Freddie, his friend in the
floppy cap, took him by the arm and said, "Hey, Ronnie, guy
here wants to know why you're called Fast Eddie. Tell him,
Ronnie."

Fast Eddie laughed. "Shit," he said. "Thought everybody
knew that. I'm called Fast Eddie cause I shoot fast, talk fast,
and bet fast. Know what I mean? I'm the best one-pocket player
in this country. Bar none. I'm so good I can't even get a game
less'n I promise to give it away first. I'll play anybody for
anything. Long as it's for up-front cash."

"What about the Fat Man?"

"The Fat Man?" Fast Eddie laughed. He turned to the man
in the floppy cap. "Hey, Freddie, this cat's asking about some
dude called the Fat Man. Ever hear of a fat man?" Freddie
smiled and looked blank.

"I knew a fat man once," Fast Eddie said. "Played a little
pool and said he came from Minnesota. But that couldn't be,
'cause this fat man couldn't even spell Minnesota. This fat man
was gabby, real gabby, talk your ears off. Got a bit hot once

'cause I beat him in some movie. Said it was all wrong, said he'd never lost a cash match in his life. But I beat him in real life too. Beat him real bad. He won't come near me anymore. He won't even talk to me anymore. He's gotten so old and fat, he couldn't get closer'n three feet to the table anyway. Is that the same fat man you had in mind?"

Fast Eddie sipped his beer. "Hey," he said, "did that fat man ever tell you about the time he outdrew the Beatles? The time fifty thousand people came to see him play? No? That's what he told me. Did he ever tell you he was the best pool player in the world? He always tells me that. Don't he, Freddie? But he won't play. He sure as hell won't play. You'd think a man as fat as that would have a few guts inside him. You'd think so, wouldn't you? But it's nothing but air. Wind and air.

"They tell me he was good forty years ago. That's what they tell me. They tell me Jesse Owens was the fastest man alive, too. But, hey man, that dude was running in 1930. I wasn't even thought up in 1930." Freddie laughed. "Don't get me wrong. I always liked that fat man. He had a great sense of humor— when he wasn't losing. He never laughed a lot around me. Did he, Freddie?" Freddie shook his head.

"Hey, did he ever tell you about the time he won a quarter of a million dollars on one game? No? That's what he told me. I always liked that story."

Freddie laughed. Fast Eddie sipped his beer. "That fat man could really get it on," he said. "Woo—ee."

## II

The shot appeared to be impossible.

Telling a story of how he had once whacked out Zsa Zsa Gabor, the Fat Man circled the table chalking his cue. He talked loudly; he had the voice of a deaf man. Now and again he peered down at the pack of balls; interrupting himself, he explained to the crowd that the five ball, which appeared to be firmly lodged in the pack, would soon inhabit the corner pocket. The Fat Man was giving an exhibition of his skills to mark the opening of Gimbel's new department store in the Yorkville section of New York.

Leaning over the table, the Fat Man aimed and drove the cue ball toward the far rail. He continued to talk of Zsa Zsa Gabor. The cue ball sped down the bright green table; banking off the rail and swerving, it shot back up the table, skirting the pack to strike the near rail and bouncing back into the pack to nudge the five ball so that it rolled slowly but directly toward the corner pocket. When it fell the crowd applauded loudly. The Fat Man grinned and wiped his face with a handkerchief.

Turning round, he said to me in a vibrant undertone: "Listen to that. I've had ovations all my life. Ovations beyond compare. Most of them hustlers are nobodies. You could write their life stories on a match box. Most of them two-bit mooches don't even know the war's over. They don't even know they're alive. They couldn't beat nobody. And that Allen guy you mentioned that calls himself Fast Eddie? That guy I never heard of? That Allen couldn't beat a drum. He ain't never won enough to keep him in chewin' gum."

The crowd continued to applaud. The Fat Man stepped back to the table and began to demonstrate a series of intricate trick shots—hitting the ball on the wing, causing a ball to reverse direction unexpectedly or knocking five balls into separate pockets on the same shot. Like any conjurer, Fats worked economically and with almost glib assurance. That which to the crowd appeared impossible was mere routine to him.

Fats looked like a man more used to the confines of an easy chair than to strutting back and forth before a table. And yet, despite his bulk, he had the movements of a thin and nimble man; he was always in transit, forever en route. His heavily jowled face somehow emphasized his small, bright eyes, eyes which invited trust, and more, belief. He had the accomplished charm of an old successful trouper, but there was about the Fat Man a sense of lingering regret, as though certain of his youthful dreams had not come true.

When the exhibition ended, the kids swarmed round the table thrusting out programs and scraps of paper and shouting for autographs. Reaching into the jacket pocket of his beige silk suit, the Fat Man extracted an ink pad and a little silver stamp. He began stamping his signature—"Minnesota Fats"—on every paper and program in reach. "I've got sixty million fans in this country," he said. "I know, 'cause I've signed at least sixty million autographs."

The next day we flew to St. Louis, the nearest major airport to the Fat Man's home in Dowell, Illinois, some hundred miles to the southeast. He more than justified his name. Of average height, he weighed about 260 pounds. He required two adjoining seats for the flight and demanded that the stewardess produce an emergency belt extension to accommodate his fifty-one-inch waist. His right shoulder twitched continuously and he had a habit of wiping his forehead with his handkerchief. For the trip home he had changed into a silk suit of another color. His alligator cue case matched his alligator shoes. On his left hand he wore a ring of green diamonds—"a high-class ring, that's all"—and a silver diamond-studded watch, "which I beat a guy out of once."

Between snacks and constant Coca-Colas, he continued his rich harangue against his fellow hustlers. He talked swiftly, immoderately, in the way a hungry man eats. He wanted, he said, to relieve the public of wrong impressions. He did not want them nurturing misguided notions of the Fat Man's place in the nature of things.

"Why should I enter them tournaments?" he said. "I don't play for trophies. I don't play for bubble gum. If I want a trophy, I'll go out and buy one. It's ridiculous, ridiculous beyond compare, for them pool hustlers getting dressed up just because it's a tournament. Putting a tuxedo on a hustler is like putting whipped cream on a hot dog. You better believe it. What I tell you now, you could bet your life on.

"I've had the world by the nuts for fifty years and people are jealous of that sometimes. They all tell these elegant lies about me. Some of them hustlers are fabulous liars, really fabulous, when it comes to talkin' about who they beat and for how much cash. It's a congenital disease. Some of them guys would derange a lie detector, drive it stark raving mad. That Allen couldn't break an egg. I recently turned down a hundred and eighty thousand dollars for a ninety-minute special on television. What do I want to play Allen for six thousand for? Y'unnerstand?

"They all like to talk about me losin' all the time. That'll be the day. I can't give you any first-hand information on the subject, 'cause I ain't never had any experience in that line. Any information about losin' I give you would be outright lies, would be hearsay, just what I hear round and about. When I play pool, there's only one beneficiary." He paused and wiped his forehead. "I came close once," he said, and he closed his eyes, as though trying to recall some obscure childhood memory.

"I came close, I remember, about thirty years ago, yeah, about thirty years ago, I guess. I had to call on the patron saint of impossible propositions. I was even heavier than I am now. Must've weighed in around two seventy-five. I was *heavy*. I remember whenever I walked around that pool table, the floor took to creakin' and groanin' same as if it was haunted.

"Anyhow, to make a long story short, y'unnerstand, I am playin' banks with a guy called Lou Russo, a real good player outta Port Reading, New Jersey. We are playin' for some big money and the action finally winds down to this last shot. Everything in the world is ridin' on this shot. Russo's pretty confident, pretty cocky. He thinks he left me with nothin' to play with. He thinks he left me beat. I look over the situation and I see that there is just no way I'm not gonna sink that ball and take all of Russo's gold. I line up, say, 'One ball, cross-side,' let go, and whatta ya think happens? The floor falls in and I drop like a boulder. I am going right through the floor.

"Now, you can never trust them pool hustlers. Not even in

emergencies. Y'unnerstand? It's automatic. So, as I am goin' down, I look over the lip of the table and whatta ya think I see? I see that cue ball comin' off the rail like Citation on a good day, hit two cushions and then just nudge that one ball toward the appointed pocket. Like I knew it would. Some of my bank shots are so accurate they look like they're on automatic pilot. That's on the square. I probably fall ten, twelve feet, but right away I shout up I don't wanna hear no stories when I come up outta that cellar. And I don't get none. When I come up I collect the gold, and that's the closest I ever come to losin'. Some guys gotta tear the house down to try and stop the Fat Man."

In St. Louis at the airport garage, Fats introduced me to his car. MF 1, he explained, was a custom-built Fleetwood Cadillac costing $13,500. The interior was decorated in velvet. Fats claimed to own MF 1 through MF 9. Unlocking the trunk, he pointed out a few of the awards, trophies, citations, and plaques he had received over the years. There were also two pistols on the right-hand side—unlikely accessories, but Fats spluttered at my surprise. "Sure, I carry a gun," he said. "These days you need a gun in church. They've tried to heist me a dozen times."

The trunk of the Cadillac also contained four cue cases—in alligator, lizard, crocodile and python. He had, he said, shoes to match each case and his wife had shoes to match his own. But these were incidental bric-a-brac. Most of the trunk was filled with neat piles of personal newspaper and magazine clippings and a book or two, including his autobiography. The Fat Man never traveled without them, presumably in order to educate the ignorant along the way. "Take whatever you need," he said magnanimously. "I'll give you whatever you need and you can change 'em around as you please. Y'unnerstand? I've been tellin' the exact same stories for forty years. I never change a word. You don't have to talk to me and waste your time. I don't like wastin' time. I believe in killin' three, four birds with one stone."

The Fat Man seemed genuinely perplexed that I should wish to accompany him to Dowell. Indicating the trunk of MF 1, he seemed to say: but it's all here. I've already made my statement. It's right there in black and white. There's nothing more to say. I've said it all before. And to some extent he was right. In the course of the next few days, hearing his buoyant tales of his vagabond life was like listening to a man who had memorized long passages from some rags-to-riches melodrama. The Fat Man remembered too much and he remembered it too well.

Dowell is a town of about three hundred people in that part of southern Illinois called Little Egypt—where pyramid-shaped mounds of coal used to dot the countryside. The Fat Man has lived here since 1941. Dowell is a ramshackle town highlighted by the Kathleen Mine, formerly the largest strip-mine in the world, and now the site of an abandoned junkyard. The town contains a post office, two taverns, a bait shop, the dilapidated quarters of the local branch of the American Legion and the cheap and cheerless homes of its residents. Most of them are out-of-work miners, and those who are not unemployed have to drive nearly forty miles to the nearest mine. The land beneath Dowell is riddled with abandoned shafts and tunnels. "Everybody here is on relief," said Fats. "They wouldn't do nothin', these people, they wouldn't turn on the tap for you."

According to Fats the area had once been a popular gambling center, "Las Vegas without the ballyhoo," but obviously nothing happened now. The dominant noise was the shrill whistle of passing trains speeding west to St. Louis or north via Springfield to Chicago. "There used to be about eight hundred people here," said Fats, "but they've gone away. Everybody would've gone away if I hadn't stayed. I saved this cocksucker of a town. Could've bought the whole jurnt for three hundred dollars at one time."

When Fats was not away on business, selling personalized pool equipment or giving exhibitions, he liked to hibernate in Dowell with his wife Evelyn, which he pronounced Evaleen, and Orbie, his mother-in-law. Given the drabness of the town, the Fat Man's house announced itself like some loud and unexpected gaucherie; it was too obviously the seat of the resident potentate. Not that there was anything architecturally remarkable about the house; it was little more than an outsize tinder box, but it loomed over Dowell like an exclamation mark. There was only one approach—an unpaved, cratered road that skirted an empty field. "I stopped them from paving the roads," said Fats. "It'd be too easy for the tourists to find me then. Dowell was always a good place to lie around in and hide."

Inside there was an odd air of abandonment, as though the occupant had died some years before and everything had been left just as it was at the time. It was as sparse and tidy as a museum. The large main drawing room was dominated by four objects. A large color television, on which a bouquet of multicolored plastic flowers had been arranged, occupied one corner; a "Minnesota Fats" pool table commanded the center of the room like a shrine; and in the opposite corner were two giant refrigerators containing the Fat Man's chocolates and his ice cream. The Fat Man claimed to eat about a hundred dollars' worth of candy every day. "At one time," he said, "I could eat eight gallons of ice cream without batting an eye. But you cut down when you get older."

There were no books anywhere, a fact that called attention to itself because of the prominence given his autobiography. This book, *The Bank Shot and Other Great Robberies,* was mounted on a gilded easel on a corner table, like a small but rare incunabulum.

The Fat Man was proud of his possessions and insisted on showing me his vast collection of clothes. He was particularly pleased with his wardrobe of silk suits, the cheapest of which cost four hundred and fifty dollars. There were the dozens of Italian shirts at forty-five dollars apiece, the expensive slacks and overcoats, the python, lizard and crocodile shoes. He also displayed his wife's fur coats and evening gowns, ticking off the sums as he pulled them from the closet. Plainly, prosperity pleased him. Yet, whenever he referred to it, he spoke loudly and with a certain flimsy familiarity, as he might have referred to some celebrity, a starlet perhaps, to whom he had once been introduced but had never seen again.

Although he and his wife had no children, some forty vagrant cats and dogs lurked round the place. A tall bird house stood on the front lawn, which Fats called "a thirty-room hotel." But what kind of birds made use of it he could not say. "They're high-class birds, that's all. My animals live like the King and Queen of England. Every one of them." At the back of the house a small cement blockhouse had been converted into a communal dormitory. "Let me show you," said Fats with the air of a man who is about to give you a tour of the east wing. He threw back the door. "Look at that. A palace beyond compare, the lap of luxury. These cats and dogs play together. They even sleep together," a fact he explained by adding: "Animals surpass humans on all counts."

When the Fat Man first came to Little Egypt the area was fairly prosperous. It was here he met his wife, a waitress in one of the local eateries. Fats had been told that she was "about the best looker in the whole of Little Egypt" and two months after meeting they were married and settled down in Dowell. Before his marriage Fats had weighed about 260 pounds, but he soon shot above 280 and sported a waistline of fifty-five inches.

His obesity obsessed him. "It's no wonder I'm fat," he explained. "I eat enough for ten big eaters. I'm a world champion with a knife 'n fork, in the Olympic class. I can eat whole chickens and hams. I used to eat thirty quails at a time and when I was done with those birds there wasn't enough left for a ravenous dog. I'm the biggest eater the world has ever seen. I can still drink more Coca-Cola than any human alive. I remember oncet I was eatin' against this guy, a real big guy, must've weighed four hundred and fifty pounds, in an eatin' competition and before we got started I grab a ham when we sat down and swallow it whole. Told him I wouldn't count it, y'unnerstand? He takes one look, gulps, and quits right there.

"Right now I'm five eight or so and weigh about two forty. I useter be five ten, but I gained sixty or seventy pounds overnight and as I spread out I came down in height. For sixty years

I've eaten anything I felt like eatin' any time of the day and night I felt like eatin' and I ain't never been on any diet. I have a tremendous consumption rate, tremendous. I've ravaged tons of food in my time. Tons. I wouldn't know a calorie from a cantaloupe. I'm the only fat man in the history of the world who was completely perfect.

"I've always been eighty, a hundred pounds overweight. It don't mean nothin'. I remember about ten years ago in Hot Springs I had a physical check-up. That doctor couldn't believe his instruments. He was sure there were about a hundred and four things wrong with me, but when he put the joint on my heart, he was dumfounded. Dumbfounded, y'hear? 'My God,' he says, 'your heart sounds like a Rolls-Royce.' The same thing happened in Chicago. They called in a jillion doctors and they all stood around looking dumbfounded. I was checked outta this world twice and made medical history. Ain't never been nothin' wrong with me that a lot of food and sleep wouldn't cure."

The Fat Man was proud of the fact that he neither smoked nor drank. "Every livin' human is disturbed," he said. "Everybody who smokes and drinks is a disturbed person. A sucker needs them props. Not me."

The Fat Man liked to imply that he was perfect in every way. He spoke of it with perfect assurance, perfect certainty. Only his reputation seemed less perfect than it might have been, less generally upheld, and it nagged at him accordingly. He was the greatest money player in the world after all. That much was clear. Yet he was still set upon by lesser men—him, the Fat Man, subjected to scorn and snickering contempt by players he had murdered a million times before. News of each fresh insult struck him to the core. It was amazing, amazing beyond compare. He nursed his reputation like a sore tooth.

"I've been haunting poolrooms from here to Zanzibar for almost fifty years," he said in his autobiography. "I've played every game in the book and some fantastic propositions you wouldn't believe. I whacked out every top player in the game, including all those fun players who dress up in tuxedos and play in those big tournaments for trophies and four dollars in prizes. The only trouble with those fun players is that they wouldn't bet fat meat was greasy if they had to put up their own cash. They wouldn't play for a grape if they owned a vineyard. But I've beaten 'em all."

Given his favorite grievance, the Fat Man tended to become wild and voluble. He churned his chubby arms. His words multiplied like bacilli. "Some of those mooches developed serious inferiority complexes playin' with me," he shouted. "Not only did they have to have their bankers with 'em, but they had to have a doctor standin' by. Just in case they went weak in the knees and their eyes began to roll. You had to give them guys tranquilizers to get 'em into the same room with me. Foolin' with me is like catchin' a fatal disease.

"I've turned men gray before their time, put 'em in a state of permanent grief. I was a deadly killer. When it came to pool, Dillinger had nothin' on me. But there's nobody left now. Who's left? Nobody. All the great players have given up for lack of competition or they died. All you got left are those mooches at the tournaments. Most of 'em aren't even included in the census. Strictly speaking, they don't exist. They might as well be in Timbuctu.

"And they say they wanna play me? You don't catch me goin' for that kind of dodge. Not for a whole barrel of gold. I'm wise to their skulduggery. Me play them? The King don't socialize with the mob. They want the gold and the glory, the glory and the gold. If they beat each other, all they get is a little gold. But if they beat me, they get a ton of gold and all the glory. Me play them? For what? They might get lucky and the news'd be in Zanzibar and even Timbuctu. It happens. Automatic. I'm the champion of the earth."

## III

In a world of fat men obesity would not exist. There are no giants among giants. Thus, because the Fat Man's world was

so outlandish, he had come to see himself as its sole inhabitant
—a man who had inexplicably strayed into this altogether pint-
sized world and was forced to tiptoe cautiously lest he crush its
natives underfoot. So long as one was in his company he made
such things almost credible. He reminded me of Alice, who,
advised by the March Hare to say what she meant, replied: "I
do. At least—at least I mean what I say—that's the same thing
you know." Likewise the Fat Man meant what he said and to
hear him talk was to enter Wonderland. It was surprising, then,
to learn that he had been born in the more prosaic confines of
the Washington Heights section of New York—and admitted
as much.

He was born Rudolph Walter Wanderone, Jr., on January
19, 1913. His parents were Swiss immigrants—his mother from
Basle, one of eighteen children and a devout Catholic; his father
from Suhr, one of sixteen children, a huge man of 6'2" and 275
pounds. They, in turn, had four children of whom Roodly, as
he was called, was the only boy.

In the old country his father had been a mercenary, or as Fats
put it "a soldier of fortune," a man who "fought all over the
world on whatever side offered the best proposition and the
payoff was always in gold." America, however, where they had
come in the Nineties, was another proposition—neither so prosperous nor so transparently romantic. His mother worked in a
knitting mill for twenty cents a day and walked the six miles
to work and back. His father worked at what he could find—
as blacksmith, plumber or piledriver heaving a twenty-pound
sledge for twenty-five cents a day. But he hustled at other jobs
on the side and gambled more than was good for him. He liked
to play cards and taught his son poker and clabbiasch before
he was three.

Fats was born at 167th Street and Amsterdam Avenue in a
predominantly Swiss-German neighborhood. The six members
of his family lived in a three-room cold-water flat with a communal lavatory down the hall. At home they spoke Schweizer-
Deutsch, occasional French and English, though Fats remem-

bers nothing but English now—his accent a rough blend of the Bronx and Lower Broadway. His is the upstart voice of the Bowery Boys modified by the clipped and semi-literate accents of one of Runyon's characters.

Young Roodly's father was often out of work and it was from him that Fats acquired his guiding principle—to be happy, work must be avoided at any cost. His mother, however, believed that to be unemployed was merely to be idle, a sin against God. But his father's dictates prevailed and Fats grew up believing that to work was to back a bad proposition, resulting in unhappiness, anxiety, and an early grave.

The family moved around the Washington Heights area about once a year. Fats was transferred constantly to different schools. Always large for his age, he remembers having to whip the bully of each new neighborhood in order to be left alone. For a time he became involved in a protection racket, protecting, for payment, the weak boys from the strong. At home he was always "the boss" and his autobiography is full of references to himself as "the young Sultan, sprayed" by his sisters, "with exotic perfumes and lilac water." Despite what must have been a dark and difficult youth, the book is the account of a spoiled and coddled boy.

Roodly was introduced to his life's work at an early age. "About two or three times every summer," he said, "the poor from the neighborhood, mostly Swiss or German, useter get together and have picnics in the park at places like Royal Point in Jersey across the river. Each family brought eggs, deviled eggs, whatever was easy, or big salamis and other foods and got into the subway, the kids goin' for nothin', and we'd all gather in the park and eat and listen to the singin' and the yodelin' or take part in the contests and the races and the rides. There were these long tables and at the end of them were these huge barrels of beer. And we'd all sit and eat and drink. Now, after the food came the gamblin', sort of like bingo or raffle wheels. There were cards from one to forty and you'd go up and lay a nickel or a dime on one of those numbers and whatever number come up in the basket won. Now, I was always pretty lucky and I'd mooch dimes and nickels off of my relatives and lay 'em on the numbers. The prizes was always things like huge salamis or liverwursts or hams or turkeys.

"But the time I am talkin' about, there was this goose, a ganz, like we said in Swiss. Well, when I won it, my uncles started sayin' what a great dinner they were goin' to have and my dad, who felt like I do about animals, said, 'If anybody touches a feather of Roodly's ganz, I'll kill 'em.' Well, we took that ganz home and it became just like a member of the family. It was practically human and it followed me everywhere. The ganz also loved whiskey and wine and beer, but whiskey was its favorite and it got drunk a lot. When it was drunk it would waddle back and forth across the room. Now, they walk funny anyhow, ducks, but when they're paralyzed, they walk even funnier. That ganz loved its drink. You'd better believe it. It was always the life of the party.

"Anyhow, to make a long story short, y'unnerstand, that goose changed my life. One day, when I was about four, on one of those outings in the park I been tellin' you about, that goose darted into some pavilion in the amusement park, which had card tables and a few pool tables down at the end of the bar. I went right in after it, but when I saw them balls with all them colors, I forgot about everything else. It was amazing, absolutely amazing. You've never seen anything like it. I climbed right up on that table and began to push them balls around till the manager threw me out. But I came back and from then on out I practically lived in poolrooms. I began to shoot one-handed when I was four and by the time I was six I was playin' for medium stakes and could run a rack of balls. That's on the square. When I was ten I was playin' for the serious cash. I owe it all to that drunken ganz."

In 1923 Roodly was ten years old. He was 5'5" and weighed nearly 150 pounds. "I only had to wear long pants to get into most of the jurnts in the neighborhood," he said. "You could be a six-year-old dwarf and get into them saloons so long as you wore long pants. But I wasn't no dwarf. I was as big as a mansion. Everybody else thought I was about eighteen." He was supposed to be at school, of course, and he did attend P.S. 132 in his spare time. But he gave it up at the end of the eighth grade when he was, as he likes to put it, "a thirteen-year-old man."

"I was a man from the word go," he said. "I was born full grown and kept on growin'." He admits to a lack of running-around money, but he hustled for gumdrops and peanut brittle, for ice skates, for nickels and dimes. Occasionally professionals of the day would come up to Washington Heights and give exhibitions and Roodly went along to watch. Playing pool was all he wanted to do. His father preferred other professions for his son—wrestler, circus strong man—but Roodly was obstinate and held out for pool.

"The local jurnts useter be real elaborate," he recalled. "But they were locals, there weren't no stars. Mostly we played Balkline and three-cushion billiards. In my neighborhood there were at least three guys that could run one hundred balls without batting an eye, but they weren't stars. The stars were all downtown on Broadway.

"When I was a kid I lived in them sawdust saloons and ate all of them free lunches. I'd eat with both hands and take the rest home with me. I never had any ambitions at all. I was born in the environment, I just wanted the cash. When I was a kid I never believed any of that shit or any of them slogans about if you work hard and be good, you'll make a success of yourself. When you're poor you don't expect nothin' from life, and when you don't expect nothin' everything that happens is a picnic. Everything is a bonus for nothin'."

In 1926 Fats left home, taking the subway down to Broadway, where he had heard the action was. "Thanks to my old man," he wrote, "I was already wise to the propositions and gimmicks, but I got my postgraduate training on Broadway." At thirteen or fourteen, he was running around with the smartest proposition men of the day. He met Titanic Thompson,

Nick the Greek, Hubert Cokes and George the Greek, Arnold
Rothstein, George McManus, Nigger Nate Raymond and
Nicky Arnstein. "Those were the faculty deans of my Alma
Mater."

"Round about that time," said Fats, "I was in a lot of neighborhoods—Delancey Street in the Bowery, Park Row, 186th
Street and Broadway. There were dozens of neighborhoods and
a jillion poolrooms—McGirr's, Doyles, the Gaiety, the Strand,
the basement of Loew's State and Willie Hoppe's place above
Roseland. I went everywhere, but Broadway was my beat, from
Forty-second to Fifty-first Street."

On Broadway he listened to the gamblers cutting up jack-
pots, talking over their propositions, examining the angles and
he adopted the Broadway argot. "Broadway," he said, "was
like going to Harvard *and* Yale, only better, 'cause the academic standards were higher. The generals on Broadway knew
things them professors would never know. I never got any of
them magnas or cum lauds, but I studied under the Grand
Masters of the Game. They knew the ins and outs and the this
and that of all the propositions in the universe.

"I was what you call wise to the comings and goings, like a
good cop," he wrote. "If a cop is worth his nightstick he has
to be what they call street wise. He not only has to know the
area, but he has to know the situation. He has to know the
people and know what they're going to do before they do it. It
was the same thing in gambling. You have to know the situation, understand the proposition, so you will know what the
other guy is going to do and then beat him to it. That's why I
was always so cold-blooded when I took a proposition to the
pool table. I had already studied the situation from every side
and I knew I had the Hungarian nuts or I never would have
gone for it in the first place.

"I useter meet the gamblers in Lindy's or just outside of
Lindy's. Or it could be in Hector's Cafeteria. On Broadway in
the summer you saw 'em on the street. I knew every human
there, every type known to man—Ed Sullivan, Walter Win-

chell, Damon Runyon, that was their beat too. Little Miss
Marker and Benny the Book was all right there, all authentic,
though he might have changed their names. Runyon always
changed the names. He based the story of the eating contest on
me. That's what he said. But I never read that stuff."

In 1926 Fats believed Broadway to be the most exciting place
in the world, "a nonstop merry-go-round," and he spent most
of his time in Louis Kreuter's, the poolroom he came to call
"the center of the universe. All the stars were there," he said.
"That was their office. They had a fabulous Jewish restaurant
in it and everybody received their mail there. Damon Runyon
lived in the Forrest Hotel next door."

It was in Kreuter's that Fats met Ralph Greenleaf and the
other star players of the day. Despite his claims of beating them
regularly, it is more likely that he simply hung around the
poolroom and watched them play. He learned a little from each
of them and used his knowledge to earn his living by playing
marks—businessmen, out-of-work actors—playing under his
speed, losing a few games and then when the stakes were raised,
shooting them down. "I never believed in doing a lick," he said.
"I never even practiced, I just played.

"Double-Smart Fats is what they useter call me," he said.
"And later, after I broke all them other smarts, every human
useter call me Triple-Smart Fats or just plain Triple. I lived
high off the hog whether I was broke or not. I went first-class
and I mixed with all the sociables and the top top-drawers. Hell,
I needed a hundred dollars a day just to eat. I needed money.
Listen, I was driving Duesenbergs when Nick the Greek had
holes in his shoes."

As Fats tells it, he spent most of his fourteenth year hustling
pool throughout the Midwest. But he is vague on the matter.
He had an uncle in Iowa with whom he spent some time, but
after Broadway, it is difficult to imagine him traveling to Iowa
for fun, much less to further his pool education. But he is filled
with tales of high-rolling times in small Midwestern towns—
particularly how he learned one pocket in Oklahoma City

from the game's inventor, Jack Hill.

Jack Hill ran the billiards parlor in Huckin's Hotel in downtown Oklahoma City. One pocket is considered the supreme game of pool, a game of defense and strategy. Fats called it "the most elaborate, the most scientific pool game in the world." Fats spent six months in Oklahoma City, at the end of which time Jack Hill informed his pupil that he now played the game better than anyone in the world excepting himself and his protégé—one Hubert Cokes.

In 1928 Fats returned to New York. With his newly acquired knowledge, and the money he won at one pocket, he bought his first car, a blue Stutz Bearcat, and tooled up and down Broadway with a tomato at his side. "I was the Maharajah of the Great White Way," he recalled. "A high-class guy. When I talked, people listened. I talked good enough to get several nominations for the Academy Award," he said. "Several. I talked so good they wanted to put me in vaudeville. Top billing on a big stage. But it was a dead-end proposition. I already had top billing. I was the smartest guy on Broadway, twice as smart as the smartest mooch around. Bein' smart was always my strongest suit.

"My best shots were the bank and the kick-in," he said, "but every shot was my best shot when I was playin' for the gelt." He claims to have added a new dimension to the normally defensive game of one pocket by running out the balls first time around. "I banked them off two and three cushions and got so I could run out the first time I came to the table. Nobody could touch me. Some of those players developed rigor mortis just lookin' at me." Before long Fats could not get a game unless he gave outrageous odds—gave away the break or spotted a ball or two or agreed to play left-handed. "Jack Hill invented that great game," said Fats, "but I made it more beautiful than the Taj Mahal."

Fats lived in New York during the early days of the Depression and remembers the brokes lining up for soup and bread. Few businessmen came into Kreuter's anymore. Business, as they say, was slow. The whole town was in hock. Fats decided it was time to leave New York and in 1931 he headed for Chicago.

"Now in 1931 I leave New York like the Admiral of the Fleet," he recalled. "I'm decked out in the most fabulous clothes money could buy, I'm drivin' a beautiful big Cadillac, I've got one, maybe two of the most gorgeous tomatoes in the world with me and a roll the size of a pumpkin in my pocket. I'm ready for anything. No more splendid sight than Triple-Smart Fats was ever seen on the Seven Seas, not in the whole of history. It takes my breath away just to think about it."

Fats was eighteen and ready to take on the best players in the country. At that time the greatest tournament players were Ralph Greenleaf, Willie Mosconi, Jimmy Caras, Erwin Rudolph, Andrew Ponzi, and Irving Crane. "But none of 'em," said Fats, "except Rudolph and Ponzi would ever play for the cash. The greatest cash players were James Evans, Marcel Camp and me."

Curiously, Fats failed to mention his old friend Hubert Cokes. But Cokes remembered him. "In 1930," he said, "Fats was a nine-ball and lemon pool player. That means, find a sucker who had a million, convince him to back you and then when you play you get a bug in your eye, or something, and you help the sucker relieve himself of his money. That was Fats. He always had a bug in his eye in those days."

In Chicago he was known as New York Fats, a name he would keep for thirty years. That year in Chicago Fats won the single biggest money game of his life. He was playing at Augie Kieckhefer's poolroom on East Randolph Street and a match was arranged between himself and the then three-cushion billiards world champion—Arthur Thurnblad. It began as a fifty-point match for one hundred thousand dollars.

"He didn't have a bean," said Fats, "not a bean, but he was heavily backed and before the betting was through the stakes was raised to two hundred and fifty thousand. He always thought the match was for one hundred thousand though.

There was no point in excitin' him more than he already was. I laid my money out in cold cash, in one-thousand-dollar bills which I had in my coat pocket. The gelt was held by a bookie in a suitcase, y'unnerstand. Now, they figured they were onto a sure thing. I'm always hollerin' and screamin' about playin' high and they thought this was their big chance. My long suit was supposed to be pool, but my long suit was actually billiards. I had a pretty fair reputation as a pool player, but as a billiards player I was a total unknown. He was the world champion. He was an idol. All those great big generals out there wanted to play for as much money as I could find. And they were cocky. If Cassius Clay was to fight a total unknown, wouldn't you go out and bet on him? That's what it was like, the same thing, identical.

"We started about ten, eleven at night and the match lasted little over an hour. There were about a hundred people in the room, bookies, gamblers and gangsters and the top rounders of the world. Everybody was bettin' each other, no tellin' how much money changed hands in side bets, but most of 'em was bettin' against me. They were all bettin'. There were no stiffs in the jurnt that night. I started real good, which I don't usually, y'unnerstand. I got the lag, broke, and runnin' six, seven balls at a time, I had him beat by ten or fifteen points the whole time. You shoulda heard the bookies squawk. It was pitiful, pitiful. The final score was fifty to thirty-two. It was real brutal play. He never had a chance. There was just too much excitement for a fun player like that. It went to his head and paralyzed him. I was never excited. Excitement's for suckers. I never get excited. I just played the game. When it was over, I stood around and talked for a while, collected my money and went out and got something to eat. That's all there was to it."

By excitement, Fats meant fear. Fear was one of his specialities. Fats looked on fear as a disease, worse than any cancer: one he had never suffered himself, of course, but had often observed in the fevered eyes of his adversaries. In his autobiography he said: "When a mooch gets carried away, he starts thinking about the big steak he's going to put away that night and he even begins to contemplate a move to a better-class hotel. But then he considers the other side of the proposition —if he loses, he ends up sleeping in the park. And right there, the deadly fear takes over. You can always tell fear in a man's face, first in his eyes, then around his mouth when his lips start to tighten and dry. A man with a deadly fear has a face like a cash register."

"I never got excited," he said. "I never got emotionally involved over cash. I've lost fortunes at craps and the horses and I just go out and get something to eat, jump in my car and go away like nothin' ever happened. Just the same as if I won. It's automatic."

During the Thirties Fats played up and down the country. In such great pool towns as Chicago, Philadelphia, and Detroit, he played one pocket, three cushions, nine ball, banks, rotation and straight pool for days and nights on end. There was a regular circuit to which the hustlers generally adhered. In October they drove south to Miami for the remainder of the year. New Year's Eve would find them at Joe Brown's place in New Orleans, then on to Hot Springs, Arkansas. In the early spring they drifted down to Shreveport or Lafayette, to one or another of those Southern coastal towns before driving north again.

"I'd play anybody for money, marbles or chalk," said Fats, "and we had some brutal shootouts then, real brutal. In the olden days you never knew what kind of table you were going to get. You take Liberace, you put him in a bar jurnt, he ain't goin' to play like he had a thirty-thousand-dollar piano. It's the same with pool. So I had a lotta close shaves. Some of them tables were so uneven, it was worse'n playin' on a raft in a tidal wave." But Fats, according to Fats, continued to win. He made a lot of money, bought a lot of clothes and drove through the country's capitals in long low flashy cars. He recalled Pierce-Arrows and Packards and La Salles and Duesenbergs and Auburns with three tires on the side and fluted horns.

This despite the fact that the country was in the midst of the

Depression and pool itself was at its lowest ebb. The great days of pool had been the Twenties, the era of Ralph Greenleaf and Willie Hoppe. Fats likened the great pool halls of that time to palaces; the Recreation in Detroit, for example, had nearly one hundred and fifty tables and teams of golden girls racked the balls. The pool halls were always crowded. During the Depression they remained crowded—filled with the unemployed. "Pool Hall Burns Down—3,000 Men Homeless" was a common joke of the time. By 1940 the pool halls across the country were closing down and with the war professional pocket billiards nearly disappeared. There may have been a Depression, there may have been a war, but they were the Fat Man's salad days. He challenged everyone. Even Willie Mosconi, who had won the World Pocket Billiards Championship fourteen times, fell to the Fat Man. In an agitated voice Fats will tell you of the time he "gave the bum the bum's rush," causing Mosconi "automatic and total sorrow. Mosconi's probably the greatest tournament player there's ever been, next to Greenleaf," says Fats. "But when it came to playin' for the cash, you can't have two players of my class in the same class. I shut him off like he was a Victrola."

Ralph Greenleaf was the only player Fats ever spoke of with any real affection and with a certain awe, though even Greenleaf was not entirely excepted from his scorn. "He's been dead for forty years," said Fats. "Forty years. And the last nine of his life he couldn't beat a drum. You coulda put a ball on the beach at Atlantic City and he wouldn'ta been able to hit the ocean."

There is little point in enumerating the number of his victories over the great players of the time. Suffice it to say Fats never lost. Not sometimes, not rarely, never. And not only at pool. Trying, for the record, to recall his life and times precisely, he will admit to losing occasionally at craps, the horses, roulette —suckers' games requiring no post mortems. But at pool and at cards he was invincible.

"My card games were clabbiasch, stud, skin, pitch, coon-can

and gin," said Fats, "and I was fabulous at all of 'em. Most hustlers play both pool and cards, but generally a pool player's weakness is cards and a cardplayer's weakness is pool. Now with me that just ain't so. I'm known as the greatest short-card player on this whole entire earth. Ask old Titanic and Hubert Cokes. Once, out in Evansville, I ruptured them two. Put 'em both in the hospital."

During the Thirties and Forties Fats was at the top of his game and his stamina, he remembers, was the talk of the town. "My longest session with one man," he said, "was about a hundred and twenty straight hours back in the Thirties. I felt like I was wrapped inside of time. But I was used to it. A habit, y'unnerstand. I played a lot of guys for almost a week with no sleep. I missed so much sleep I could've kept coffee awake. Stayin' awake for days on end is a mortal cinch, a habit like anything else.

"I'm the greatest athlete the world has ever known. I can stay up for a week. I can do it today and I'm over sixty. You can take all those athletes like Jim Thorpe or any of 'em and put 'em all together and they couldn't stay with me for a week. Now, some of 'em can do it on pills, but after the third day they wouldn't recognize their wife if she walked into the room. I don't need pills. I only eat. And I've got all my facilities.

"Listen," he said. "You might not believe this, but it's on the square. I useter be known as the greatest outside man in the world. I remember once Nick the Greek and me went out to Las Vegas. El Rancho and the Last Frontier was the only two jurnts in town then. All the rest was sand. They offered me a job in a casino at seventy dollars a day. If I'd taken it I'd've been in with the people and probably owned a casino today. I'd of been a peer over anyone else on earth. I'd of perfected percentages. There I would've been, the top banana on this here earth, but I turned it down. And I was broke at the time—I had the shorts pretty bad. But I was also against work since I was born. I'm an outside man. I do what I want to do."

In 1941 Fats was married and more or less in residence in

Dowell, Illinois. Twenty-eight at the time, he somehow managed to avoid the war. "I wasn't drafted because I wasn't asked," he explained. During the first eighteen months of their marriage Fats and his wife remained in Dowell, but in 1942, seduced by tales of serious play in Norfolk, Virginia, he and Evelyn drove south, where they were to remain on and off for nearly six years.

"There wasn't anything extra special about Norfolk, Virginia during the war years," he said in his book. "It was like every other port city hit with an overnight boom and all the quick money that went with it, only Norfolk had a tremendous shipyard and Naval Base and when the shooting started in Europe and the Pacific, right away Norfolk was a round-the-clock proposition. The suckers came from all over to snatch the high-paying defense jobs and when it came time for recreation, they wanted to cut up worse than the Whoopee Set back in Prohibition. Norfolk back then was a lot like movies about wide-open towns during the Gold Rush and the Oil Boom days. It was exactly like that. It wasn't the suckers that attracted me to Norfolk. It was the high rollers. Every big action man in the country had converged on Norfolk and wagering was nonstop, unlimited and gargantuan beyond compare."

The action was what pool hustlers call a jamboree—a sort of high-roller's convention, which lasted throughout the war. Bucky Phair, who hustled pool in Norfolk, said, "You wouldn't believe it, so there's no use saying. The gamble was so big down there then that guys who never bet over ten bucks felt as though they had to bet a hundred so as not to be cheap."

The Fat Man claimed that he would have ended the war as a millionaire had it not been for his craving for craps. In the beginning it did not matter since it seemed the action would last forever. "Opportunity never knocked at my door," he said. "It kicked it down." But shortly after the war ended, through the efforts of Senator Estes Kefauver, much of the gambling, not only in Norfolk but throughout the country, was shut down and gradually the players went into an enforced retirement. By 1949 the action was at a standstill and wide-open gambling, Fats recalled, "was a basket case. After that you couldn't get a real smart roller to bet on a pool game any more than you could get the Daughters of the American Revolution to quit having tea parties." Fats and Evelyn returned to Dowell, where he suffered "almost a total eclipse. Big gambling," he said, "had been taken to the cleaners by the generals and would not be back again."

For the next ten years Fats did little but stay in and around Little Egypt. They were lean years for him and for pool. There were occasional jamborees in obscure Southern towns, but they were few and far between. Fats contented himself with his animals. Now and again a few of the boys would come to town to play pool at the St. Nicholas Hotel in nearby Du Quoin. Fats particularly remembered one of these occasions in early 1951.

It always began in the same way. A hustler wanted action; the calls went out round the country and within the week the hustlers had converged. It was just like old times. Daddy Warbucks drove over from Evansville, Weenie Beanie flew up from Virginia, Squirrel took the train from Tuscaloosa, and in no time at all there were fifteen hustlers living in the St. Nicholas Hotel. The hotel's owners dismantled the kitchen in order to turn it into a kind of private poolroom. After dinner they began to play. Having the advantage of home ground Fats reckoned himself an odds-on favorite. About three in the morning, he remembers, he was far ahead, when he turned from the pool table to see six masked men entering the room carrying Thompson submachine guns. "I'll never forget it," said Fats, "like it was yesterday."

Ordering the hustlers to remove their trousers and stand against the wall with their hands above their heads, the gunmen spread a blanket on the pool table. Daddy Warbucks' driver was so frightened he pissed in his trousers, greatly angering one of the hijackers when he came to collect them. "Fats," said Daddy Warbucks, "whined that he couldn't hold his hands over his head for long and promised to behave beautifully if he was allowed to sit down. He was told to stand as he was."

Fats did not remember that. He remembered only that one of the bandits recognized him and said: "Say, Fat Man, you've robbed a lot of people in your time, haven't you?"

"I've robbed 'em all," said Fats.

"In that case," said the bandit, "we won't take your dough. You're one of us."

"They took all the money they could find," said Daddy Warbucks. "Including Fats'. You should've heard him howl, but only after they left. A couple of schoolkids could've held that place up. Them heisters was plain unlucky. They only got five or six thousand. Any other night they would have had a sure twenty-five thousand. But they were lean times."

"When the gendarmes came," said Fats, "we all said, 'Oh, I lost ten or twenty. I was kinda short.' " Thirty minutes later they were all playing pool with markers.

The year 1961 was a turning point of sorts in American pool and many a fading hustler was given a new lease on life. Pool had been dormant for nearly twenty years and many hustlers had been forced into learning a trade and abandoning the game altogether. "The cash prizes and the side money were so small in those days," said Fats, "the players were going broke just catching the subway to the game. The game was stone cold dead. I mean dead enough to call in the embalmers."

But in 1961 the first Johnston City Hustler's Jamboree was staged by George and Paulie Jansco, who described themselves as "sportsmen and pool enthusiasts." They built a twenty-five-thousand-dollar structure to house the tournament and called it the Cue Club & Billiards Academy. The tournament was to be held for a three-week period each October. Johnston City is a town of less than four thousand people in the coal country of southern Illinois, some sixty miles from the Fat Man's front door. "Johnston City's so small," said Fats, "I could show you where it is and even then you couldn't find it."

The Janscos replaced the traditional rotation and straight pool with the hustlers' favorite game—one pocket.

"One pocket is the game that kept pool alive," said Fats. "It was about time somebody shot down straight pool. Straight pool was about as obsolete as washing clothes on a rock in the river. When they quit crankin' automobiles they should've quit playin' straight pool. But they didn't. There's still a dozen jack-offs tryin' to keep it alive. They had a straight pool tournament in California recently and they couldn't draw flies—nobody. Straight pool's pitiful, pitiful, a joke. Playin' straight pool and expectin' people to come is like openin' a lipstick factory in the middle of the Belgian Congo. Who would you expect to come?"

At that first tournament in 1961 only fourteen players appeared—Eddie Taylor, Jersey Red, Tugboat Whaley, Iron Joe, Cowboy Jimmy, Atlantic City Red, Connecticut Johnny, Boston Shorty, Daddy Warbucks, Weenie Beanie, Johnny Irish, Handsome Danny Jones, Tuscaloosa Squirrelly and Rudolph Wanderone, Jr., who was still known as New York Fats. Of the really serious and accomplished hustlers only Wimpy Lassiter and Irving Crane failed to appear. So it seemed the good old days had come to life again.

The top prize was five thousand dollars, but, as always, it was the side action the boys had come for. Fats declared himself an early favorite, but he was eliminated from the tournament by Daddy Warbucks, the man he had "ruptured" so many times before. The other hustlers needled Fats, saying that he was washed up, that he should seriously consider taking up a game he could actually play. In a high-stake one-pocket match, Handsome Danny Jones, backed by Daddy Warbucks, beat the Fat Man decisively. The Fat Man raged. The hustlers smiled, making wry and sympathetic noises.

The Fat Man was only forty-eight, but the long interlude at home with his cats and dogs had done little to improve his game. He had lost his edge and admitted, hesitantly, that he might be past his prime. But five years later, when he came to write his autobiography, he claimed he had lost because there had not been enough money on the matches and he elevated his placing in the tournament from fourth to joint third.

He had not lost his tongue however; he continued to amuse reporters with florid tales and tart denunciations. "I've been buried alive for ten years, boys. It puts a man off his game. I'm playin' so bad I've forgotten how good I really am. Ten years ago I'da knocked you bums into the bleachers. I could still if I bothered to practice, but I'm a very lazy person."

When the competition ended Fats returned to Dowell like a man whom time had deprived of exhibiting his real superiority. Plump and pessimistic, he looked like a cherub who had been declared ineligible for higher orders.

Before the Johnston City tournament in 1961 the pool hustler was a man who preferred the relative obscurity of the underworld. To be in the limelight was tantamount to being arrested for vagrancy. On any traditional social scale the hustler occupied a station not far removed from that of the pimp or the pickpocket and so, for reasons of security, he tended to favor a strict and guarded anonymity. Such secrecy did not apply to the professional tournament players—the Greenleafs and Mosconis, "the fun players," who, according to Fats, "came on like they'd sung in the school choir and had been raised in the YMCA." They were billiards players, the aristocrats of the game. The pool players, on the other hand, made no assertions of aristocracy. They would not have admitted their pseudonyms; they were the sort of men who lurked in the lobbies of bus depots when they could not afford a rented room. The Johnston City tournament helped to alter their position—the tournament and a film, released earlier that year, called *The Hustler.*

*The Hustler* was the first film to portray something of the circumstances and the character of the professional pool hustler, scuffling cross-country in pursuit of the big score. The film's main dramatic focus centered on the confrontation between a young, ambitious hustler called Fast Eddie and an old master called Minnesota Fats. Fats, as played by Jackie Gleason, was well-fed, well-heeled, well-spoken, and, presumably, the finest pool player in America.

Toward the end of 1961 New York Fats, who rarely saw a film, sat through *The Hustler* and promptly threatened to sue its makers and one Walter Tevis, on whose novel the film had been based. The Fat Man was appalled. The film, he claimed, not only plagiarized certain episodes of his life and stole his thunder, but it actually showed him losing a marathon match to a nobody—he, the Fat Man, who had never lost a cash match in his life. It was a public insult. It was defamation of character. The Fat Man breathed fire.

In turn Walter Tevis threatened to sue Fats. "I wrote the book while I was working nights in a poolroom and going to school to get my degree," he said. "I completely invented the character of Minnesota Fats. He doesn't exist. I resent anyone capitalizing on my imagination. I once heard of a second-rate pool hustler named New York Fats," he added, "but I never saw him play."

Fats fumed but did not sue. But a curious phenomenon occurred, a mysterious identity transfer. People actually began calling him Minnesota Fats; people in the street, complete strangers, began telling him how much they had liked *his* film. Not through his own efforts, he claimed; no, this pseudonym was being thrust upon him by those who had seen the film and had recognized that cheap caricature of him. And because the film lifted the pool hustler to the level of folk hero, it also gave pool in general and Fats in particular a status he had not enjoyed before, a certain romantic notoriety.

But not according to Fats: "*The Hustler* didn't give me no lease on life," he said. "It made me familiar to housewives and children, y'unnerstand? It got me into the limelight. But I was already well known. It gave me sixty million fans when I would've had ten or fifteen million anyway. Respectable? It didn't make me respectable. I was born respectable. Listen, the lowest pool hustler in the business is four times more respectable than some of those humbugs in Washington."

Toward the end of 1961 the offers began to trickle in. Magazines and newspapers began to write about him; he began giving exhibitions and in 1964, at the age of fifty-one, he was offered and accepted his first job—he who had always prided himself on being strictly an outside man. He was to be vice-president of a billiards firm and explains his acceptance with a kind of puzzled innocence. "The only way anybody'd get me to work," he says, "was to make the hours from one to two with an hour off for lunch. They did and they laid this company on me and made me a general. I couldn't get out of it, y'unnerstand? But they knew what they were doin'. I jived up this game of pool. I draw the crowds. Them other mooches couldn't draw nothin', they couldn't draw breath. I've drawn bigger crowds than the Beatles ever did. Pool's a fabulous environment now."

Thus he started work with Rozel Industries, a company that markets an extensive line of billiards accessories. "I've got billiards factories in Chicago, St. Louis, Taiwan, Hong Kong, and Tokyo. All over the world," he said, waving his arms. "And I never had a gray hair in my head till I went to work. It's pitiful, pitiful."

There were additional perks. During the late 1960s, he had two television shows—*Minnesota Fats Hustles the Pros* and *Minnesota Fats Hustles the Stars*. Most of his old pool cronies appeared on the former and such stars as Zsa Zsa Gabor and James Garner competed against him on the latter. Fats turned hustling into an industry. He even acquired his first Social Security card in the name of "Minnesota Fats." Brandishing the card, Fats declared he now existed—officially.

For the next few years his work occupied most of his time —to such a degree that he had few opportunities for any serious pool. Not that it mattered; there was no money in the game anymore. It had become respectable. It was riddled with fun players, tuxedo and trophy players. Even so the Fat Man was lured back one final time—to Jansco's tournament at the Stardust Hotel in Las Vegas in 1968. The tournament was nearly over; all the hustlers were there and when the Fat Man walked in the door the catcalls began to rise and burst like little explosions throughout the room.

"Well, look boys, it's the old Fat Man," said Weenie Beanie. "I thought they'd given you a life sentence, Fats. Put you out to pasture."

"Not Fatty," said Boston Shorty. "Didn't you know? Fatty's taken over the world. He's one of them executives, a tycoon or something. Fatty's a busy man, ain't you, Fatty?"

The other hustlers laughed. The Fat Man grinned, laying down his crocodile cue case. He was wearing one of his loose silk suits and crocodile shoes.

"You wanna play some pool, Fatty?" said Boston Shorty. "Is that why you come out here?"

"Sure, I wanna play, squirt. But I wanna play for cash. I didn't come all the way to Vegas to gawk at chorus girls. Not at my age."

"Okay. Spot me two balls and I'll play you three outta five for a grand. Okay?"

"Listen," said Fats, "I was fixin' propositions before you could add. You don't wanna play. You wanna free ride. Only you're on the wrong train. Show some respect for your elders, sonny boy."

"You're sure old, Fat Man. What happens to old pool players, anyway?"

"They die," said Fats.

The Fat Man walked over to the table and picked up the eight ball. "Listen, boys, I've come to shoot some pool." He looked around. "You shoot pool here?"

"Quit talking like you were in the movies, Fats," said Weenie Beanie. "This isn't some cheap flick. What makes you think we want to play with a has-been, anyway? Everybody knows you haven't shot any decent pool since the war. Before that maybe. This isn't the movies, Fats."

"Weenie Beanie, I know that," said Fats, "and I'll tell you what I'll do. You're supposed to be a smart man, so I won't have to tell you more than twice. I wanna play some pool. I'll play you for anything you can afford. But the gold has got to be up front. I only play for the up-front gold."

A tall handsome man in his early forties, Weenie Beanie's real name is Bill Staton. His nickname sprang from a series of Weenie Beanie Drive-Ins he owned in Washington, D.C. He considered himself a cut above the hustling classes and dressed accordingly—in the flashy garb of the Florida country clubs. "I'm no hustler," he liked to say. "I'm an educated man. I graduated from North Carolina. Choo-Choo Charlie Justice was my fraternity brother." But he had come from the poolroom, a fact he now preferred to conceal. And he worried lest the "exclusive Virginia country club" he had joined or his children discover his real diversions. Weenie Beanie stood there in his white suit and white shoes scrutinizing the Fat Man, as though trying to decide if he was as much of a has-been as rumor believed him to be.

"I'll tell you what, Fats," he said finally. "I'll play you one game of one pocket for five hundred. Just one. I mean, you're old and it's late and that seems fair. One game and we go home. Okay?" Weenie Beanie grinned. "I'd spot you a ball but I don't want to offend you. So we'll play even. Okay?"

"Rack 'em," said Fats. He pulled his cue case open, screwing the two halves of his Rambeau together. "You just bought me another suit, Weenie Beanie. I think I'll get me one in beige this time, with a special soft silk lining maybe. Yeah, I think it'll be beige."

"You're really putting on weight, Fats. I could buy two suits for that kind of money."

"Cheapskate," said Fats.

"Hey, Fatty," shouted Handsome Danny Jones, "I hear you're a big television star now. I hear you spend a lot of time with Zsa Zsa Gabor. Is that right, Fatty?" He winked at his friends. "Tell us the truth, Fatty."

"The truth?" yelled Fats, rubbing talcum powder onto his hands. "What would you bums do with the truth? You don't score no points for the truth in this game." He indicated the group of hustlers busily making side bets on the match. "You think these mooches is some sorta Boy Scouts?"

The Fat Man won the lag and prepared to shoot. The hustlers crowded round the table. "Back up, boys," said the Fat Man. "Give me some air. I can't shoot in a vacuum." The crowd moved back. Leaning over the table, the light catching the green diamond ring on his little finger, he stroked the ball gently down the length of the table so that it nudged the pack, pushing it fractionally to the left, rolled on and kissed the rail near the corner pocket, where it remained. The Fat Man swore and moved away from the table. "Amazing," he said, "absolutely amazing. It ain't possible to miss that shot." He glared at Paulie Jansco. "Turn off the fan, Paulie, it's blowin' my ball off course."

Weenie Beanie strode swiftly to the table, his left hand in his trouser pocket. "It's a shame you can't play as well as you talk, Fats," he said. The hustlers laughed. Weenie Beanie had no option but to make a safety, however. Sighting carefully, he hit the six ball at the corner of the pack; the two balls caromed off the rail and returned to the safety of the pack on the Fat Man's side. It was almost a perfect safety and would cause Fats trouble. Weenie Beanie strolled back to his stool, a tight smile on his face. The hustlers clapped desultorily.

The Fat Man walked to the table. He chalked his cue. He pulled a handkerchief from his pocket, dabbing his forehead almost daintily. "Your game's sure improved, Weenie," he said. "That's a shot in a hundred. It sure is. But Weenie, you're goin' to have to shoot a lot better'n that to beat Minnesota Fats. A lot better." He peered down at the table, looking carefully, as though he had lost his way.

"Fats, you ever been to Minnesota?" said Weenie Beanie. "You ever actually been there?"

"I colonized the place," said Fats, without looking up from the table. "I got a million fans in Minnesota alone."

He leaned suddenly over the table and struck the cue ball so that it almost hopped. Spinning round the seven ball down to the low rail, it swerved back up the table and buried itself in the pack on Weenie Beanie's side. The hustlers clapped and

Weenie Beanie tapped the floor with the butt of his stick. Fats had put him in a bad spot.

He sauntered to the table. "You sure left me a lot, Fats," he said. "You're a real mean player. What do you suggest I do with this?"

Fats smiled and said nothing. He sat on his stool drinking Coca-Cola from a paper cup. At the table Weenie Beanie examined his position. It was bad. There was little chance of making a safety and only the hint of a shot. He was in a tight spot and he knew it. On the sidelines the hustlers watched and waited. Weenie Beanie chalked his cue nervously, looking round the table for an opening. Leaning over he began to shoot, but straightened up and backed away. He approached the ball from a different angle. Sighting, Weenie Beanie banked it off the high rail; it skipped back into the pack and the two ball, as though pulled on a string, broke from the midst of the pack and ran smoothly into the corner pocket. Cheers split the silence; the crowd rose, applauding wildly. The Fat Man raised his paper cup. Weenie Beanie stood back from the table and grinned.

"That was some shot, Weenie Beanie," said Fats. "Got an encore?"

"Several. I got several, Fat Man."

He was now in a commanding position. But, despite the shot, there was little left for him on the table. There was a possible bank with the eleven ball and Weenie Beanie looked it over. It was a dangerous risk. If he missed it would leave the table open to the Fat Man, but he seemed to feel the risks were reasonable, that he was now in stroke, since he looked at it again, calculating the angles and where his cue ball would be when the eleven ball had dropped. Drop the eleven ball and the game was over. He leaned down. The hustlers fell quiet. The Fat Man stared impassively ahead. Weenie Beanie stroked two or three times and then drove the cue ball through the pack, slid it between the four and the eight to kick the eleven ball; caroming off the rail, it headed for the corner pocket. One or two of the hustlers rose to their feet and began to cheer, the Fat Man grimaced and looked down to the floor, and the eleven ball, hanging on the lip of the cup—remained there. The cheers were stifled and a gasp of disappointment burst from the crowd. Weenie Beanie shook his head and moved away.

The Fat Man got up from his stool and walked across to the table. Chalking his cue, he looked around the table. His right shoulder twitched constantly and he massaged it. He swiveled his head and wiped his face with his handkerchief again.

"Don't miss," said Weenie Beanie.

The Fat Man did not look up. "I ain't gonna miss," he said. "The Fat Man don't make mistakes." He turned round and looked at Weenie Beanie. "Only suckers make mistakes," he said.

There were one or two nervous laughs and the crowd fell quiet again. "Weenie Beanie," said the Fat Man, "you just weren't happy makin' all that money, were you? Three ball." The three ball shot into the Fat Man's pocket. "Tell you what I'm gonna do. They say you got eight of those hotdog stands up there in Washington. Nine ball. I want all eight of 'em. I figure there is one dingy old place up there that's all hot and greasy among 'em. Six ball. That's where I'll put you to work after I win 'em tonight. You'll be the short-order cook in the dingiest and dirtiest one of 'em all. On the midnight shift. Twelve ball. And after you've been workin' in there one night during the summer for about ten hours and figure it's time for you to go home for the night, I'm gonna come in and order two hundred and fifty fried eggs. Fried over light. Four ball. Yeah, two hundred and fifty of 'em. I'll say, I don't want nobody cookin' these eggs but Weenie Beanie himself, the egg-cookin' champion of the world. Fifteen ball. Then as you cook 'em, one by one, I'll eat all two hundred and fifty of 'em. One ball. And, my boy, I will then get up and walk out and not leave you one red cent tip. Seven ball." Stretching across the corner of the table, the Fat Man drove the winning ball into the corner pocket. "Not one red cent," he repeated. Looking up, he grinned and wiped his face with the handkerchief.

Slowly, almost reluctantly, came the lazy noise of polite applause. Weenie Beanie rose, pulled his roll from his pocket, stripped off five bills and handed them to the Fat Man. He smiled. "You're the goddamnedest Fat Man," he said.

"Yeah. Well, how'd ya make out against the Fat Man, Weenie Beanie?"

"Well, Fats," laughed Weenie Beanie, "I guess I came out second best."

Fats looked round the room. "Some of these hustlers ain't even that lucky," he said.

## IV

In one of his films, *A Night at the Opera* perhaps, Chico Marx played an improbable piano. Beginning on the lower keys, he performed a complicated run, sweeping rapidly up the piano, off, and running on, continued to play in mid-air. It was his speciality. Whenever the Fat Man spoke of his high-rolling days "in olden times," Chico's music came to mind. Like Chico, the Fat Man always went past the end—his recollections as improbable as music produced in thin air.

Even so the Fat Man inspired a kind of conditional belief. He *seemed* so sure. He gave an extraordinary impression of believing everything he said and assumed, of course, that you believed him too. The Fat Man spoke authoritatively—in headlines—and so he was able to convince without appearing contradictory.

Throughout his autobiography, for example, he claimed to be the most intelligent man he knew. "The more I hang around you pool hall imbeciles," he said, "the more I realize I am the most intelligent man I know. I could spot Einstein the ten ball. I know everything that everybody else knows and nobody knows what I know."

During my days in Little Egypt, he spent much of his time belittling his former colleagues. Pool, of course, produced his best harangues. "Stupid? Most of the hustlers I know would get lost in the Automat. I'd give some of those mooches a million dollars' wortha conversation and they'd understand less'n a nickel of it. When some of them bums locked horns with me they was never nothin' but natural-born losers. One of them high-class colleges shoulda given me a doctor's degree, 'cause I diagnosed them as sufferin' from incurable failure. It was pitiful, pitiful. When I played pool I was like a good psychiatrist. I cured 'em all of all their daydreams and delusions."

On my last night in Little Egypt, the Fat Man, his wife Evelyn, and I had dinner at the Perfection Club. The Perfection Club is on the main highway between Dowell and Du Quoin. Thirty years before Evelyn had worked here as a waitress. Here she had met and been wooed by Fats. The place held a special significance for both of them. It was the Fat Man's favorite eatery.

"The food here's better'n Toots Shor's," he said. "In every way. Sit down and have a couple of steaks. They're outta this world. You wouldn't believe it."

Everyone knew the Fat Man in the Perfection Club. During dinner the owner and passing guests stopped by his table and between mouthfuls of steak Fats acknowledged each of them with innocent vulgarities. In other parts of the room, those diners who did not know him personally looked furtively across, speaking in the hushed tones of those who unexpectedly find themselves in the presence of real celebrity. The Fat Man seemed not to notice. He was used to it after all and had often explained to me that he was something of a hero among the Little Egypt locals.

"It useter be that ten, fifteen people a day would come to my front door looking for handouts," he said. "I'd give 'em money and food and clothes, anything they wanted. A house burned down across the way the other day, everything in it. The family canvassed the town and collected about thirty dollars, twenty-six dollars, I dunno. I gave 'em a hundred. In cash. Just like that. I didn't even know 'em. Before that I'd taken 'em a pile of clothes, big as a store, boxes filled with shoes and dresses and coats and belts. You ain't never seen anything like it."

Cash was one of his favorite words. A sucker, he believed, was fundamentally a man without cash. "Cash never mattered to me," he said. "I could always get money when I was empty. In any town in the country. In the middle of the night. Then things were all right." Fats believed in cash and happy endings.

"All of them players had to scuffle at one time or another. Even Ty and Hubert. And we're all that's left from the old days —Hubert, Ty and me. I'm the only one who never had to work a day in his life. Not once. Work and I were never what you call close. Why, I'm the greatest hustler who ever lived on this whole entire earth." He ate another mouthful of steak. "Ain't that so, Evaleen?"

Evelyn nodded absentmindedly.

"Today, the word 'hustler' doesn't mean what it did in the olden days," he had written. "Today, if somebody says you're a hustler, right away everybody figures you robbed the suckers blind. Back in the olden days we called that kind of operator a shark, because back then a hustler was something altogether different. If somebody called you a hustler in the Twenties or Thirties, they meant it as a compliment. Mrs. O'Riley might say to Mrs. Murphy, 'Sure, Katie, that young, blue-eyed Joe O'Dowd, who married little Ruby Walsh, is a real hustler— why he's been working at the bank for only three years and already he's a cashier.' So Mrs. Murphy would say, 'Why, bless Patty, he is a real hustler.' That's exactly the kind of hustler I was, only instead of working in a bank, I worked the poolroom, and I ended up the cashier who took everybody's money."

"Listen," said Fats, "only a hustler gets hustled. You're not goin' to get anything from the Johnny Straight citizen, because he don't want nothin' from you. It's the greedy little guy who wants to get his hands on your boodle who's the easiest target for a hustle."

The Fat Man ate hurriedly and ordered another steak. Despite his many references to style and class, he had the manners of an esurient truckdriver. Between mouthfuls he made anxious trips to the kitchen to check that the meat he had ordered for his dogs was being properly prepared. Back at the table he continued to talk. Like most lonely men, the Fat Man's conversation rambled. While talking he tended to exclude his wife, who, in any event, seemed uninterested. Occasionally he turned to her for confirmation and she would nod in the manner of one who has heard the joke before.

"Hustlers are good for the economy," he said. "I don't know why people bother 'em. They're distributors. They keep the currency in circulation. They distribute other people's money around, which otherwise would be stone dead. They buy clothes and cars, live in hotels and whoop it up. Those multis, the suckers, they keep their money in a bank where it don't do no good. They don't spend. What good to anyone is a deadbeat sucker? Ninety-nine outta a hundred of 'em is lookin' for a bargain. Those multis will travel twenty miles to save six cents on a loaf of bread.

"You think them multis know how to live? Do you call that livin'? Everybody's got these definitions and things. It's a joke. It's pitiful. You call workin' twenty-four hours a day to make a million and then spend twenty years holdin' on to it livin'? That's for suckers. They're dead. Doornails. Livin' is eatin' and sleepin' and havin' fun. Enjoyin' yourself. What good's a million if you can't do that?

"I don't play no more. I wouldn't give a quarter to play for nothin'. When I played pool it was for five hundred, a thousand a pop and on up. Y'unnerstand? My long suit was gettin' the cash. Y'unnerstand what I'm talkin' about? I don't miss playin' pool. I don't miss nothin'. That pool table of mine at home could be there for four thousand years and I might not touch a ball. Like I told ya, I'm not a pool bug the way most of 'em are.

"I'm an entertainer. I can entertain everybody. Kids, their mothers and fathers, the police, an old people's home. Now Sinatra can't do that. Dean Martin can't do that. I jump generations.

"I ain't never regretted nothin' in my life. I always done what

I thought was right. I ain't got no skeletons in my closet. I don't owe nobody a match. I'm on the square. I could always sleep and eat real good and that's all I ever demanded outta life. I can do that without owning companies or winning championships. That don't mean nothin'. I live like the King of England anyway. Ain't that so, Evaleen?"

Evelyn nodded.

"Wantin' things outta life, those big plans, never entered my head. Never entered my mind, y'unnerstand? A beef tongue sandwich and a box of strawberry chocolates. I don't want nothin' else."

The Fat Man looked around the restaurant. "People round here," he said, "the generals, they asked me a million times to go into politics. I could be a senator tomorrow. Voted in in two minutes. Hell, the people love me. I'd give 'em something, not take it away. They want to change the name of the town, name it after me, but I don't want any of that. I wouldn't give a nickel for politics. Too much like work, y'unnerstand?"

Eating another mouthful of steak, he suddenly looked up, a fierce look on his face. "I'll tell you something you ain't never heard before," he said. "I'll tell you something no other livin' human could tell you. You can fool an awful lot of people, but you can't fool yourself. That's the nuts, the mortal cinch. I'm tellin' ya like it is, y'unnerstand? I'm in the clear. I ain't got no problems. I'm ten times purer than the Pope of Rome." A piece of steak fell from the corner of his mouth to the table. "Ten times, y'hear?" He wiped his mouth with his hand. "Ain't that right, Evaleen?"

Evelyn nodded.

The Fat Man said his wife understood him very well.

# Tim Holland

Money is like a sixth sense
without which
you cannot make a complete use
of the other five.

W. SOMERSET MAUGHAM

Tim Holland had laryngitis. He had it bad. Christ, he couldn't
even cough. From beneath the awning of Claridge's Hotel he
scowled at the bleak and ragged sky and lit a cigarette. Christ,
it was cold. In any other part of the world, he thought, it would
be just another fucking winter day, but here in London they had
the gall to call it April. Well, it had stopped raining anyway.
He looked at his watch. Turning up his jacket collar he left the
hotel and walked down the street into Berkeley Square. Suddenly it began to rain again. Christ, he thought, good bloody
Christ.

He began to run. Moments later he reached the Clermont
Club and hurried inside. He was out of breath. He should never
have given up golf, he thought, he should never have let it slip
away. It made him angry to think about it. The girl at the
reception desk smiled. "Good afternoon, Mr. Holland," she
said. He nodded wearily and signed his name in the register.
Brushing the rain from his jacket, he walked toward the club's
main ground floor room; already he could hear the loud garbled
whir of voices, the dry clack of shaken dice.

The club's annual spring backgammon tournament was in its

second day. The elegant Georgian room was crowded with players, their girlfriends and hangers-on, the attendant press. He stopped at the door and lit another cigarette; for the moment he didn't care if he never spoke again. He had come early this afternoon in order to play a quarter-final match and to see a reporter who had wangled an interview the day before. He ordered a cup of coffee and sat down in a corner of the room. Despite his lack of breath, he was at forty-three in relatively good condition. Tall and tanned, he had the slim and balanced build of an athlete. He might have passed for a businessman, a stockbroker perhaps, but there was something too contrived, too flamboyant in his dress for that. Sipping his coffee, he crossed his legs, smoothing the crease in the right trouser leg. He wore a dark-blue suit and a blue shirt—the TH monogram visible just below the heart—with a red tie. A red handkerchief mushroomed from his breast pocket. On the small finger of his left hand he wore a large gold and lapis ring and round his wrist a matching gold and lapis watch. He also wore dark glasses. There was about him an entrepreneurial air, the arrogant air of a man who controlled some dark and complicated enterprise.

He looked round the crowded room. Christ, he was bored. What's wrong with me, he thought. He was bored with crowds and backgammon. Sometimes it seemed so superfluous. Strange to think that it had been his chief obsession once. How many tournaments had he attended in the past fifteen years? A hundred? More? Through how many long nights had he played, in how many high-stake games? They were uncountable. How often had he seen these same players before? They were recognizable landmarks in an all too monotonous terrain. The women were different, the women changed, though they always *looked* the same—like plastic ornaments. He had seen them perched prettily behind the players' chairs in Biarritz and Monte Carlo, in Gstaad, in St. Moritz, Southampton, Palm Beach, Las Vegas, the Bahamas. Yes, they were always there, he thought, thrilling to the sound of the dice and the uninhibited play. But they interested him no longer. He had been playing too long at the top. He had worked hard at backgammon and had taken his share of its rewards. He had been world champion for three consecutive years. That was a record no one would equal in a hurry, he thought. But what else was there to achieve? The fun was gone. No, not entirely. The fun was still there, but the deep, competitive urge had gone, the desire to dominate. Besides backgammon was a business now and he had become one of its most successful executives. He had written a book on the subject for beginners; he had invented and marketed a game called Autobackgammon. At present, when he was not playing in tournaments, he toured the country promoting his products in department stores, lecturing at wealthy resorts and country clubs. He had even hired a public-relations man. Christ. He looked suddenly round the room with the air of one whose thoughts had been overheard.

A few minutes later his match was announced. His opponent was a young Englishman whom he had played before. Sitting down at the table he nodded but did not speak. His opponents rarely interested him. They were impediments, no more, obstacles to be removed as ruthlessly as possible. He had no real feelings on the matter. It was a job like any other, a means to an end. He ordered a drink and prepared to play.

As the game began a small crowd gathered round the table. He was unaware of them, playing fluently and with a kind of rapt indifference. He did not speak; he did not smile; his eyes rarely left the table. There was a palpable arrogance in his play. He rolled the dice and moved his men about the board with the poise of a man who knows that victory is only a matter of time. Less than an hour later he had won. Removing his dark glasses he seemed to notice his opponent for the first time and reached across the table to shake his hand. He felt no pity for his victim nor pleasure for himself. He felt empty. He wanted a drink. Perhaps a drink would soothe the irritation in his throat. He pushed through the crowd to the bar.

"Congratulations," someone said behind him. He turned around. It was the reporter and he wished now that he had not agreed to talk to him. The day before the reporter had referred to him as a gambler; but he was not a gambler and resented the name. He was, he believed, an expert at the art of winning games. Winning was his business. That's no more gambling, he thought, than a man who investigates the corporate structure of a business, satisfies himself as to its solidity, then buys ten thousand shares of the company stock. Is that gambling? But the reporter wouldn't understand. No, he did not much feel like talking. He wished he were home in New York. He wished he were in his bathrobe sitting in the den—beyond the reach of people and the telephone, watching baseball on television.

"I don't have much of a voice," he said.

"What was that?"

"I said I don't have much of a voice."

"Don't worry, it won't take long,"

"No, it won't," he said. "I don't have very much to say."

Talking to the reporter now he recalled the house in which he was born in the spring of 1931. The four-bedroom house in the borrowed Tudor style in the wealthy enclave of Rockville Centre on Long Island—then considered *the* place to live in that part of the island. His father was forty when he was born, his mother being some fifteen years younger; their only child, he was christened Simeon Harold Holland. From the beginning he despised his prissy Christian name and winces still when he hears it. His family was of that approximate rank known as upper middle class. "We lived like millionaires," he said. "Even if we weren't." There was usually a maid, a nurse, and a handyman in residence and the family ran at least two cars—a Chrysler Roadster, a La Salle perhaps, invariably a Buick. Until he was seven his parents also maintained a home in Fort Myers, Florida, where they preferred to spend their winters. It was a tranquil existence, undisturbed by the more mundane and presumably middle-class adversities. Money was treated neither with respect nor with disdain. It was unimportant and was never discussed within his hearing.

Money had never been an embarrassment. His mother was wealthy when she married. The role of housewife did not interest her and she decided to work while Tim was still a child. She opened up clothing shops in the Rockville Centre area, wrote several best-selling children's books and ultimately operated factories, manufacturing such goods as playpen toys and Button Dolls. Less versatile, his father worked as a public-relations executive for Buckeye Pipeline, a subsidiary of Standard Oil of New Jersey. He was the sort of man who rose at seven every morning, drove the car to the station, took the train to work, returned at four and drove to the Rockville Centre Country Club, where he played golf with the boys till dinner time.

His father loved all sports and games, and bridge was the first the young boy learned. At the age of eight, while his friends devoured Mickey Mouse and Superman, Tim was reading Ely Culbertson's *Contract Bridge Complete*. His parents normally played bridge two or three times a week and whenever they were unable to find a fourth the maid was dispatched upstairs to bring the sleeping child down. "I learned bridge by watching my parents play," he recalled. "It wasn't difficult. Sometimes I just sat on the staircase so that I could watch the game through the balustrade. Since my mother was the better player they had frequent arguments. One would refuse to play with the other and invariably I was sent for. I never learned to play poker; it was thought to be a game for the downstairs crowd. No, bridge was *the* card game and my mother always gave me my share of the winnings. Listen, my bridge earnings were more than my allowance. And it was easy money. I was being paid for something I found pleasurable. By the time I was eleven I was earning almost twenty dollars a week at the game."

In his youth his father had been a semi-professional boxer, basketball and baseball player, and he persuaded Tim that excellence in sports was one of the few really worthwhile aims in life. He spoke of sports as others might speak of literature or politics. In those pre-television days his father took him to Madison Square Garden, sometimes as often as three times a week, to any sporting event there. "When I was ten," he recalled, "I knew all the batting averages of all the batters and all the pitchers' records. I wasn't interested in anything else—unless it was another sport. By the time I got to high school I was good at every sport I played—baseball, basketball, football and golf. But I was best at golf, better by far than anyone I knew. My sole childhood ambition was to be the best golfer in the world."

The Rockville Links, then called the Rockville Country Club, was only a block from the Holland home and it was there that he first learned to play. His father and Joe Turnsea, the local pro, coached him constantly and, except during the baseball and basketball seasons, he was to be found on the course every day after school and every weekend. He was able to devote his entire summer to golf since, unlike most of his friends, he was not expected to work during the holidays. "When school was out I was a loner," he said. "I was the only golfer among my friends. Out of six hundred students at Southside High only two or three belonged to the club. I spent most of my time playing with the caddies for a quarter a hole." He never gambled at anything other than bridge or gin or golf during his high school years and only rarely for high stakes. "When I was fifteen I lost about six hundred dollars one afternoon at golf against a few of the older players and it took me two months of caddying to pay it off. It had a bad effect on me, but even then I knew the competition was something I really enjoyed. I knew the returns would be good, that it was a good investment. Money was important because it was a symbol of winning, but had the prizes been in yen, I wouldn't have cared. It was what hurt the *other* guy that counted."

For twenty years golf was to be his chief preoccupation. He won his first championship at the age of seven, a father-son tournament, and another with his mother in the same year. In high school he won the New York Scholastic and the Long Island area championships three years in a row. "I must've won thirty-five local tournaments before I left school. Until I was twenty and met Sam Snead, I thought I was the best golfer in the world. I thought I was invincible."

He had grown up idolizing Sam Snead. "The first book on golf I remember reading was Snead's *Winning Golf,* which he'd autographed for my father. I copied all of his mannerisms, how he addressed the ball, his grip, his walk, even his clothes. I was always a very loud dresser on the course, but when I saw that Snead tended to blacks and sedate grays I changed my ways. He had a terrific influence on me. He was the most beautiful golfer that ever lived."

In 1947 he decided to attend Lehigh University, but not for academic motives. Lehigh, in his view, had two strong attractions. It was not too far away—in Bethlehem, Pennsylvania— and it boasted one of America's great golf courses, the Saucon Valley Country Club. The club's pro, Ralph Hutchinson, attempted to help Tim with his game, with little or no success. "I thought he might help *a bit,*" he said, "but I thought I knew it all anyway. I was as cocky a kid as you'll ever see, but I was also good." He remained at Lehigh for only six months however. Later that year, in order to be closer to a girl, he transferred to Adelphi University. The following year, tiring presumably of both Adelphi and the girl, he transferred again— to the University of Miami in Coral Gables, Florida.

He arrived in Florida at eighteen, ostensibly to attend college, in reality to play golf. "Florida was great for golf. All the great American golfers came from the South, most of them from Texas or Florida. And I believed that I could be the best golfer in the country if I were not interrupted by such activities as school." His mother had seen that he received an allowance of a hundred dollars a week and a car. In his spare time he studied law, reserving his real affections for golf and gambling. "In college," he recalled, "life was beautiful. Golf opened the door to all walks of life. And it was an excellent way of making money. Why should I have studied in order to make two hundred a week one day when I could play golf and make more right away?

"The first person I met in Florida was Al Besselink. I was driving into Coral Gables and I passed a driving range and there was a crowd watching a tall blond man hitting the ball. It was Bess. I stopped the car and began to hit some balls myself. I suppose I must have taken some of the crowd away because he came over and introduced himself. When he discovered I was at the university he suggested on the spot that we become roommates, that I move in with him. I told him I already had a place. 'Okay,' he said, 'good. I'll move in with you.' And he did. That afternoon he got his car and his clothes and moved in." Besselink was the captain of the Miami golf team and when Tim arrived he had been at the university off and on for some six years. He was nearly ten years older and well known in amateur golfing circles. The two men roomed together for nearly three years—until Besselink turned pro.

They became friends, but from the beginning theirs was an erratic relationship. By nature a solitary man, Tim could not avoid being influenced by the older man's impetuous and more extroverted nature. Despite his abilities Besselink was the sort of man who was perpetually without; he took to borrowing Tim's clothes, his car, or lured him into foolhardy propositions for which Tim was expected to pay. During his junior year, for example, Bess suggested a golf match between themselves and two pros from Cincinnati who had come to town the day before. "It's a sure thing," Bess explained, "a dead cinch. I watched them play, they're terrible. And incidentally," he added, "we're playing for five hundred dollars. You'd better put it up, I'm a bit short. But don't worry, it's a good investment." Reluctantly Tim agreed. He had made these sorts of investments before with not altogether satisfactory returns.

The next day the two men played well—Bess shooting a 30 on the front nine and Tim a 31 on the back nine, but coming up to the short eighteenth hole the match was even. Worse was to come. Bess hit his ball into the woods and Tim drove his into the rough. The position seemed hopeless. Bess averted his eyes and Tim vowed never to be seduced so easily again. Taking his second shot Tim lofted the ball toward the green. It fell just on the edge and rolled to within six inches of the hole. The putt was unmissable and they won the match. When the two pros had paid Bess he shouted to Tim, "I told you, didn't I? It was a sure thing." Tim smiled and shook his head.

They returned to the clubhouse. Tim went to take a shower and when he came back to the locker room he discovered Bess in the middle of a poker game. "Just as I walked in," he recalled, "Bess was pushing all our cash into the pot. I looked at his hand. I didn't know very much about poker, but I knew it wasn't any good. He had nothing. Not a thing. Fortunately everyone else folded and Bess won about twenty-five hundred dollars. I asked him for my original five hundred back but he refused, assuring me that the least he could do was to triple it for me. We got dressed and Bess insisted we drive down to the Fronton in Miami Springs to watch the Jai Alai games. He felt like a winner, he said. Well, Bess bet and bet on what the locals said were sure things and he lost and lost and lost. Each time I asked him for my five hundred back he said, 'I'll pay you, I'll pay you in a minute, Tim. Can't you see I'm onto a good thing. I'm going to make our fortune tonight.' But an hour later he was down to our last three hundred dollars. He was furious and he turned to one of the knowledgeable punters, a man who really *knew* the game, and said, 'Listen, which of those teams out there can't possibly win?' and the man pointed and said, 'That team, the one in the yellow. If that team wins I'll give up gambling in the morning.' Well, Bess put our last three hundred on the yellow team and it won. Bess won three thousand dollars. It was incredible. And even then he refused to give me back my five hundred. He wanted to end the evening at the dog races to increase our stake some more. And so we went. As soon as we arrived Bess bet twenty-seven hundred on a dog called Beachcomber. Beachcomber was famous in Florida. He had won twenty-two straight races that year. I don't think he had ever lost a race. Bess was beside himself. At last, a certain winner. As the rabbit set off and the gates were released a great howl went up from the crowd. The mighty Beachcomber had his leg lifted up taking a leak. By the time he'd finished his business the rest of the pack must have had a forty-yard lead. Beachcomber set off after them slowly closing the gap and coming into the stretch he was only a few yards behind the leader. That dog had heart. But he was nipped by a nose and Bess lost the twenty-seven hundred. He had only three hundred left, less than I had started with. Now Bess was what most people think of as a *gambler*. He was the sort of man who bets in the evening and then can't afford to buy breakfast in the morning. He was a gambler, a chancer. He'd risk money at anything."

Thus Holland's college days were passed. He remembers spending considerably more time on the course than he ever did in the classroom. College for him was an unending series of golf matches played for higher and higher stakes. He knew he was good and had little desire to improve. He didn't have to. In those days he always seemed to win. In 1950, for example, at the age of nineteen, he won the club championships at the Rockville Centre Country Club, the La Gorce Country Club and the Miami Country Club. He had gone to Florida to study golf and felt he had passed the course with honors. He graduated, in fact, in 1952 with a degree in Business Administration and spent the next two years in the University of Miami Law School.

"I learned a lot," he recalled, "and one of the main things I learned is that you must make people play for more than they like to play for. You have to put pressure on the other guy. Take a man who has a six handicap and claims he has a ten. A man like that will tell me he'll play for a twenty-five-dollar nassau if I give him ten strokes. And I'll say, I'll tell you what, we'll play a hundred-dollar nassau and I'll give you twelve strokes. A man like that, I'll have him beat going off the first tee. Let's be honest. It all comes down to brains in the end. It all comes down to being a little smarter than the next guy.

"In those days golf was my whole world. You must remember how much the game has changed in the last twenty years. When I left the University of Miami in the middle Fifties there was no money in golf and very little glamour. It wasn't until Arnold Palmer and television in the early Sixties that golf became a monetarily rewarding game. The largest purse of the time would have been about five thousand. And even as late as '56 or '57 there was a social stigma attached to the game. I remember when I suggested to my mother that I join the pro tour she was appalled and assured me that I could do a lot better than being a golf bum.

"Another major difference was that there were no young men playing the game. In 1957 when I was twenty-six I was considered very young. Golf was dominated by men in their thirties and forties. Cary Middlecoff was thirty-six or thirty-seven and the three best golfers of the time, Ben Hogan, Byron Nelson and Sam Snead, were all forty-five. There aren't many great forty-five-year-old players around today.

"I began to play serious golf against the pros after I left school. But I was a maverick. The American Golf Association didn't believe in gambling. They didn't want me competing in calcuttas. I felt they couldn't tell me how to run my life. They wanted me to be a good boy and because I wasn't they kept me off the Walker Cup team. It was a hypocritical organization and they tried to railroad me. It didn't matter. It was more fun playing in the real world anyway."

In the middle Fifties the real world meant Florida and specifically La Gorce Country Club. La Gorce boasted more than a hundred millionaires as members and among the gambling golfers it was known as Hustler's Haven. "All of the really big action in the country took place at La Gorce," he remembered. "It was the gambling capital of golf. They had such colorful players as José Dorelis, who was called the Count because he wore a monocle, Bobby Riggs, Danny Miller, Marty Stanovich, Mike McClaney, Chuck Sheldon and many, many others. La Gorce attracted the best professionals and the best hustlers of the day.

"Dorelis couldn't play golf very well, but he was part of the group I was in and he was a great high roller. When I graduated from college I used to give him thirty-six strokes and still beat him. Hell, I was better than scratch by then. The Count was always trying to hustle me into giving him a bigger and bigger edge. I remember one match particularly. The Count said to me, 'I'll bet you five hundred I can beat you if you wear a monocle. We'll play even, but every time the monocle falls out you lose a stroke.' Well I took the bet immediately of course and the Count said he'd bring a monocle in the morning. But that night I bought my own monocle and practiced with it, but in squinting to keep it in my eye I couldn't hit the ball or else the monocle kept on falling to the ground. I finally decided to hit the ball with my eyes closed. I could afford thirty-six strokes after all. The day of the match a lot of side bets were made. There was a lot of action. By the time we reached the ninth green, which was near the clubhouse, I was three or four strokes ahead. I wasn't worried. As we set off for the next tee the Count said, 'I'll give you four ninety now,' and I said, 'I'll take it, Count.' "

In 1955 at La Gorce he met Danny Miller. "I didn't know who he was. He was just one of a group of sixteen or so who always played each other. Everyone bet. I was the kid. I played Danny a lot. I was giving him twelve or thirteen strokes and I beat him all the time. He was the world's worst golfer. But he liked to play, he didn't seem to mind losing, and after every match he'd always settle—though we never played for much. He was really terrible and I advised him a couple of times to give it up. There was no hope. He was that bad.

"Well one day we got up a foursome and it was me and Miller against the other two. They were betting among themselves and they really didn't care about my ball. I was betting against Miller as well. The others were playing for a lot of money— forty or fifty thousand that day alone. The other two were a little better than Danny, but for the first seventeen holes the match was pretty even. We got down to the eighteenth, a par four, and Danny hit his ball into the woods and then just chopped it out onto the fairway. The other two had hit their drives cleanly, which meant that Danny's total equity was riding on his next shot and he was in big trouble. I didn't pay too much attention because Danny was so bad. There was no way he could win anyway. And I think he must have known it; he looked like he was going to cry.

"There was a strong wind blowing from right to left that day. The green was about a hundred and ninety yards away. The pin was on the right side of the green, a trap on the right and another trap in front. It was an impossible shot, but Danny hit the ball curving through the wind to within five feet of the hole to win the match. I lost two hundred because of that shot and he collected the rest of the money too. The two big losers bitched about Danny's luck. It looked like a lucky shot, but I'd seen it and I knew it couldn't have been. It was one of the most beautiful shots I'd ever seen. Afterwards, driving me home in his El Dorado Cadillac, I turned to him and said, 'Danny, just how good are you?' Danny smiled and said, 'Tim, for a sharp kid, it sure took you a long time.' "

He remembered almost every match he played, and one of his favorites took place at the Diplomat Golf Course in Fort Lauderdale in 1956. It had been arranged that Tim and Cary Middlecoff would compete against Al Besselink and Lloyd Pitzer, a Chicago businessman. The stakes were high and he and Middlecoff gave Pitzer a stroke a side. "I shot a thirty-two on the back nine and Cary shot amazingly well and we won. The next day we gave each of them a stroke a side and beat them again. At this point Bess suggested he find himself another partner and that the stakes remain the same. 'I don't care who you get,' said Middlecoff, 'as long as it's not Snead or Hogan.' The next day Bess showed up with Dutch Harrison who had just won three consecutive tournaments on the pro tour and we killed them. Then Bess got Bob Hamilton and we beat them twice. At the end of the week he turned up with Doug Sanders. We massacred them and Bess was furious. He wanted to play again but on another course. Sanders just looked at him and said, 'You dumb son of a bitch. It doesn't matter where we play them. We could play them up and down U.S. 1 and they'd still beat us.' But Bess talked us into another match, this time at La Gorce. There was a terrific gale. I shot the course in sixty-six. The next best score was seventy-seven. It was the goddamnedest round of golf. It was like shooting a fifty-eight on a good day. Cary told me that I was the best wind player he had ever seen."

In 1957, Holland entered the British amateur championships held at St. Andrews in Scotland. In the quarter-finals he set a course record of 65, but was knocked out in the next round. He traveled on to Deauville for the French amateurs where he lost again, this time in the finals. Although he did not know it at the time his serious golfing days were over. He continued to play and just as fervently, but somehow it was not as important as it had been. And he had found another interest.

In the spring of 1958 at La Gorce, he noticed a group of the more elderly members playing an unfamiliar game in a corner of the clubhouse. He had never seen the game before, but asked if he could play. "You don't know anything about it," he was told. "You'd better stick to golf."

"It doesn't matter," he said. "I'll pick it up as I go along."

After he had played a few games one of the players said, "Tim, give it up, it'll take you a lifetime to learn this game."

He was indignant. "I'll bet you a thousand I beat you all when I come back from the tour," he said.

The game was backgammon. While on the tour he looked, as he had always done when attempting to learn a new game, for a book on the subject. Apparently, none existed, but a few weeks later, in a New York store selling nothing for more than twenty-nine cents, he chanced on Walter Richards' *Complete Backgammon*. He read it as carefully as he had read Culbertson's book on bridge and Snead's book on golf. He carried it with him wherever he went. A bet was a bet after all.

When he returned to Florida he was shocked by the fact that men who had been playing the game for forty years still did not know *how* to play. He despised inefficiency in game playing. "I was drawn to the game immediately. I liked it because it moved quickly, it was fast. Backgammon is an inductive game. This will happen because that has already happened. It became obvious to me after only five games that it was a matter of mathematics. It was not very difficult to relate a theory of percentages and probabilities to the game."

To begin with backgammon conflicted with his golf since at La Gorce, at least, both games were usually played in the afternoons. "My golf began to suffer. But I soon realized who the best backgammon player in the club was. I told him I had to run a few errands and said, 'I'll do what you do except when you're in the box.' And then I went out and played a round of golf. In that way I had the benefit of winning with the best player, and never had to play against him. I'd go out and play a little golf and when I came back I was always ahead."

He habitually spent his summers in Long Island playing golf at his old country club, traveling infrequently into New York itself. During the summer of 1958, however, he found it increasingly difficult to leave the city. He had taken to going to the Cavendish Club in pursuit of his new passion and could not tear himself away. "The highest backgammon action was there," he recalled. "The Cavendish was in the basement of the Ritz Towers on Park Avenue and Fifty-seventh Street. It was basically a bridge club, but they also played clabbiasch, word games, high-stake scrabble and backgammon. The regulars were people like Oswald Jacoby, Johnny Crawford, Teddy Bassett, Bud Simonsen and Nicky Sergeant. They were all serious backgammon players.

"That year I lost almost every penny I had at backgammon. I had to borrow from my parents. Those boys really knew the game. There were three or four of them who used to wait for me at the club. Sharks. It was never a question of them winning, it was a question of just *how much* they won from me."

He would often spend whole weekends at the Cavendish, playing for seventy-two-hour stretches. "There were no tournaments of any kind in those days, well, there may have been some that no one turned up to. There was only the Cavendish if you wanted to learn. I just played and played and lost and lost. I was a kind of tax-free donation to those players. I entertained them. Backgammon became an obsession to me, a kind of disease. Worse than taking the needle. I really came to need it —or thought I did."

He gradually abandoned golf. "I never had the drive to become a top player anyway. I used to be on a par with Arnold Palmer, who is only two years older than me. But he had the desire, I didn't. It's no more complicated than that."

In 1958, the year he returned to New York, he lived in his mother's brownstone on Fifth Avenue and Eleventh Street, occupying the top two floors. Occasionally he went out to Rockville to play golf, only to rush back to the Cavendish at night to play backgammon. It was an unsatisfactory life; during the winters particularly he had little to occupy him during the day. In 1960 he married for the first time, and became a partner in a small stockbroking firm. It was the first job he had ever had. He worked from home, selling shares on the telephone before they came on the market. "I did a lot of introducing—introducing a man who wanted to sell to a man who wanted to buy. I did a lot of that." Eighteen months later, dissatisfied with himself and the firm, he sold his equity in the company. "Business bored me. There was no personal confrontation. And stockbroking, well, stockbroking was ass-kissing, a terrible trade." On leaving his firm he occupied his days by selling the occasional pension, inventing something called Jeeves with Collar Trees (a kind of heart-shaped expandable sponge that prevented shirt collars from becoming creased while traveling), and he wrote a series of illustrated golf lessons for the New York *Post*. But it was backgammon that continued to obsess him.

"Backgammon is a queer compulsive game. It's the luck factor that seduces everyone into believing that they are good, that they can actually win. But that's just wishful thinking. To become good, really good, at backgammon could cost several

years of your time and twenty, maybe thirty thousand bucks.
But only if you had a talent for the game to start with. It cost
me. It cost me a lot. But I learned. I took a lot of punishment
at the Cavendish Club, but I learned to play. And let me tell
you, it took a little time, but I got it all back and I got it back
from the sharks that took it from me. I got it back and more.
I got it back in spades. I extract a fat interest on my losses when
I win. And I usually win in the end. Like I said before, winning
is my business."

He could not remember what he had said. His throat was
swollen now. His next match was not till later in the evening,
but he could not decide whether or not to stay. He wondered
if it had stopped raining. The reporter had gone some time ago
and now he sat in a corner of the room staring at his empty
glass. He had not taken a drink till he was thirty-five. He could
not remember why.

He looked around the crowded room; there was a game at
almost every table and the players sat or stood around in stiff,
hypnotic poses. They leaned across the boards as though they
heard a kind of broken music in the dice. Like acolytes, the
women stood behind with pinched expressions of concern.

Christ. He was sure his voice had gone completely now. He
should not have talked so long. He should not have talked at
all. The reporter had almost certainly gone away with the
same improbable views on gambling that he had held before.
Derring-do and high romance. It was always the same. Gambling, he thought, if you called it that, was merely a just remu-
neration for your time and devotion to the game. It meant that
you had put in, say, four thousand hours of work for which you
expected to be reimbursed at so many dollars to the hour. The
equation was simple, unchangeable. You were not rewarded
every time of course. You lost occasionally. But that was unimportant. A good player was one who was not influenced by
adversity. He had learned to divorce his feelings from the game.
He accepted his losses with equanimity because he knew that

in the long run his gains would be much greater. And would always be. The law of averages was as infallible as the law of gravity.

He felt sick. He rose from his seat and walked slowly down the corridor to the front door of the club. It was still raining. Christ, he thought, good bloody Christ. He returned to the backgammon room. Approaching one of the other American players in the tournament, he suggested they get up a game for sizable stakes. "And let's get a couple of English pigeons in the game," he whispered in a dying voice. "They've got a lot to answer for."

# Johnny Moss

The next best thing
to playing and winning is
playing and losing.
The main thing is to play.

**NICK THE GREEK DANDOLOS**

## I

He wanted, he said, to speak his mind, to say his piece, to set the record straight. "Do you know," he began, then yawning he turned to the bedside table and reached for a cigarette. It was five o'clock in the afternoon and the old man lay on the rumpled bed in baggy undershorts. He had been playing poker till well past dawn. "Do you know," he said, "if one of them fellows was to make a book about *my* life, it would be a real book, a crackerjack, not one of them made-up books, y'unnerstand, not one of them fancy books you read and don't believe." He yawned again. "And it wouldn't be dirty neither." The old man's eyes were full of sleep and memories.

"I'd hate it," he said, "bein' dirty I mean." Sprawled on the bed, the pillows bunched behind him, Johnny Moss continued to smoke, occasionally stroking a small tattoo high up on his left arm. It was not an exceptional tattoo. He had had it done when he was twelve. It was faded now, but even then it had lacked imagination, had failed to achieve the appropriate grotesque effect. And yet, illuminated by the bedside lamp, that small and perfectly ordinary pink rose seemed somehow alive. A sudden wind rushed through the open window; he clutched his arm as though to make certain the rose had not been blown away.

Moss looked toward the window with half-shut eyes. He had the listless face of a tame hound. Benign, mild-mannered, he spoke in a soft and convoluted Texan, the accent so dense and difficult as to make it sound like another language. "Never did like all them bad words folks use today," he said. "Ain't right. See what I'm sayin'? Y' know, if somebody was to make a book about my life, all the hotels along the Strip would take it on. They'd display it everywhere 'cause they all know I'm a respectable gamblin' man. They know I ain't never cheated, ain't never connived. It'd sell too." He sat up. "'Cause folks would know that's the way things really was. No highfalutin make-believe. None a that. It'd be kinda like a history book, like real life."

Moss spoke of his life in the passionate way men refer to some single intense and unforgettable experience—a place, an encounter, a woman, a work of art. It was perfectly remembered, perfectly formed. Hesitantly at first and then with rising confidence, he embarked on a tale he had already written in his own mind and seemed almost surprised that I had not heard it before. Oddly, there was nothing brash or ostentatious, none of that arch complacency one tends to associate with Texans in his point of view. Rather, there was an understated gentility, a certainty of bearing and belief. He had turned his life over and over in his mind like a boy examining some small and hitherto uncaptured animal—with joy and fascination.

From the window of his room at the rear of the Dunes Hotel in Las Vegas, one could see the bleak expanse of the desert stretching toward the distant mountains. The view did not appeal to him and he kept the curtains closed. The room itself was strewn with lumpen heaps of clothes, dirty glasses and coffee cups, keys, a watch, loose piles of change and dollar bills, the trifling bric-a-brac of a man accustomed to being alone and on the road. He had inhabited hundreds of such rooms in his time. His needs were few—a stake, a bed, a bath, and company to while away the nights at poker. It was the room of a traveling salesman.

He had been closeted in this one room, however, for three years. In 1971 he had taken over the management of the card room in the Aladdin Hotel farther down the Strip—his first formal employment in nearly forty years. It had been for him a tolerable change. He was tired. He was sixty-seven. He had spent too much of his life on the road. Here he had only to bide his time and the action invariably came to him. Only tomorrow, he pointed out, the World Series of Poker was being held in town; every high roller in the country would come. Pug Pearson, of course, actually lived in Vegas; but Amarillo Slim had arrived the night before and Adrian Dolly Doyle, Treetop Jack Strauss, the Wizard and Crandall Addington, all of them good old boys from Texas, were bound to drop into the Aladdin that night. Moss had the optimistic air of a man about to attend a class reunion.

Johnny Moss was a practical man and at his age he sensed that this might well be his last big tournament, his final chance to prove to himself that he was still the best poker player in the world. He had not played in last year's tournament; he had just not felt up to it—the long hours, the concentration, the intense play. But he had won the first two tournaments in 1970 and 1971. He was, where world poker championships were concerned, undefeated. There were others, however, other younger players, who believed he was now too old, too old and too irresolute. He shrugged, then smiled, and stroked his pink tattoo; it was the smile of a man who had punished heretics before. There was not a player in Vegas whom he had not, at one time or another, broken and sent home. "I killed 'em," he said, "I made 'em misers." Yes, he had broken them all, the best of them.

He was fond of recalling the first time he had come to Vegas back in 1951. Rising from the bed and walking back and forth across the room, he told me of the telephone call he had received from his boyhood friend, Benny Binion, who now owned the Horseshoe Casino in Glitter Gulch. "Johnny," Binion had said, "they got a fellow out here calls himself Nick the Greek. Thinks he can play stud poker. Johnny, I think you should come out here and have some fun."

"So I packed up and went, y'know. I was in Dallas at the time. The game was staged at the Horseshoe, right up in front so's the crowd could watch. It brought the entire Strip down. They was apushin' and acrowdin' around that table with their eyeballs hangin' out. Now the Greek, he had a real big reputation. You see what I'm sayin'? They say he won something like sixty million dollars in his time and I reckon he lost a little more. He must've been 'bout seventy then, yeah 'bout seventy, but he was still a real smart player. Age hadn't done much to bother him none.

"Well, I come on up from Dallas. I wasn't the best player in the world, y'know, but I could play real good and I reckoned I had it in me. I'd already been up four straight days and nights aplayin' cards in Texas and when I come into town that Sunday night, well, we set right down to play. No point in puttin' it off when there's money to be made. We played five-card stud from Sunday straight through till Thursday. On Thursday night I told him I was tired, I told him I was wore out and was agoin' to bed. 'What's the matter?' that ole Greek says to me, 'can't you take the pressure?' Well, I slept for about twenty hours and y'know that Greek didn't even go to bed. Seventy years old and he just sat around playin' craps awaitin' for me to come back to the table. And I did and we played through till Sunday night again and I went back to sleep. We must've played stud like that for two months or more and I come out a couple of hundred thousand winner.

"During that session, I played the biggest pot of my whole life. I remember there was an ante of a hundred dollars and the low card had to bet two hundred. We had us one card down to start and mine was a nine. Course I didn't know then what that Greek had in the hole. To start with I had a six up and he had a seven, so I bet two hundred. Nick, he raised me a thousand right away. I called. He then caught an eight and I caught another nine. I bet four thousand. And then, cool as can be, he raises me sixteen thousand. Now, I could've taken that pot right then and there with my two nines. He couldn't a had better than a pair of eights. But I didn't want to shut him off. I was asettin' a trap, y'unnerstand. And that ole Greek, he closed his eyes and jumped right in. I wanted to take that other eighty or ninety thousand layin' there in front of him. I wanted it all, every nickel of it. Now he didn't think I had two nines, no way, so I just call him. He then catches a three spot and I catch a two. I'm still high with the nine and I bet thirty thousand. And he calls, which is just what I want him to do. I got this hand oiled and tuned like a fine machine. I mean it's as pretty a time-bomb as you ever saw.

"Well, there's only one card to come. And I catch a three and he catches a jack. Now that jack is the only card that can hurt me, y'unnerstand, and I reckon Nick's not dumb enough to bet high money just so's he might outdraw me. Now he's high. Well he stalled and stalled, apuffin' away at that seegar of his, and finally he pushes forty-five thousand into that pot. Well now I think there's somethin' wrong with this pot. It don't smell right. He don't have no two jacks. Besides, he couldn't have another jack or he would have bet more. But I don't care what he caught now. I've played this hand a certain way in order to break that Greek and that's all I'm thinkin' about. The money isn't important. I rarely raise back into a cinch, but I bet everything I had left, which was about twenty-five thousand. He's not agoin' to steal this pot. He's not agoin' to make me dog it and lie down. He's got to beat them two nines a mine or leave the table. He was in a bind. I could see that. There must've been more than two hundred and fifty thousand in that pot by now. The crowd, they was dead quiet. The town could've been burnin' to the ground and they'da stayed to watch the outcome. And then, quiet as can be, the Greek says to me, 'Mr. Moss, I think I got a jack in the hole.' Well I look at him and I says, 'Greek, if you got a jack in that hole, you are able to win yourself a damn big pot.' Well the Greek reached down and turns over the jack. The jack of diamonds. I'll never forget it. Damndest thing I ever saw. I trapped him and he went and outdrawed me.

"You see what I'm sayin'? I was riled. I was riled, but I never said nothin' and just as soon as I raised me another stake we went to bettin' again, switchin' to seven-card high split, deuce-to-the-seven, Kansas City lowball. Stud, y'unnerstand, was my worst game, but I can win playin' stud. We played about two, three weeks. I beat him outta seventy, eighty thousand, I dunno. Stayin' up four, five days at a time, sleepin' for twenty hours, then playin' again. We laid low for a while. Then we played draw poker. Now, draw was my best game and he only played me three, four days. I must've beat him outta four hundred thousand. Might've won more, I dunno. The entire game must've lasted four months, maybe five. And then, when the end comes, that ole Greek smiled, got up from the table— we was playin' ace-to-the-five, I remember, and I had him against the cold nuts—and he says to me, 'Well, I guess I got to let you go, Mr. Moss.' I had broke him, y'unnerstand. I had cracked him wide open. But that Greek was a real gentleman. He never said nothin' else. He just got up and he smiled and he set off to bed."

Moss lit another cigarette. He stood at the window absent-mindedly watching the setting sun. It was an excellent tale, an excellent souvenir, and as he smoked that slow shrewd smile crossed his face again. His memories refreshed him. He would play an elegant game of poker again. Standing at the window he seemed contented, confident even. But something puzzled me. Not his show of confidence; no, his confidence was conta-gious. It was the utter absence of any outward evidence of money, of accumulated goods, that set my mind in circles. During those long late afternoons I found it increasingly diffi-cult to equate the extravagant accounts of gambling gains with this tired old man who had chosen to make his home in a hotel room. Expecting, I suppose, the customary clichés of affluence

—spacious suites, tailored suits, champagne and Cadillacs—I came at one point to suspect that all the tales were tall, that this was not to be the "history book" to which he had referred. But he was not that sort of man nor did he have the usual pretensions. "I don't have much regard for money," he said. "Money's just paper to gamble with and when I leave the table I don't pay it no nevermind."

He explained that his attitude toward money stemmed, at least in part, from his beliefs in the old Southern Baptist ethic of goodness and the golden rule. There was, for him, nothing complicated, trite, or even sentimental in such a belief; it was what his people had taught him and he held onto it even now. He believed in what he liked to call a good man, by which he meant that it was a sin to cheat, to steal, or to kill, unless you had to, to protect yourself or your family. A good man was one whose family came first at all times. "My people are in good shape," he said. "I never touch our house money. I'd rather borrow from a bellhop than ask my wife for a penny. I don't have no comment to her about gamblin', win or lose. I'm a spender. Most people are savers. Savin's not in me. Never has been. My only obligation is to my family. I don't have none toward myself.

"And that's what I mean about the money," he said. Picking up a pile of loose change from the bedside table, he dribbled it from one hand to the other. "Me and my wife was born poor, we had good times and bad and we been married near to fifty years. She runs our home down in Texas, y'know. Now I may be broke," he said, "or as near to broke can be, but Virgie, my wife, well, Virgie's a millionaire."

John Hardie Moss was born in the poor prairie town of Marshall, Texas, in 1907. His was a family of itinerants and before he was a year old he, his older sister and brother and his parents pushed on to Fort Worth by covered wagon. The two-hundred-mile journey through East Texas took nearly a month. Shortly thereafter his mother died and the family moved on to

Dallas and settled down, selling the wagon and the horses to the local fire department.

He remembers little of those days but for the fact that his family was always poor. "I didn't know nothin' else," he said. "Far as we was concerned, there had always been a Depression." Work was difficult to find, but his father was finally employed as a line repairman for the Dallas telephone company. It didn't last. "When I was about five, one of them telephone poles fell on my daddy's leg. He got the gangrene poisoning and they had to cut his leg off. So my daddy was a cripple and he run outta money. There was no work anywhere, y'unnerstand, and so we moved on over to East Dallas. Daddy went into the grocery business after that, but it didn't work out any better than the time before and he went broke again."

The family lived in one of the poorest sections of town in what was called "a shotgun house." "They called 'em that," said Moss, "'cause you could open up the front door and shoot right through the place with a shotgun." The house was a ramshackle three-room affair. His sister slept in the middle room, his father in the front and Moss and his brother camped out on the back porch. It was the only home Johnny Moss remembers.

"In East Dallas," he said, "none of us kids could afford to keep in school. When I was about eight I had to leave and go to sellin' newspapers in the street. Daddy stayed at home and did the cookin' for the rest of us. I got hold of a bicycle, second-hand, and took to deliverin' papers for the Mackay Telegraph Company. I did that for a spell and then I took a job from one of them drugstores in town.

"Benny Binion and Chill Wills, the actor, we was all gamblin' on the streets of East Dallas when we was kids. Chill was sellin' papers and so was Binion 'fore he went into bootleggin'. I really learnt gamblin' as a newsboy—shootin' dice in the alley and sellin' newspapers in the domino halls, and the men there learnt me how to play real well. I was a pretty good dice man then. I learnt to play poker by teaching myself mostly. By the time

I was fifteen I was a full-growed man. I made a livin' at dice 'fore I was fifteen. You run around with fast company, y'unnerstand, and they teach you how to cheat, how to fade the dice and mark the cards, but they always cheat you outta your money. I quit runnin' around with 'em when I was about fifteen. Before you can be a gambler you got to be able to protect yourself. And I learnt how.

"There wasn't much easy money in Texas in them days and gamblin' was a way out. When I was a kid all the money I made I gave to my daddy and he give me back a quarter. Well, we needed it. But I never asked people the price of nothin' as far back as I can remember. I just went in and bought anything I wanted. We didn't have money and I decided to get me some one way or the other. That's all, not for me, for my family. I can get along on nothin'. But you got to take care of your obligations win or lose. We needed money real bad at home and my daddy told me I had to stop work or stop gamblin'. And I said, 'Daddy, if I don't work how can I get money to gamble?' And Daddy, he said, 'Son, that's what gamblers got to figure out.' So I quit work."

When he was sixteen, Moss went to work in a Dallas gambling house at three dollars a day as a lookout for sharps. "The owner of that place," he said, "was the best draw man around and the first thing you know, I learnt myself to be a real fine draw player. I hung on there for about three years and then moved on to the Elks Club 'cause there was some shrewd players in there who could learn me hold 'em. I lied about my age to get into the place. It was two-dollar-limit hold 'em. During the day I made enough money at the domino parlors to support my hold-'em lessons at night."

In 1925 he married Virgie Ann, and the following year, still only nineteen, he took to the road as a professional poker player. Moss headed for the East Texas oilfields; Virgie traveled with him watching him play and keeping an eye on the money. "It was the time of the East Texas oil boom," Moss recalled, "in places like Gladewater, Tyler, Longview and Kilgore. More

oil wells there than you could see. I played dominoes and poker
in them towns with the roughnecks and the drillers. I used to
play with people who had money. You have to work with 'em
and know 'em to gamble with 'em, y'unnerstand, so I become
a roustabout alayin' pipelines for a time.

"It was a violent world, y'know, and I was just a fresh kid.
After I got money I started to carry a gun. I used to carry a
.38-Special with no hammer, so's you could get it outta your
pocket in a hurry. The road was real rough in them days goin'
from town to town. You always had to worry 'bout hijackers
and the Rangers. All those road gamblers and thieves and
cheaters. You have to know them cheaters in advance. I got me
a rundown on most of 'em. They never slipped up on the blind
side a me. Wasn't always that way, y'unnerstand. Used to be
that gamblin' was an honorable profession, a means a holdin'
your own in the world. But dope runners, pimps and hijackers,
when they was picked up by the Rangers, they always said they
was gamblers. They put a bad name on gamblin'. See what I'm
talkin' about? They wasn't gamblers. It's because they can use
that word and get away with it that put a bad name on gamblin'.

"In them old days in East Texas there were a lot of cheaters.
More cheaters than oil wells. They were pick-on people. They
always tried to take my pot, even when I'd won it square.
They'd say, 'What do you have to take this pot?' and I'd say,
'Two sixes,' and pull out my six-guns—when I had them handy
that is. I stayed for about five years in that territory and then
around about 1932 I lit out for places like Breckenridge and
Graham in West Texas. I wandered all around West Texas in
the Thirties and whatever they played in that town, I played.
I don't have no pet games. I play everything and everybody,
long as no thieves is involved. Every time I see a game where
people want to be staked, like in pool, I didn't want to learn how
to play. To be any good at all you've got to use your own
money. And you've got to play a heap a games.

"I remember once when I was livin' in Graham, foolin' with
drillin' oil and oil leases and mixin' with a rich oil crowd and

big ranchers and they used to go abowlin' at the bottom of that main hotel there in Graham. They used to bowl for twenty-five hundred, five thousand dollars a game. And that was in the middle of the Depression. I used to bowl with 'em. Now I don't even know hardly nothin' 'bout bowlin'. But how it was was that I drove every day from Graham to Wichita Falls, 'bout sixty miles away, atakin' lessons from a pro there. And do you know in two weeks I made about three hundred thousand offa them oil people. I got to where I could average 175–180 a game. Them rich ole boys. Tell you somethin' about 'em. Don't care what the game is—cards or bowlin' or golf—I've seen 'em when they have the money and the nuts, when they have it all agoin' for 'em and they still lose. At golf, y'unnerstand, I always shot what I normally shot, even if I lost, but double the stakes and I shoot my normal game and them rich ole boys'll shoot two, three shots above their average every time. You can bank on it."

Moss added golf to his repertoire in 1937. The times were lean and he was working as a cowboy, doing, as he put it, "a little ropin'. One day I ride by the golf course out there near Breckenridge and spy some players gamblin' up on the green, so I picked me up some clubs and taught myself how to play the game, case it ever came in handy. But I never said nothin', I never let on I could even spell the word. What folks are bettin' on you learn to play, that's all." Within a year he was good enough to shoot in the high 70s and entered the New Mexico Amateur Golf Tournament.

In the first round he was matched against a local schoolteacher called Buggs. Moss checked him out and learned that he normally shot around 80. "Now, this Buggs was a skinny little guy," said Moss, "and I thought, hell, I can shoot eighty. I guess I can shoot eighty. I hadn't even played the course. And I was abettin' ten thousand dollars with the sheepherders that I could beat this guy. Now, one good way to beat on a man is to bet him. He was only a schoolteacher, y'unnerstand, a real one, I mean that was his occupation, so I tried to bet him just fifty cents a hole to give him something to think about, but he wouldn't go for it, he wouldn't bet. So I tried him for a quarter a hole and he says to me, 'I give you the unnerstandin', Mr. Moss, I don't never gamble.' I even tried to bet him a Coca-Cola a hole and he says, 'I think you take my meanin', Mr. Moss, I ain't bettin' nothin'.' All right. Well, we started out and he kept ahittin' that ball down the middle of the fairway and apoppin' it up on the green next to the hole and he was killin' me. I mean he was *killin'* me.

"Now my caddy was a real good boy by the name of Elmo Baring outa Paducah, Texas. And Elmo, well, he was one of them boys that could really irritate you, y'unnerstand? Get right in under your skin. And I says to him, I says, 'Elmo, now goddamn it, you go out there and *irritate* that schoolteacher.' Now Elmo had a piece a my play, a good piece, and at the very next green we'd both knocked our balls pretty close to each other, Elmo got down on his knees and looked at them balls real careful and he says, 'Mr. Insects, it's your shot I believe.' Well, this skinny ole teacher just looked at him and says, 'I give you the unnerstandin' my name's not Insects. It's Buggs.' And Elmo looks up, like he didn't have no idea what that teacher was atalkin' about, and he says, 'Johnny, what's the difference between insects and bugs?' 'Hell,' I says, 'damned if I know the difference.' Well, for the very first time that teacher misses his putt and I didn't have no trouble with him after that. He just couldn't keep his mind off'n his own name. I made me a bundle that afternoon."

Despite his winnings during those Depression years, Moss had stonier days than he now cares to recall. The night before his first and only child, a daughter he called Eleoweese, was born, his wife took a room in the local hospital for which there was a thirty-five-dollar charge. But that night Moss lost all his ready cash in a poker game. Eleoweese was born at home and Moss acted as midwife. On another occasion he won one hundred thousand at poker and instructed Virgie to go out and buy a house. Before she could choose one Moss was broke again. Throughout the Thirties and the early Forties Moss's fortunes ebbed and flowed with alarming regularity. What he won at golf he lost at cards and what he won at cards he lost at other less familiar games and propositions. It must have been during this period that Virgie Ann began to manage his money. It is a subject about which he remains reserved. Standing now in his hotel room in the Dunes Hotel, he shrugged, turned away and lit another cigarette. "Sure, I had my ups and downs like anybody else," he said. "You win and you lose, that's all. But the losin's not very interesting and besides, I know a lot more about winnin', about playin' and winnin'. It's what I do best. It's all I want to do. You see what I'm sayin'? Look here, we're all right now. Not long ago Virgie, she said she'd pay me a thousand a week if'n I was to come and lie around the house in Odessa and drink whiskey all day. One thousand a week." He smiled. "But what would I do with all them dollars if'n I couldn't put them to some good use? What would I do with a thousand a week if'n I couldn't gamble? What's the use in that?" He shrugged again; he didn't expect an answer. For him, the game was the sole attraction, the game for itself.

He liked to talk about his wins, particularly when they overcame what appeared to be insuperable odds. He remembered one such match in 1939 in Lubbock, Texas. At Meadowbrook, the local nine-hole course, it was proposed for a wager of $5,000 that he could not shoot a 46 using only a four-iron. Moss agreed, and on the day of the contest Titanic Thompson suggested an additional $3,300 bet that he could not shoot a 45. "You had to hand it to Ty," said Moss. "He always seemed to know just where your weak points was and how to lean on 'em. Ty knew that we was next to broke, that eighty-three hundred dollars was all the money Virgie and I had left in the world. Virgie, she begged me to hold out enough to pay the hotel bill there in town, but I was determined. I shook my head and bet it all. Besides, it was always a pleasure to go up against Ty. Now I'd practiced, I'd practiced two or three days with that four-iron. I'd never shot better than a forty-six, but I knew when the money was down I could lick it.

"The day of the contest there must've been a couple a hundred people, gamblers and the like, awalkin' around and watchin'. On the first hole, a four-hundred-and-twenty-yard hole, I knocked that ball a whack and I was alayin' about three feet from that ole hole in three shots. A cinch. I stroked the ball and that putt rolled straight for the hole and then just before droppin' in like it should've it bent off. Well as I walked over to the second tee, I got to wonderin' how I could miss an easy putt like that. My caddie, he said the ball must've hit a rock, a pebble or something, but hell, there wasn't no pebbles in that part of the world. I'd even given the greenskeeper a hundred to keep the cups where they'd been when I was practicing. I thought I'd thought of everything. I couldn't figure it. Couldn't figure it at all. And, y'know, the same thing happened on the next green. At the last moment that ball just bent away from the hole. It was a strange thing, I can tell you. Then it dawned on me. Couldn't be but one thing. Someone had crept out there early and raised them cups, raised 'em just an eighth of an inch or so, so's the ball would kick away. Well, I sent my man ahead to the third green to stomp that cup back down. You see what I'm sayin'? Some conniver's on the fourth green raisin' 'em up and my man's right behind him on the third astompin' 'em back down again. It went like that for a hole or two and finally, round about the fifth, Ty stepped outta the crowd, that boyish grin of his spread all over his face, and I says, 'So, it was you?' Ty just grinned, the way he does, and I told him if he calls off his man I'd call off mine. Well, we agreed to that and when I'd done with them nine holes, I'd shot a forty-one and took all the bets.

"When it was over Ty paid me off and he said I was the best four-iron player there was. But, I'll tell you, Ty was the best golfer I ever knew of or heard of. I watched him once at the Ridgelea Golf Course there in Fort Worth beat Byron Nelson outta a thousand by shooting a twenty-nine on the last nine. He was that good.

"In them days I played a heap a golf, guess it was about all I ever did then. I told you there was a lot of cheaters around.

Remember once down in West Texas, Dick Martin, a fine golfer, he was my caddy. We was playin' for a pile of money and this boy I was playin' against kept on amovin' his ball. Dick kept sayin' I should do something about it, but I says, 'Let him move it. He'll hurry his shot so I won't see it and I'll bet he misses it. The same thing with the putt, let him move it. I'll speak to him about it the first time the putt goes in.' You see, cheatin' works on a man's mind, stirs it up. I've had cheaters against me who was so worried about their cheatin' they had difficulty with their play. In golf they'd cheat at anything, move balls, change scores and use that old Vaseline trick. I mean they'd smear your clubs with grease when you wasn't around. That way your ball don't get no English, y'unnerstand, no hooks and slices.

"Well, funny thing happened once. In them days it use to didn't cost nothin' to kill niggers. In them days they used to caddy and they never wore shoes. Now there was alot of cheaters, remember. And if one of 'em hit their ball into the rough, them nigger caddies would walk in lookin' for the ball and pick it up with their toes and drop it at the edge of the fairway. Now, I could see that plain as day. Because we carried a lot of cash with us we always toted our guns in our golf bags. And I finally says to one of them caddies, I says, 'Nigger, you pick up another ball with them toes of your'n and next time I'll shoot 'em off. All five of 'em. And another thing. Tomorrow, you all wear shoes.' Well, next day, sure enough, they showed up in shoes and on the very first hole one of them cheaters drove his ball into the rough, but by the time we get to it it was alayin' on the edge of the fairway. That really fooled me and I began to worry my mind over it. What them niggers had done, I reckoned finally, was to cut off the soles of their shoes so's they could still pick the ball up with their toes. I got my gun out then and there and fired about three inches away from his big toe. Oh that nigger jumped. Did he jump. And I says to him, 'Next time, I'll take off your big toe, nigger,' and he says back to me, jumpin' up and down and wavin' his arms around, 'Oh, Mistah Moss,

Mistah Moss, next time I'll wear my sole, honest I will, Mistah Moss.' He did too." Lighting another cigarette, he smiled. "Maybe you oughtn't to call 'em niggers," he said. "Don't want to offend nobody. It's just that back in the Thirties that's what they was called."

During those years golf became his chief obsession. He continued to play cards but it had become a comparative sideline. And as late as 1947 he was still playing for as much money as he had. He could not describe the feeling with any accuracy, but he implied it gave him some queer and buoyant pleasure to play as close to the edge as he was able. "I remember we was aplayin' the summer of that year at the Stevens Golf Course in Dallas, a tight little municipal course, me, George Barnes, and four or five others. Well they all bet me about nine thousand for a nine-hole match," he said, "and I went and lost. As we walked away from the ninth green George, he says to me, 'How much money you got left, Johnny?' Well I had about eight hundred dollars in my pocket and Virgie begged me not to bet it all, but George wanted to bet the whole eight hundred on one hole. I mulled it over, it didn't take long, and I agreed. We teed up at the tenth, a short hole, and George drove his ball to within four, five feet of the cup. Virgie, she just looks at me y'know, as if to say, see, I told you it would happen, you just can't leave well enough alone. And I looks at her and I says, 'Honey, at least let me take my first shot 'fore you upset yourself.' Well I lined up that little ole ball and, do you know, I hit for the pin and that ball hit the edge of the green, bounced once, maybe twice, and rolled right into the hole. Barnes must've had a heart attack. We agreed to go double-or-nothing on the next hole, which I birdied, and I won the next at par. I now have sixty-four hundred dollars. We agreed to finish the last six holes at a thousand a hole and another five thousand on the whole match. It was a great afternoon. 'Fore we had done I had 'em all broke. I won twenty thousand plus my nine thousand back. And y'know, Virgie just smiled and never said nothin'."

Following his marathon card match with Nick the Greek in

1951, he remained in Las Vegas. The next year on the course of the Desert Inn he played for the highest stakes of his career. A few of the local high rollers bet Moss that he could not break 80 using only irons. Chief among them, Moss remembers, was one of Frank Costello's collectors. "It just happened one day," he said. "We was asittin' about the clubhouse and they put up the proposition offerin' to bet one hundred thousand dollars. I'd been shootin' some golf with them, shooting in the mid-seventies. We'd been aplayin' for a few weeks and I won a lot of money. Well they thought they was on to a good thing, y'unner-stand, and so did I, and I says, 'I couldn't shoot eighty if you fixed it, but I'll tell you what I'll do. I'll bet ninety-four thou-sand 'cause that's all the cash I got on me.' They liked that real fine and some of the people from the Flamingo, they put up the other six thousand to keep the numbers even. Everybody in town must've come out to see that match. It was a tough bet, but I thought I could shoot it for that much money. I couldn't have shot it for fun, that was sure. I used a two-iron to drive with and things went pretty well, all considered, and at the end of the first nine I was three, four over par. It was a par-seventy-two course. I was aholdin' my own. But one bad hole and I was gone. I knew that. I picked up a few strokes here and there and on the eighteenth I shot a low hook into the wind and it fell just into the rough. I had a bad lie, but I was a pin shooter, not a green shooter. What's the difference whether you're short or you go over. There's no point in underclubbing. That's why I was good. I'm thinkin' all the time about that little ball, what it's up to and where it's goin'.

"As I say, I had a bad lie and I didn't catch my ball real good comin' outta the grass. But I hit for the pin and there was a lot of overspin on that ball. It hit the grass first and went over the back side of the green. I had to par that hole to win and before that shot I'd've bet anything I had that I was going to par that hole and win. Well I was in bad trouble now. I didn't think about it. I just pitched that ole ball up. I didn't want to pitch it up, be short and have to run down. So I hit for the pin, but it rolled eight or ten feet to the other side. It looked like it was a mile away and I had to sink that putt to shoot a seventy-nine. Now choking is a funny thing. It doesn't affect me much. I looked over that there putt and I thought, I ain't playin' no break, I'm agoin' to stroke it straight in. I was a good putter and I laid seven-to-nine against that I would make it. One thing, it wasn't agoin' to be short. I looked up just to see what the boys was thinkin', and they was deathly still, bitin' their fingernails. Well I just stroked that ball and kind of accidentally, y'know, it went in and I won.

"Now when I made that putt, them guys asked me if I could do it again. They thought I was tired, you see. 'Do you want to shoot at it for two hundred thousand?' they said. And I says, 'Sure, if you put your money up. Only one thing though. I can't bet but a hundred eighty-eight thousand, that's all the cash I got on me.' We was walkin' toward the number one tee and I remember Uffner sayin', 'Jesus, this guy's gonna bet the two hundred grand he can do it again. This guy's just plain crazy.' And they all backed down.

"Golf was a great game," he said, that sleepy smile crossing his face again. He was getting dressed now, getting ready to go over to the card room at the Aladdin Hotel. "I was always in great shape. I used to play forty-five holes a day and walked 'em all. I always played for money. If you didn't play for money you didn't play, that's all." But in 1954, as a result of a car accident, he was forced to give up golf. It was a bad accident and Moss was not expected to live.

"I was laid up six, seven months," he said. "During that time my daughter Eleoweese, she's a strong Baptist y'unnerstand, she went and called the preacher in. Now I don't go to church none and that preacher, he leaned down over my bed and I said just offhand, 'Preacher, do you think it's a sin to gamble?' And he says to me, 'Are you tryin' to find out somethin' for nothin', son?' 'Well the only thing I ever did for a church,' I says, 'was to give 'em money and not go. I don't need no preacher and I don't need no prayin'. I never got nothin' for nothin' and I never asked nothin' for nothin'. Now the best thing you can do, preacher, is to get up and leave my house.' I never did like hypocrites much.

"I don't believe you gotta be a good man to go to church," he said. "There are a lot of hypocrites in the church y'know. They used to look down on Virgie 'cause they knew she was married to a gamblin' man. But I had some publicity once and Virgie, she says to me, 'Since you had your picture made and was written up in the papers and all and it was printed that you was a millionaire, they started sayin' hello and good mornin' to me in church.' You see my meanin'? Hell, I got a million dollars worth of property down in Odessa, all paid. Funny how money changes people's opinions of you."

Forced to give up golf, Moss took up cards again and between 1954 and 1968 he returned to the road. He always knew where the action was. "You get telephone calls, that's all," he said, "and you go. I spent a lot of time on the road in them days. Before Vegas we was all road gamblers. I went anywhere and everywhere. I remember once in 1967 or 1968 old Amarillo Slim, he asked me to come with him to London. Said there was a lot of high hold 'em bein' played and we could make us some easy money there. We went and we played a few times in some gamblin' clubs over there and we won. Then I began to notice we had us a companion in tow. Every club we went to he was there. He was with us everywhere. I point this out to Slim and he explains to me that this guy is from a London gamblin' gang that had cut themselves in for thirty percent of our action. He was a collector. And I says, hell, we don't have to stand for that 'cause everybody knows nobody in England carries guns. And Slim, he says, 'Well maybe this guy don't have no gun, but he carries this hatchet that he uses to nail your hands to the floor if you don't come across with the cut.' That was the information. I don't know nothin' about it. I just listen to people talk. But it was then I decided I'd just go on back to Texas. It wasn't *civilized*. Besides there wasn't any real *high* action there. To win money you got to play with money. You can go huntin'

with a gun and you can either shoot a rabbit or you can shoot
an elephant. Now I never did like rabbit huntin'."

By 1968 he had been on the road continuously for nearly
fifteen years. That year his wife urged him to retire. He was
sixty-one. "And you know," he said, "I upped and retired, just
tired of livin', I guess. I went home and I lay around there in
Odessa for a spell. I got big and fat and was afixin' to die, so
I decided to unretire myself. Can't do that y'know, can't lay
around doin' nothin' with yourself. Can't do that. There was
still a heap to do, y'unnerstand."

The card room in the Aladdin Hotel is in the hotel's large
main room on the ground floor directly across from the Sinbad
Lounge. On the wall behind the sea-green poker tables is a sign
that says: POKER—24 HOURS EVERY DAY. Above the sign is a
spread royal heart flush and just below is the notation—*Johnny
Moss, Manager.* On this particular night the card room was
crowded with loud flamboyant men in Western dress who sat
around or milled about the central poker table. There was a
look of tense anticipation in their tanned and weathered faces.
They looked like ranchers who had ridden into town for the
annual rodeo. Large, brutish, heavy men, they might easily
have come from Central Casting: they might, if appearances
meant anything, have said such things as "Reach for the sky!"
or "Saddle up!" or "Howdy, stranger!" but hunched around the
poker table they talked instead of cards and propositions.
Mainly Texans, they had come to Vegas to compete in the
World Series of Poker which was to begin the following day.
Around the table were Pug Pearson, Texas Dolly Doyle, Treetop Jack Strauss and Amarillo Slim. When Johnny Moss
walked in they looked up from the table, greeting him with gruff
and repetitious welcomes.

"Hey, Johnny."

"Hi, Johnny."

"Howdy, Johnny."

"It's sure good to see ya, ya son of a gun."

"Hullo, boys, hullo," said Moss. He nodded and smiled. The boys returned to their game. Ordering a drink, Moss sat on a chair against the wall and watched the others play. The poker limits in the Aladdin begin with a ten-cent ante and rise to the highest poker in the world. Moss obtained his license from the State of Nevada "because they know I don't do no business with nobody. I leased this card room just so me and the boys could play real high. I run it real well. I make the boys toe the line. I ain't a tough guy or anything. I couldn't lick a sick whore, don't misunnerstand me, but I'd take 'em outside anyway. They have to act like gentlemen in here," he said, "or at least as well as they know how."

He nodded toward the poker table. "These guys here is all high rollers," he said, "an' I got nothin' against 'em, y'unnerstand, but they don't play like the gamblers twenty, thirty years ago. See what I'm sayin'? There's poker players comin' up today that only have one game. Now when I'm playin' poker, I'd used to go to a place, they'd be aplayin' lowball. All right, I'd play along with 'em. I'd go to another place they're playin' draw, I'd play draw, to another place they're playin' stud, I'd play stud, go to another place, they're playin' hold 'em and I'd have to play hold 'em. And ace-to-the-five and deuce-to-the-seven and pitch and gin. You have to play all them games to be a *professional* gambler.

"Remember once when I first came to Vegas, for about forty straight days I flew from here to Los Angeles every day, hired a car and drove to Gardena to learn to play ace-to-the-five at the local joints. It was no higher than twenty-dollar limit. At five o'clock I'd fly back to Vegas, sleep for a few hours and then go to the Flamingo for sixty-four-hundred-dollar-limit ace-to-the-five. Takin' planes to Gardena to play with a lot of god-damn old men and women. But it was worth it. I learned the game at a tenth a the price.

"To be a professional gambler," he said, "not only means you have to know how to play all them games, you have to keep your eyes open for two dangers, the hijackers and the law, specially in the old days. They're both after the same thing, the cash, and they'll do almost anything underhanded to get their hands on it. You see what I'm sayin'? You got to learn to duck and dive, keep your ear to the ground and your eyes peeled. I'm tellin' you, it's like livin' in the jungle."

In 1956 Moss was subpoenaed for fraud and income-tax evasion and brought up before a federal grand jury hearing in Fort Worth. "It was a very confused and messy trial," he recalled. "Twenty-three jurors, the district attorney and me. They wouldn't even let my lawyer in the courtroom. The trial went on for a long time, a two- or three-hour session and that was after the jury had listened to several federal men for three weeks beforehand tellin' 'em what a bad man I was. I mean it was real boring and by the time that attorney got around to questioning me most of the jury had either fallen asleep or they were anoddin' and adozin'. Hot day too, a real hot day.

"Well at one point during the proceedings that attorney he asks me if it was true that I had played golf for eight to ten thousand dollars a hole and a few of them golf-playing jurors begun to perk up. I guess he must a heard tall tales about that match I had at the Desert Inn a couple a years before, 'cause all the rest of them jurors woke up when he asks me if I had played a match for a hundred thousand. They woke up. They were real interested now. Well then what happened, that attorney he suddenly comes out with a putter. He wanted to learn how to putt, I guess. He got into a kind of putting stance and asks me how I had made that putt for so much money. He asks me how did I putt. He asks me to show him how I had done it. 'Well,' I says, 'I just sort of stand like this,' and I showed him. Now I had to be a dog, y'unnerstand, I had to be their dog. I had to put myself in the place of them jurors, just like they'd been there taking that putt, just like a sucker would feel about it. It was a ten-foot putt, but I told 'em it was five. I didn't want to seem supernatural or nothin'. I says to them, 'Up close the hole looks this big, but when I step back it looks this small. I know that even if I get that ball over there, the hole would be too small for that ball to get in.'

"Then one of the jurors says, 'But you made that putt?' And I says, 'Well I was plain lucky, I guess. I had a good line, a good stroke, and I just shut my eyes, stroked it and lucked it in, I guess.' And that juror says, 'I believe you, son.' All them jurors looked as though they did the same thing every day. Hell, I didn't want to tell 'em I was one of the best putters there is."

Moss laughed and looked around the room. "Then that attorney asks me if I choked and I said sure I choked, sure, even the pros choke. The fear just grabs ahold of you. 'Listen,' I said, 'I once saw Ben Hogan miss a very important two-foot putt. Ben Hogan. Everybody chokes. It's only natural.' I didn't tell 'em I never choke, that I play for the cash and you don't choke for the cash. I wanted to be just like them suckers in the jury.

"Well all along it looked like I was agoin' to get twenty years, five for sure. In the end I asked 'em if they would acquit me. A man could be in the corner about to cut off my head, I says to them, and I wouldn't ask him not to, but I asked 'em not to indict me. I said I never asked for nothin' in my life. This is the first thing I've ever asked for. I ain't exactly beggin' for mercy, but as far as I know I ain't guilty of what you say I am. And, y'know, they let me go." He got up to answer the telephone. "But hell," he said, "I declare everything anyway."

At the main table the boys are laughing and making bets among themselves as to who will win tomorrow's tournament. Amarillo Slim, who had won the year before, tells Pug Pearson he would be smart to take a piece of him. "Do yourself a favor, Puggie," says Slim. "I'm even *more* ferocious than last year."

Pug grins, rolling his cigar from one corner of his mouth to the other. "I ain't takin' a piece of nobody but me," he says. "Wouldn't make no sense, Slim. You ain't luckin' by me again this year."

Standing just behind Pug is a large impassive man in dark glasses. He looks like the house detective. He has not moved for an hour. He is the only man not playing cards. When Johnny Moss returns from the telephone, I ask him who he is. "Him?

He ain't no player. He used to be a hit man down in Texas. Killed thirty men, maybe more. But he's all right now.

"Listen, I know fifty thieves and fifteen, twenty killers," says Moss. He looks at me, an ironic smile on his face. "Well, *maybe* I know 'em. Up until I come up here to Vegas, you always carry your pistol with you. Not that you're tough or anything. It was just the way it was. People know you carry guns, they don't pick on you. They don't pick on you much. After me and my wife was hijacked down in Alabama I bought me a four-ten scatter gun and I'd carry it with me whenever I played poker. Kept it in my lap. When I come back to my hotel room, well, I got it cocked 'cause how many folks you know gonna stay in a room with me when I come in the door with my shotgun cocked? No sir, nobody's gonna play stick 'em up with a shotgun around.

"You can't never be too careful in this business, y'unnerstand. It used to be worse than it is nowadays. I remember once in 1965 I heard about this game in a house that's supposed to be hijackin'-proof. It was in Beeville in Texas about a hundred miles from Houston. They were playin' hold 'em there, a lot of good ole boys. First time I went I took away about a hundred and ninety thousand and the second time about twenty-two thousand. I thought I'd found me a gold mine, a place where I could win me some real easy money. Place was built like a pillbox, y'unnerstand, I mean there was just no way anybody could get in or out less'n they asked. But after the second time I had a phone call from some guy in Dallas, who said, 'If I was you I wouldn't go back to Beeville no more.' I don't know who it was on that phone, but I sure knew what he meant, so I waited for about three weeks till a friend a mine who was aplayin' in the game tells me, 'Johnny, there musta been two hundred thousand on the table last week. You're sure missin' out on all this money.' So I decided it was safe to go back. Nothin' had happened, you see. I went back the next week and we was aplayin'. There musta been nineteen of us boys in that room. Titanic Thompson was in the game too.

"Now, as I said, you can't never be too careful. We had an

outside man aguardin' the place but they must've taken care of him. And they cut the telephone wires. All I know, all of a sudden they shot tear gas in through the peephole. We looked outside and there were five or six thieves carryin' scatter guns, wearin' fatigues with socks over their heads and gas masks on. Like men out of space. There was gas everywhere in that room. I says to ole Ty, 'Ty, I'm gettin' sick and these guys ain't leavin' till they get in.' And Ty says, 'Johnny, let's stroll out there and get us some clean air.' And we did. When I saw 'em, I knew every one of 'em. One of the players in the game hid out in the toilet. He was wearin' a big diamond ring on his hand and the leader of the hijackers says, 'If he don't give up that diamond cut it off'n his finger and kill him.' They was pros those boys, real pros.

"Well we'd hid our cash inside. I hid my money up in the divan in the coils but they found it. Ty hid his in the freezing compartment of the icebox and they found that too. Only guy to save his money hid it in the plunger on the inside of the toilet. Had a rubber band around it. Saved himself about twenty thousand. That's why you keep a rubber band around your roll, so's you can throw it in the bushes case you're hijacked. In the bushes or the tall grass. A rubber band's saved me about six times from being heisted.

"But not that time. They made us keep our hands on our heads. And when they got the money, must've been near to two hundred thousand, they locked us back inside and lifted all the keys to our cars. I just lay down on that divan and waited. And sure enough the Rangers come and the FBI outta Dallas three hundred and fifty miles away. And one of them Rangers come up to me as I was alayin' on that there divan and he says, 'What your name?' And I says, 'Joe Miller,' and he says, 'What you lose?' The door was open and I look out there and see this ole farmer astandin' out there by the truck and I says, 'I didn't lose nothin'. I just come over here with Uncle Jim and I had a heart attack and I was alayin' down restin'.' Then I walked outside slow as you please and tole that ole farmer, 'Now, you tell 'em you're my Uncle Jim and let's make like shepherds and get the flock outta here.' You see, you can't tell them Rangers nothin'. They'd as soon take you in for pitchin' pennies."

There is loud laughter from the main poker table. Amarillo Slim has told another of his interminable Texan tales, this one concerning a low lady called Dago Mary. Moss has heard the tale before. He sips at his drink and smiles. He knows all the high players in the game. Although he refers to them as friends, gamblers tend not to socialize; they rarely spend much time in one another's company when they are not in competition. There is, among them, little more than an amiable commercial contact. Moss takes their money or they take his and they remain, as he puts it, loosely, curiously, "friends."

He prefers to play with familiar players. "You see," he explained, "when the stakes are high I'm in a better position to read their shows and tells. Y'unnerstand? I know when they got hands and when they ain't got no hands. Eight outta ten men, I play with 'em long enough I can tell when they're abluffin'. They got a tell. You get a tell by the way they move their checks. You get the reaction, the conversation. You like to play with people you've played with before; you know where you are. You have to learn what kind of hand this guy shows down, watch that one's moves, watch the veins in his neck, watch his eyes, the way he sweats. See what I'm sayin'?"

He lit another cigarette. "I don't rate many players in the game no more. There were some great ones," he said. He looked away and the names began to trickle out—Little Man Popwell, Lone Wolf Gonzales, Society Red, Nick the Greek. "There's Red Wynne, but he's too old. Nigger Nate Raymond, but he was a cheater. There was Tommy Abdo, a regular player, a great high roller. But two or three years ago he got up from his chair one night, they was aplayin' in the card room at the Dunes, he walked off a few feet and dropped to the floor with a heart attack. The rest of them players rush over to him and all he says was, 'Somebody count my checks.' Then he went and died. There ain't many like him left."

Toward midnight Jimmy the Greek Snyder walked into the room. The Greek, a large and crafty man, formerly a gambler, now produced a syndicated newspaper column listing the odds on most of the country's sporting and political events. He also ran a public-relations firm. Born Demetrius Synodinos, the Greek was the tournament's official bookmaker. His starting prices made Johnny Moss, Jack Strauss and Pug Pearson the co-favorites at 5–to–1. The Greek smiled and said hello to the assembled players. "Hey, Greek," said Pug, "with three of us as equal favorites it sounds to me like you couldn't make up your mind."

"My mind's set firm Puggie," said the Greek, "it's a good price." He turned to me. "Got the best hold 'em players in the world in here," he said. And then, as though he anticipated a contradiction, he added, "Well maybe there's somebody in Texas playing in a cigar store or something, somebody that plays really well, but nobody knows about him, see? Other than that the best players in the entire world are sitting at that table."

At the far end of the table, Treetop Jack Strauss, so-called because he was 6'7", peered at his cards. In his late forties, he had the heavily jowled face of an aging bloodhound. A Texan from Houston, he had been a history teacher and basketball player but had renounced these occupations in order to devote himself to gambling. He was a compulsive gambler, gambling on everything from football to cockfights. Pug recalled how Strauss, two years before, was down to his last $40 after a black run in Vegas. One morning playing blackjack he increased his stake to $500, ran it up to $4,000 playing poker in the afternoon, up to $10,000 at craps that evening and bet it all on the Kansas City Chiefs to win the Super Bowl the following day, collecting $20,000. "He'll bet on anything that moves," said Pug. "Christ, he'd bet on a *cockroach* race."

Pug himself had been beaten by Amarillo Slim in the finals of the tournament the year before. He did not like hold 'em very much. "It's a Texan game, a cowboy's game," he said. "But it's sure tough. When I first heard tell of it, it was called 'hold 'em and fuck 'em.' I couldn't play this game a lick last year," he said. Pushing his straw hat to the back of his head, he grinned. "But I'm a sponge," he said. "I learn."

"Well, you ain't done with your education yet, Puggie," said Amarillo Slim. Amarillo Slim Preston straddled his chair at the opposite end of the table. Six feet four and 170 pounds, he wore a white ten-gallon Stetson, a $550 red suit and a pair of $5,000 anteater-hide cowboy boots, "which were poached from some exotic game preserve," he said, "but not by me, neighbor." He cupped his cigarette in his hand as though protecting it from a high wind. "Hey, Greek," he said, "lookee here. I'm the world champeen at this here game. The world champeen. How come you're only makin' me eight-to-one? Ain't you read my book? It says right there on the cover in plain English—Amarillo Slim, the world champeen of poker shows you how he beats 'em all. Can't you read, Greek? Hell, I'd get better odds in a spelling bee."

"That Slim," said Johnny Moss, "he always had a lot of country con. I been aknowin' Slim since the Forties. That book of his is a joke. He may have won last year, but he was lucky. He's good, but he ain't great. He ain't gonna last out this tournament."

Moss sat there against the wall. When he was not talking he seemed almost to be asleep. "I'll tell you," he said, "people playin' in this game are good ole boys, mostly Texans. I been knowin' 'em for years and years. Strauss is a strong player and unpredictable. He's a great ring player, great in a seven- or eight-handed game. Keeps you on your toes. Puggie's an aggressive player, always movin' in on you. He's a fighter, a killer, and he's dedicated. You gotta be. And he'll never play partners with nobody. He's always alone. The Greek's right. Them two are the ones to watch." He paused. "And me. You can't count me out yet. I'm sixty-seven and I'm still in there with a fightin' chance. Virgie wouldn't want all that money to go nowhere but Texas. And when I say Texas, I mean Odessa. You get my meanin'? When it comes to winnin', I got me a one-track mind."

## II

The following afternoon thirteen of the country's sharpest high rollers sat down to play poker—the game Nick the Greek liked to call "the art of civilized bushwhacking." It was a $10,000 buy-in, the winner taking everything—$130,000. The tournament was being held in the main card room of the Horseshoe Casino down in Glitter Gulch, some five miles away from the Strip. The Horseshoe was once the only family-owned casino in Las Vegas, owned by Johnny Moss's old boyhood friend, Benny Binion. It has the world's highest limits at craps and for certain people there are no limits at all. Built in 1937, the casino was sold in 1954 when Binion was dispatched to Leavenworth federal prison on a five-year tax-evasion rap. It was repurchased by his son Jack and others in 1960.

Benny the Cowboy Binion has a long record in Dallas of bootlegging, theft, carrying concealed weapons and two murder raps, for one of which he received a two-year suspended sentence, the other being dismissed with a notation of "self-defense." He left Dallas hurriedly, coming to Vegas in 1946. "I had to get out," he said. "My sheriff got beat in the election that year." Now sixty-eight and retired, Binion is still known round town as a boss gambler and when questioned about his lurid past he is fond of saying, "Well, boy, tough times make tough people."

In its time the Horseshoe has attracted most of the country's high rollers and not a few of its eccentrics. Jack Binion likes to tell tales of a certain Murphy, an elderly millionaire from New Jersey. Murphy insisted the bed be removed from his room, preferring a mattress which he covered with a beaver sheet. He greeted early morning visitors in an overcoat. He demanded the drawers of his dresser be refilled daily with sand and freshly cut flowers. He was observed by night fishing for crocodiles in the swimming pool of the Sands Hotel. Murphy revealed that he possessed an infallible craps system. With such a system he intended to break the entire town. Binion told me that in one eight-week period Murphy lost more than three million dollars. Each Monday morning at eleven o'clock, he paid his creditors in crisp one-thousand-dollar bills. Binion shook his head and smiled. "One Monday morning Mr. Murphy paid his bills, packed his beaver sheet and just disappeared. Went back East," he said, "New Jersey, I guess."

Glitter Gulch is the commercial center of Las Vegas. In Fremont Street the neon-covered casinos stand side by side like giant nickelodeons—the Horseshoe, the Jackpot, the Four Queens, the Mint, the Golden Nugget. At the rear of the Horseshoe is its showpiece—a gigantic Plexiglas horseshoe suspended from the ceiling, containing a million dollars in ten-thousand-dollar bills. Tourists, or what Jack Binion calls "the nickel 'n dime folk," are permitted to photograph the cash and, for a small consideration, their film is developed in the drugstore across the corridor. The use of Polaroids is discouraged.

The casino itself is decorated in a kind of bawdyhouse baroque—paneled bars and balustrades, red carpet and chandeliers, mirror-stripped ceilings, crushed-velvet papered walls, and a multitude of squat brass cuspidors. The waitresses are dressed as cowgirls and the bartenders wear arm garters and black string ties. It is the sort of atmosphere one might find in any early B Western; one half expects to run across Audie Murphy, Joel McCrea, or Randolph Scott drinking whiskey at the bar.

Casino employees dust the green felt tables in the card room and set out chairs and ashtrays. The competitors would be playing hold 'em, a Texan variation of seven-card stud. In hold 'em, each player antes and then gets two down cards. The betting then begins and a player must either stay in the pot or fold. Then three cards, called the flop, are dealt face up in the center of the table. After further betting two more cards are dealt face up, one at a time. The five cards in the center of the table are community cards and may be used by all the players. From the total of seven cards, five are used to make the strongest hand. "Because there are so many concealed hands in the game," Johnny Moss explained, "hold 'em is the toughest card game in the world. Texans are best at it 'cause Texans play it. There are no poker players in the East anyway. Great gin players, bridge players maybe, but no poker players. Hold 'em is to, say, stud or draw what chess is to checkers. It's a fantastic game."

The main hold 'em event was the culmination of a series of preliminary tournaments held the day before for lesser stakes. Joe Bernstein had won the ace-to-the-five, Jack Strauss had taken the deuce-to-the-seven, and Pug Pearson had picked up thirty-two thousand dollars by winning the seven-card stud competition. There had also been a razz tournament (a seven-card stud low game), which was won by a squat, ebullient man called Sam Angel. A player of mediocre merits, Angel was usually to be found in the lobby of the Dunes Hotel hawking diamond rings and necklaces, which he dredged from his pockets or from a sample case he carried under his arm. He was known up and down the Strip as Sam the Diamond Man.

The players drifted into the room and stood around in little groups talking to other gamblers, listening to the dull interrogations of the press, or nodding to well-wishers in the crowd who had gathered behind the rail. The spectators jostled back and forth angling for optimum positions, while the players seemed alert but curiously at ease.

Other than the three favorites, there was Adrian Texas Dolly Doyle, a huge, amiable man of 290 pounds from Fort Worth. Standing next to him was Crandall Addington, a young millionaire from San Antonio. Addington was an ostentatious dresser—white shoes, cream suits and patterned shirts. He wore gold Patek Philippe watches, gold rings and a diamond stickpin in his tie. Slouched at the table waiting for play to begin was Bryan Roberts, known simply as Sailor. He too came from Fort Worth and throughout the tournament he wore short-sleeved floppy jump suits made of rough toweling. The suits gave him the look of a man who had had to leave the house unexpectedly and so had forgotten to change. "They're comfortable to move around in, that's all," he said. "I have dozens of 'em in dozens of different colors."

The other six players were all long shots and for the most part unknowns. There was Bobby Brazil, a swarthy youth from Lake Tahoe, Jolly Roger Van Ausdale from Missouri, Jack Lanier from California, a large man called Hooks from Dallas, a former football player and schoolteacher. There was Sam Hoff, known as the Wizard; he had longish hair, a beard and spectacles and looked like the second guitarist in a country rock band. Lastly there was Jimmy Cassella, who preferred to be called Fury. Dark stubble dotted his pallid features. He had that kind of vulpine face that could only have been fashioned in New York; he was the only Easterner in the game. And for as long as he played his wife, a blond in a skin-tight mini-skirt, hovered behind his chair. That afternoon one of the reporters asked her for her full name. "Well, sweetheart," she said in bright, theatric tones, "around the house I'm plain old Mrs. Jimmy C. But you can use my stage name if you want. On the stage I'm known as Crystal Lake."

Just after four o'clock Amarillo Slim entered the room. "Let's get the show on the road," he announced. "The world's champeen is ready to play." A few minutes later the thirteen players cut cards for position and sat down at two of the large green felt tables. Each had $10,000 worth of chips in front of him—the $25 chips in yellow and green, the $100s in black and white. "I'll lay six-to-five the winner comes off this here table," shouted Slim. The three favorites, Moss, Strauss and Pearson, all of whom were sitting at the other table, smiled but did not look up. Jimmy the Greek cautioned the crowd to be as quiet as possible.

The crowd massed behind the rail was predominantly Western, mainly men, in Stetson hats and cowboy boots. Those not dressed in cowboy clothes tended to have the hangdog look of the unemployed and one of them wore a faded deliveryman's shirt with CHARLIE'S printed across his chest. The few women

among them had a cheap and unexpected Fifties flavor—
bermuda-shorted, sweatered, with teased bouffants and pam-
pered pompadours. Most of them chewed gum. The crowd
would remain there throughout the tournament, entranced,
hanging on to every play; there was in their faces the veiled
rapacious look of habitual voyeurs.

In the card room proper the bleachers were crowded with
gamblers, casino owners, and journalists. Other gamblers
prowled back and forth between the two tables. One of these
was a slight, skeletal man with gray and stringy hair. He wore
dark glasses which only emphasized the acute triangularity of
his features. His name was Fred Ferris, but everyone called him
Sarge. He looked like a consumptive and one could hear a
rough hiss of breath at the back of his soft Louisiana drawl.

"Sure, I feel bad," he said, "but not as bad as I look. Shit,
I been up all night playin' cards and I feel bad." He fiddled with
his dark glasses. "Listen, a doctor, he once said to me, 'Son, I'll
give you six months,' and I said, 'Doc, I'll take it.'"

Sarge was a Vegas regular, a great lowball and deuce-to-the-
seven player. He also played hold 'em, but had refused to enter
this tournament. "I ain't playin'," he said, "I ain't playin' 'cause
I don't like an audience and all that shit. But hell, *they* love it.
Look at Puggie. He *eats* it up. He don't care whether he loses
or wins, long as they take his picture. Shit, I'd rather play
solitaire."

To begin with the action was slow, monotonous even, as the
gamblers probed for weaknesses, for signs of uncertainty in
their opponents' play. They appeared to play intently but with
a kind of feigned insouciance, as though it were just another
game of cards. Still, there was a look of solemnity in their eyes.
Only Amarillo Slim seemed unimpressed and uninvolved. He
played, as he always did, with one eye on the cards, the other
on the crowd. Some minutes after the game began he threw a
handful of dollar chips into the crowd. Rising to his feet, he
bowed slightly and tipped his ten-gallon hat to them.

"Christ, he's thin," said Sarge. "Look at him. He looks like the advance man for a famine."

Again, about an hour later after taking a large pot, Slim rose and said, "Hard to fool is the world's champeen, neighbor," then shouted across to the other table, "Well, it looks like you and me again, Puggie." Pug smiled and chomped on his cigar.

The play did not vary much; there were few swings, few shows of strength and at nine o'clock a forty-five-minute break was called for dinner. During the break for the benefit of the crowd Jimmy the Greek listed the scores on a large blackboard: Slim—$18,325, Hoff—$17,325, Pug—$14,075, Sailor—$13,100, Brazil—$10,950, Cassella—$10,100, Moss—$8,775, Addington—$8,525, Van Ausdale—$7,500, Strauss—$6,725, Doyle—$6,700, Hooks—$6,000, Lanier—$1,900. Most of the players were already down. Slim smiled and waved to the crowd.

As the players walked in to dinner an announcement came over the public-address system: "*Amarillo Slim,* the world poker champion's autobiography, is on sale in the lobby now," it said.

"You know," said Slim, "I never did read that son of a bitch."

The Sombrero Room was very crowded. Seated round the tables were the gamblers, the hoteliers, the wheelers and dealers, the hangers-on and the press. Johnny Moss and his wife sat by themselves at the back of the room. Since most of the players were Southerners, the dinner included such Southern specialities as catfish, hush puppies, hominy grits and black-eyed peas.

"What is *catfish?*" an English journalist asks, poking suspiciously at the fish with his fork. "What?" says Pug. "You ain't never heard of catfish, son? I can't believe there's *nowheres* where there ain't catfish. Don't you have no cricks over there in England?"

Seated next to Pug is Joe Bernstein. He is perfectly tailored, perfectly tanned; the slicked-back silver hair accentuates his style. Dressed casually in blue and white, he continues to look at seventy the way Palm Beach dandies must have looked some forty years ago. "He was in the barber shop the day Anastasia got it," someone says. Bernstein wants Pug to win and is anxious to take bets even though Pug, at the moment, is behind. The two men talk of other, older gamblers; the name of Nick the Greek comes up. "Don't talk to me about the Greek," says Bernstein, his mouth full of black-eyed peas. "Pardon, you're upsetting me, bringing up the Greek like that. All he got famous for was losing. I got famous for winning. Listen, in New York in the old days we played a lot. A lot. When the town was hot the crap game floated. I remember, *personally*, one of Johnny Coakley's crap games in a loft on Fifty-fourth and Broadway. Game lasted twelve days. Arnold Rothstein was playing. The Greek lost over a million in that game. Some winner.

"Nigger Nate was there too," he said, clicking his teeth as he spoke. "Now, *there* was a conniver. Peeking, conniving, the eye in the sky. Nate once said to me, 'Joe, I'm an old man. I should be allowed to steal a little.' " Bernstein laughed.

"Shucks," said Pug, "why Nigger Nate was an ole tush-hog. No tellin' how many people he killed. Maybe thirty or forty. I saw him last year just before he died. Told me he was fixin' to die. He was eighty-two, I guess. Asked me if I wanted anybody killed. 'There's a lot of sons of bitches in the world,' he says. 'Thought I'd take one of 'em with me if you liked.' "

Johnny Moss was reluctant to discuss his own chances of victory. "Don't like to talk about it none," he said. "It's too early yet, much too early yet. We gotta get rid of the driftwood first." He looked at Virgie and smiled. A tiny woman with a round and wrinkled face, she seemed somehow bigger than she was. She, at least, seemed confident. She touched the back of Johnny's hand.

"Don't care whether it's cards or what it is," said Johnny, "to win, you gotta have confidence and know your psychology. You gotta be able to move your checks so that your opponents get in so deep it becomes just as dangerous for them to stop as to go ahead. You gotta make 'em call you and then bust 'em. Money isn't the important thing in cards. Money's just chips to me, units. I see it as four stacks against five, that's all. A poker player's best attribute is patience. Then you gotta want to win more than anything else. If you're aplayin' with your brother or your daddy, you got to break 'em. If you got something to give 'em, give it to 'em after the game is over. And you gotta have confidence. You can't pretend to have it. That's no good. You gotta *have* it. You gotta *know.* Guessers are losers. When you get outclassed it's gonna show. It's just like puttin' a lightweight fighter up against a heavyweight. Gamblin's just as simple as that. You gotta know your capability and stick to it. Ain't no secret about that."

Sam Angel walked up to the table; he looked almost naked without his sample case. "I stopped work a few hours ago," he said. "Came to watch the action." He looked at his watch. "Hey, Johnny," he said, "let's go. We been in here nearly an hour. Let's get on with the show."

Play began again, this time more seriously, and one by one the competitors were eliminated. At 10:30 Lanier was knocked out by Pug. An hour later Amarillo Slim, who had had a disastrous run, lost his last four thousand in one hand and was gone. He rose, a grim smile on his face, and waved his hat to the crowd. A woman in bermuda shorts threw back one of Slim's dollar chips to him. He kissed it and put it in his pocket. Slim pushed his way through the crowd and left the room. "Better stop the world champeen 'fore he jumps off the roof," said Doyle to Jack Strauss.

"Let him jump," said Strauss. "He's got too much hot air in him to do him any harm."

Five minutes later Doyle himself was eliminated; rising voluminous in blue like a blimp, he left the room. And so the night went on. By three A.M. seven players had been broken— Lanier, Amarillo Slim, Doyle, the Wizard, Addington, Van Ausdale and Cassella. Of those who remained Strauss was the big winner with $42,725. Pug had $41,350 and Johnny Moss lay in third with $22,000. The general opinion was that it would end up being a head-on clash between Strauss and Pug, which seemed to worry Pug. "That boy's played a jillion hours," he said. "That's all they ever do in Texas."

The players drifted off to bed or into the casino. Johnny Moss continued to sit in his chair twirling his chips on the table and talking to Amarillo Slim. The English journalist approached; he was anxious to know just how much cheating occurred in top-rank poker.

"Hell, none that I know of, neighbor," said Slim. "Leastways, not among real gamblers. Right, Johnny? Listen, I been heisted three times in the last ten years. Cheated on more than that. I can smell crooked play. Sometimes what I smelled cookin' just wasn't on the fire. But they wasn't real gamblers. A gambler's word is his bond." He waved his hand round the room. "If one of these boys tells you a goose'll move a plow," he said, "then hook him up, neighbor, 'cause he'll damn sure move it out."

Johnny Moss yawned. "Listen," he said, "there are three classes of gamblers, y'unnerstand—cheaters, cheating gamblers and professional gamblers. Now, if a cheater can't cheat, he won't play. He just won't set down less'n he's got something agoin'. If a cheating gambler can't cheat, he'll play, but they can't win when they have to play, and a professional gambler winds up with all the money. The boys playin' in here, they're professionals." He yawned again.

"Come on, Johnny, let's get us some sleep," said Virgie.

"Yeah, I'm tired, real tired," he said. "I could do with twenty hours."

"You ain't got but twelve," said Slim.

Johnny smiled; it was almost a grimace. Arm in arm the couple left the card room.

"Are you coming back next year, Slim?" the English journalist asked.

"Hell, I'm back already," said Slim. "As soon as this session is over I'm having myself a nice little game with the new champeen." He rubbed his hands together. "And that just might be Mr. Moss if he can keep his eyeballs open."

The following day, shortly before six o'clock, Johnny Moss walked into the card room of the Horseshoe Casino. He wore blue trousers, a white shirt and blue and white shoes. There was about him a kind of Sears Roebuck elegance that did little to disguise the fact that he had had a sleepless night, broken by the dawn and by dark dreams he could not now bring himself to recall. But he was ready to play; he was always ready to play. He put on his glasses and sat down in the chair he had vacated less than fifteen hours before.

The play began just after six, and as on the previous day it was slow and repetitious. Johnny Moss sat back in his chair and seemed to doze. Pug, in red, his straw hat tipped over his brow, was apparently content to let his opponents break one another before stirring himself to action, since he avoided any real confrontations. Strauss looked sullen and bored. Sailor, in a maroon jump suit today, scowled, throwing in hand after hand. Bobby Brazil was merely taciturn. Only Hooks, the former football star, seemed absorbed; but then he was winning one pot after another. There was, in fact, more action at the next table where a game of lowball had started up between Sarge and some of the losers. But that was not why the crowd had come. The crowd was impatient; they muttered among themselves and waited.

Toward nine o'clock Hooks pushed all his checks into the pot for the twelfth consecutive time and for the twelfth time the other players folded. Raking in the pot, Hooks grinned. "We'll jerk some of that ginger out of you yet," said Pug. "Why yesterday, when you were behind, you looked like a man with an ax in his head." Hooks grinned again. Five minutes later Hooks did it again, pushing in about $10,000. Only Pug remained in the pot. Chomping on his cigar, he looked carefully at his cards. Finally he pushed $10,000 into the pot and called. Pug had three tens. Hooks had been bluffing and was eliminated. Bobby Brazil was the next to go. The day before he had not entered the pot once between midnight and three A.M., simply losing his ante each time. Today, for more than an hour, he did it again and it became just too expensive. Pug broke him with two jacks. He was the dark horse of the tournament and when he rose from the table, there was loud applause. Brazil smiled.

"He's a good loser," one of the reporters said.

"A good loser's just another loser," said Sarge.

The game continued and less than an hour later Sailor too was broken by Pug. He joined the game of lowball at the adjacent table. Of the ten players eliminated Pug had broken eight of them himself. By 9:30 only three players remained in the game. Jimmy the Greek scrawled their scores on the blackboard. Pug—$62,000, Moss—$45,000, Strauss—$23,000. A break was called.

"Well, whatta you think, Slim?" said Doyle.

"I think we got us a fine horse race now," said Slim. "Play hard, Johnny," he shouted. "We gotta keep this thing in Texas."

During the break Pug wandered out of the room with Jimmy the Greek. Johnny Moss sat in a corner talking to his wife. Strauss remained at the table where he was joined by Sarge. "Now listen, Jack," he said, "whenever Puggie puts them checks of his into piles of two thousand, he don't have nothin'. I been watchin' him. When that happens you *go* for him. You had him on the ropes before, remember. You got to take a bit from him at a time. You can't bulldoze him. Take a bit at a time. He's not goin' nowhere." Strauss nodded impassively.

At the other end of the room Amarillo Slim was holding court. He was dressed in a white suit and a bright pink shirt. A white ten-gallon hat was pushed to the back of his head. He showed the English reporter his watch—made from an 1899 gold ten-dollar piece. "I bought it in Albuquerque from Dago Mary," he said. "She threw in three pairs of levis in the price." This draws a big laugh from one of the waitresses, a pert flirtatious blonde.

"Howdy, Slim," she said.

"Honey," said Slim, "I don't know what you did last night, but it sure agrees with you."

"Oh, Slim," gushed the girl, "can I do anything for you, get you some water maybe?"

"Now honey, would a country hog drink town slop?"

"Oh, Slim."

A few minutes later, Pug returned to the card room and the three men sat down to play. Pug was cheerful and exchanged quips with someone in the crowd. Johnny Moss looked at his watch; he was tired and knew that this was his major weakness. Strauss sat with his back to the crowd. He has a tendency to play to the gallery, holding up as many of his cards as he wants them to see. For the first few hands the three men played cautiously and with a kind of studied calm. But soon the pots began to grow and after an hour of play they rarely averaged less than $10,000 a hand. Pug and Strauss shared most of the winning hands and by ten o'clock it was becoming clear that Johnny Moss would not survive much longer. Through either fatigue or misfortune, his stake of $45,000 had been whittled down to $15,000. At this point the first big confrontation occurred between the three men.

The hand began innocuously enough. Johnny has to act first and antes $600. Strauss antes $600 and so does Pug. The dealer then deals two down cards each. Johnny receives two aces, Strauss gets a nine and a ten and Pug a queen and a jack. Casually, Johnny bets $2,200. Strauss, looking impatiently at his hand, calls. Pug hesitates; he feels he has a big hand but he wants to wait for the flop and so he calls. The dealer now deals three cards face up in the center of the table—a jack, a queen and a two. Still uncertain, Strauss checks and a moment later Pug checks too. Looking carefully at his cards, Johnny stalls. He has a strong hand. He does not know, of course, that Pug has queens and jacks. He believes he has the stronger hand and after a moment's hesitation he eases all of his remaining chips, about $12,500, into the pot. Knowing that Johnny could be eliminated here, the crowd falls silent and the lowball players forsake their game and move across the room to watch.

It is up to Strauss. He looks at the pot, then frowns and throws in his hand. "Well, Johnny," says Pug, "what do you got? I think you got two kings or two aces in the hole. You ain't got nothin' else, y'know. At least, I hope you ain't got three queens or three jacks." Pug looks at his hand again, then puts it down and relights his cigar. Jimmy the Greek walks up behind him. Pug turns round and whispers, "I think Johnny's a big dog here." Finally Pug counts out $12,500 and pushes it into the pot. There is now $33,400 there. Both men are waiting for the last two cards. Because there can be no further betting, Johnny turns up his hand and so does Pug. It is now clear that Pug has much the stronger hand, but if this troubles Johnny he shows no sign of it. Pulling a handkerchief from his back pocket he begins to wipe his glasses. The dealer burns one card and then turns up a nine. With one card to come Johnny is about a 5-to-1 underdog. "Get on with it, dealer," says Pug. "Deal." Hesitating slightly, the dealer turns up the final card—an ace —giving Johnny three aces and the pot. Pug whistles and the crowd bursts into excited asides and exclamations. Johnny shook his head, wiping his glasses again. "I was ready to walk out," he whispered. "I ain't drawed out on nobody in a long time."

The fortuitous ace did much to lift Johnny's spirits and with them his play. Thereafter he won hand after hand and at 10:30 came a showdown with Strauss. Pug had already folded. There was $56,000 in the pot with one card to come. Johnny had three eights. Strauss had four cards toward a straight heart flush, needing a nine to complete it.

"I'll lay three-to-two against him getting it," said Sailor.

"You'll get two-to-one," said Pug.

The dealer turned up a seven and Strauss was out of the tournament. He rose wearily from the table and walked from the room.

"Let's take a break," says Pug.

In the stands the losers are laying odds among themselves—

even money to begin with, although some are demanding 6–to–5 on Pug. Everyone, it seems, has a piece of the two men.

"The Greek's got twenty percent of Puggie," says Sarge, "and somebody else has got a dime."

"A dime?" the English reporter says.

"Yeah, ten percent."

"The Greek's 'bout ready to slit his throat," says Slim. "If I had a girl tight as his stomach tonight I'd really be in business."

"And Moss?"

"Johnny's cut up like a boarding house pie," says Sarge.

Wandering through the crowd is Eighty-Dollar Natey, one of the town's more prominent shylocks. He carries, it is said, a roll of $30,000 in his pocket. Dressed in black and gray, he has the air of a successful mortician. He does not walk; rather, he seems to move sideways through the crowd like a crab. His skin is sallow, cadaverous—the result of a twelve-year stretch in San Quentin. San Quentin is not one of Natey's favorite subjects and his dead eyes drift off to other parts of the room whenever it is mentioned. He prefers to speak of usury, describing himself as a financier. "Natey's got a lot of clients," says Sarge. "There are a lot of guys that owe him the world."

Johnny sat at one of the tables with his wife. He was tired but confident. The odds always favor the player with the most chips and at the moment Johnny had $70,400 to Pug's $59,600. Despite the odds being given in the stands, he was a clear favorite.

"Sure I'm a favorite," he said, "but this game can go any way. I'm in a good position and position is very important in poker. I've played this game a long time. Anybody can lift their checks up and down, but they can't always push 'em in the pot. That's goin' down a different street. You gotta be cold about that, real cold." Johnny smiled. "You know," he said, "some doctor, he once told me I'd have heart trouble when I was older and I says to him, 'Not me, doc, I don't have no heart.' "

At eleven o'clock that night Pug Pearson and Johnny Moss

sat down to play. A large crowd had gathered now; bunched behind the rail, they shifted ceaselessly for position. There was something greedy and apprehensive in their faces—the wanton look of men who have come to watch an execution.

At the table the two men wait for the opening deal. Johnny yawns. He appears to be listless, remote. Pug, the straw hat tilted over his brow, rocks nervously in his chair, chewing gum and aspirin. He has had a headache since dinner and now, apparently tiring of aspirin, he orders Alka-Seltzer. The two men look at one another and smile.

"Homicide and suicide, that's what this is," says Amarillo Slim. "One will gun the other down and he'll go home and shoot himself. I'll tell you, neighbor, Johnny has more experience than the other boy, but I'd know who I'd bet on if I were in there. You just ask Pug who he'd rather have in there with him. Lookee here, I'm ready to play again. I'm not goin' anywhere long as these fools have that much money."

Slim turned to the English journalist. "Listen, you play a lot of poker over there in England. What do you think'll happen here?"

"Well, I don't know who will win," he said, "but I see this as a classic confrontation between the old sentimental hero come back against a man emanating killer death-rays. I see Johnny as the gentle giant about to do battle with Pug, who is one step removed from Cro-Magnon man."

"How's that?" said Slim. He looked distinctly puzzled. "Neighbor," he said, "you *sure* have a funny way of saying things."

The two men began to play and for nearly an hour the game swung monotonously back and forth—Pug winning most of the small pots, Johnny winning $24,000 in one hand to even matters again. Both men played tightly, conservatively, and the game became a grind, the money trickling slowly, tediously onto the table. "Move it, boys, move it," said Slim. "Either throw it away or move it in." At midnight, in order to quicken the action, they agreed to play with $500 chips. "Gawd," whispered Slim, "this began as a cattleman's game, became an oil-man's game, and now it's the kind of game only South American dictators in exile can afford to be in. Now, neighbor, that's real high poker."

The increase in stakes seemed to stimulate Pug. He began to play more rapidly, more aggressively, calling and raising with an ominous authority in his voice. He took hand after hand and by 12:30, he had won $80,000, leaving Johnny with $50,000. There was something savage in his play, a cold-bloodedness. As a result the crowd's sympathies swung to Johnny and they clapped and cheered whenever he won a hand, however insignificant. "You notice how quiet it gets when I take a pot," said Pug. "I think this crowd in here is all wearing 'I hate Puggie' buttons." Despite his losses Johnny continued to play as he had played all night, all his life perhaps—quietly, impassively. He seemed more than a little bored. From time to time he and Virgie exchanged brief smiles and when he had won what appeared to be a substantial pot she would cry, "You show him, babycakes!"

A hand or two later the first major confrontation between the two players took place. After opening antes of $500, Pug is dealt a jack and a two and Johnny a jack and a six. Pug bets $500. Johnny calls and raises $500. Johnny is raising in the dark, what is called blinding it, in order to create action. Pug calls, pushing $500 into the pot. The dealer then deals the flop—the two of clubs, the eight of diamonds and the jack of diamonds. This gives Pug jacks and deuces and Johnny a pair of jacks. In order to test Pug's hand Johnny bets $2,000. Pug hesitates, rolling his cigar around in his mouth. He now knows or thinks he knows that Johnny cannot have a hand, possibly an off-breed hand, he thinks, some kind of phoney hand or he's trailing a pair of aces or another high pair, but that ain't likely. No, he thinks Johnny is going for a diamond flush or a straight if he has a nine or a ten in the hole. Pug decides to raise since with two pairs he almost certainly has the better hand. Putting his unlit cigar on the edge of the table, he calls Johnny's $2,000 and raises another $5,000. There is now $12,000 in the pot.

With two cards to come it is Johnny's play. He does not
believe Pug has two pairs, one pair in all probability, but not
jacks. He believes he has the better hand. And Johnny thinks,
I'm not just goin' to call his $5,000. I'm not agoin' to give him
a chance with two more cards comin', no more free shots. I
don't know whether he's got a hand or not, but I don't think
so, so I'm movin' in with all I got. Hesitating only momentarily,
Johnny, using both hands, pushes seven stacks of chips into the
pot, calling Pug's $5,000 and raising $26,500. Again the crowd
falls silent and once again the gamblers and the journalists
gather swiftly round the table. Pug looks carefully at his cards.
Johnny looks dreamily into the distance. The only way Pug can
call, he thinks, is with jacks and deuces, jacks and eights, three
deuces or three eights. Not likely. Besides all them checks can
frighten a man, particularly a young man. It's hard to look at,
it's like putting a cannon in your mouth, it's gruesome.

Pug stalls and stalls while Jimmy the Greek prowls nervously
behind his chair. Pug frowns and shakes his head and then with
resignation, as though the decision rests in the cards and not
with him, he slowly pushes $26,500 into the pot and calls. The
crowd gasps. There is now $70,000 on the table. Johnny contin-
ues to look across the room as though he were unaware or
unconcerned. Since the betting has ended, both men turn up
their cards. "Dealer, deal," says Pug. Burning one card the
dealer turns up a king. The king helps neither player, but it is
disastrous for Johnny. The only way he can now win is if the
final card is a six and it is thirteen-and-two-thirds-to-one
against a six coming up. Both men know the odds and Pug
visibly relaxes. The room falls silent. Even Amarillo Slim is still,
an unlit cigarette drooping from the corner of his mouth. The
dealer looks at both men, takes up the deck and deals the final
card. It is the six of spades.

The crowd broke into cheers and loud applause. Johnny had
done it again on the final card. He smiled and wiped his face.
Pug had a wan look of disbelief. Jimmy the Greek leaned down

and advised him to go and wash his face. Lighting his cigar and looking at no one, Pug left the room. The hand left Pug with $34,000 and Johnny with $96,000, making Johnny a 3–to–1 favorite with the gamblers in the stands.

"Pug'll go broke before his break comes," said Slim. "He ain't got much left and nowhere he can go. I mean where does the hobo go in the snow?"

Pug took a short walk down the street. He looked shaken but still determined. "I thought I was goin' to bust him right there," he said. "That was a real brutal draw. He runs lucky that ole boy, but when he's goin' for cards he's paid for 'em, so he has a right to get 'em I guess. But it don't matter none. It'll just take longer now and time is on my side. I'll grind him for two, three thousand a pop. I'll get him in the end. That's one *tired* man you see in there."

Johnny *was* tired. It was nearly one in the morning and he wanted to go over to the Dunes to bed. He wanted to cash in his chips, postpone the game until tomorrow. The other gamblers hovered around his chair offering tactical advice. Jack Strauss advised him to be aggressive as Pug was rattled and might break completely now. Sarge, on the other hand, advised Johnny to play safely, conservatively, and grind Pug down. Johnny did not seem to hear them. He tinkered with his chips and looked dreamily away. I'm sixty-seven, he thought, and I oughta go to bed.

Waiting for Pug to return to the room, Amarillo Slim is on the telephone attempting to arrange a challenge poker game with Bobby Riggs, who is playing an exhibition tennis match at Caesar's Palace. Finally he puts the phone down in disgust. "Can't get through to the little bastard," he says. "He's got himself surrounded by lawyers and them public-relations fellas."

The phone rings almost immediately. Slim answers it and announces that there is a long distance call for Sam Angel. The fat diamond salesman crosses the room. "All over the world people know my name," he says. "My reputation is staggering."

Taking the phone, he listens carefully, a sly smile forming on his face. "Yes," he says in a loud voice, "I've had a few challenges in a few quarters." Cupping his hand over the phone, he informs the onlookers that as the new world razz champion he is being asked to go on the *Johnny Carson Show*. "Indubitably," he says into the phone and turns to the crowd as though expecting an ovation. It later emerges that Slim had fixed the call.

At one o'clock Pug returned to the card room. Pug played quietly, almost morosely. Johnny seemed to have lifted himself for one final all-or-nothing effort. He had taken Strauss's advice, apparently, since again and again he pushed most of his chips into the pot on seemingly insignificant hands, but at a price that would have broken Pug. And again and again Pug declined to play, sullenly throwing his cards into the middle of the table. Each time, as a big hand began to build, a sudden silence and flow of tension swept through the crowd. "There he goes again," someone would say as Johnny pushed huge piles of chips into the pot, and the gamblers would surge around the table to see if Pug would meet the threat.

Toward 1:30 a big hand begins to build again. Both men ante $1,000. Pug is dealt a six and a king, Johnny a three and a nine. The dealer deals the flop—the three and queen and king of spades. Pug bets $2,000. Johnny calls and raises another $3,000. Pug merely calls. The dealer burns one card and turns up the six of spades. Every card showing is a spade. Pug now has kings and sixes and he checks, waiting to see what Johnny will do. Johnny is uncertain. He was representing a spade flush, though he did not have it. He has been forced to wait for the last card and if it had not been a spade, he could not have bet. But when the six of spades turns up he decides. Pug may have the better hand, probably does, but if I bet high, he can't call. Not in his condition. He just can't take that chance. For the fifth consecutive time Johnny pushes enough chips into the pot to cover what Pug has left—$36,000. Pug sits back in his chair and moodily chomps on his cigar. He looks carefully at his cards and at the open cards on the table. I don't need no x-ray eyes here, he thinks. I know Johnny Moss and I'm lookin' for something out of the ordinary from him, not this. Something stinks. I didn't need much, a little ole six, and I got what I needed. I think I got the nuts.

"Well," says Pug, leaning into the table, "I don't think you got spades, Johnny. You might have kings and treys or queens and treys, even three treys, but I don't think so." He shakes his head. "No, I don't think so, Johnny."

Almost casually, he pushes his remaining chips into the pot and calls. There is $84,000 on the table. Pug sits back and Johnny throws his hand over to the dealer. A kind of croaking ululation rises from the crowd and scattered applause; Pug leans across the table and pulls in the pot. Johnny asks a waitress for a glass of tea.

Pug must have won eight out of the next ten hands and at two o'clock the game was even. Each man had $65,000 stacked in front of him. The play was now open and aggressive, the pots averaging $20,000 a hand.

"What do you think now, Slim?" the English reporter asked. "What's your hunch?"

"I don't believe in hunches," said Slim. "Hunches are for dogs making love."

Wearing his enormous Stetson, the leather vest and faded levis, Benny Binion walks into the room to watch the end of the match. He admits his prejudices openly. "Sure, I want Johnny to win," he mumbles, a toothpick protruding from the side of his mouth, "ain't no two ways about it. We Texans, we stick together. Only fair, boy. In Texas, justice means 'just us.' "

Some thirty minutes later Pug goes over the $100,000 mark with two large pots from which Johnny has backed off. Johnny continues to play coolly, almost absentmindedly, and once or twice has seemed almost to be asleep. Pug exudes a kind of irrepressible confidence; he smokes and smiles, gossiping with the gamblers and the waitresses. He is playing at high speed now, pressing Johnny at the turn of every card and betting high.

"You got to watch that boy," said Sarge. "Pug's no cardplayer, he's a people-player. He's a real son of a bitch to play with once he spots your weakness. And listen to that chat of his. What a ham."

Johnny had soon been whittled down to his last $20,000. Forced by Pug, another large hand began to develop. Pug was dealt the seven and the ace of spades; Johnny had the king of clubs and the jack of spades in the hole. The dealer then turned up the queen of spades, the ten of spades and the three of clubs in the center of the table. With two cards to come, Pug needed only another spade for an ace-high flush. Johnny required one card to complete his open straight. There were only eight cards that could help Johnny—nines and aces—but one of the aces was in Pug's hand and the nine of spades would give Pug his flush.

Pug opens the betting with $1,500. He believes he has the best hand and wants Johnny to raise. He wants Johnny committed to the pot before another card comes up. At this point Johnny is an underdog, but he calls the $1,500 and raises $3,500. Pug does not hesitate. I've got him on the ropes now, he thinks and with two draws comin', I'm a favorite for a nut flush. He calls the $3,500 immediately, then raises Johnny for all his remaining chips—$15,000. Johnny looks almost distastefully at the stacks of chips in the center of the table. He seems abstracted. He knows his back is against the wall. But there are still two cards to come. He shrugs; slowly and with a kind of numb regret, he pushes the chips into the pot. Again, the crowd swarms around the table. Pug rises to his feet, pushing his straw hat to the back of his head. Johnny removes his glasses. Jimmy the Greek calls for silence. The dealer turns up the six of diamonds. The card helps neither player, though Johnny's chances are considerably reduced. "You can stick a fork in him," says Slim. "He's done." A moment later the dealer turns up the five of hearts. Johnny has lost. "My gawd," says Pug, and begins to clap, and for the first time that night the crowd applauds him.

Johnny rose from the table and shook Pug's hand. "If it had

to be anybody other than me, I'm glad it was you, Pug," he said.

"Thank you, Johnny, thank you," said Pug. "I just want to tell you, that was the best game I can remember and I'd have said so even if I lost. That's one they won't forget for a while."

Jack Binion put a large silver cup in front of Pug. It was filled with thirteen hundred one-hundred-dollar bills. Photographers and reporters crowded round the table taking photographs and asking loud and garbled questions.

"Look at all those photographers around Puggie," shouted Sam Angel. "Hell, I'm the greatest razz player in the world and I ain't had two cents of publicity."

"Well, the best man won," said Strauss. "He had bad breaks and he still won. Took guts, that."

"If the milk sets long enough, the cream will always come to the top," said Slim.

"I never took my eyes off you, Puggie," said Sarge. "If Mr. Michelangelo had been paintin' a ceiling right up there, I wouldn't have taken my eyes off you."

Within minutes of the end of the tournament a game of stud had started up at the next table. "Hey, Puggie," shouted Joe Bernstein, "bring some of that cash over here and sit down."

"I'm goin' home, boys," said Pug. "I'm all wore out."

Sarge watched Pug leave the room with an ironic grin. "I knew Puggie had it won when he started giving out all that John Barrymore shit. Pretendin' it was all a strain. But you better believe this. Johnny lost because he was tired. He was absolutely exhausted. Can't take the pace no more. Pug stole that last forty thousand. In his prime Johnny was a beautiful player. Like a machine. He could play for months and never make a mistake. His play was like a work of art."

The next night, in the card room of the Aladdin Hotel, Johnny Moss sat impassively at the corner table. Virgie sat on his right. He had not slept well and his face was creased with fatigue. He looked round the card room with dull disinterested eyes.

Most of the other players in the game have gone home, but a few stalwarts inhabit the adjacent table. Strauss is leaving in the morning for the cockfights in Louisiana. Slim says there is a big game in Fort Worth and Doyle says he might tag along.

"Just let me phone my wife," he says.

"Tell yours to phone mine," says Slim.

Toward midnight Pug walks into the room.

"Wanna play some, Johnny?" he says.

"I wouldn't mind playin' some with the world's champion," says Johnny, a sleepy smile on his face.

"How many players you bust last night?" says Joe Bernstein.

"Nine, I busted nine of 'em myself."

"You didn't bust me," says Johnny. "I busted myself."

"How'd that game of stud go last night?" says Pug.

"Crandall lost a bundle to Sarge, that's what happened," says Slim. "And Sarge lost it at the Dunes. He was drownded."

"Wow," says the English reporter.

"Strauss was massacred."

"How much?" says Pug.

"Everything."

"That's a lot."

Johnny yawned. It was commonplace conversation. He had been listening to it for fifty years. His mind was still on the tournament—plodding obstinately through the bleak narrative of his defeat, comparing, interpreting, living it out again. "A man that bets his money all the time is hell to phase," he said. "I don't care what they say. I'm not a good caller. I like to bet. Callin's nothin'. You bet to strength. I break all callers. In that last hand, y'unnerstand, Puggie can't have no hand that's a bigger price than mine. I liked my chances, that's all, and I took 'em. But after the six of diamonds was turned, I'm a big dog. Slim thought I had the double-geared nuts. But I didn't. Not what I needed anyways. I needed sleep.

"Age has affected me pretty good, I guess. I think too late. I have a good mind for my age, but it ain't as good as it was. You let plays get away from you. I shoulda called for a recess.

I shoulda picked up my money, gone home and started in again the next day. But win or lose, I keep 'em agoin'. I'm not goin' to play in tournaments no more. *Never.* I'm too old. Pug wants the glory. I just want the money. Hell, I've had the glory before."

"You was tired, Johnny, you was tired, that's all," said Virgie.

Johnny shook his head. "I could've beat him, y'know. I should've beat him. But I didn't."

Virgie smiled. "There'll be another game," she said. "There's always another game—tomorrow."

(NOTE: *The following year, in June of 1974 at the age of sixty-eight, Johnny Moss, against sixteen competitors including all those mentioned above, won the World Series of Poker and $160,000.*)

# Titanic Thompson

---

**It is when the pirates
count their booty
that they become mere thieves.**

WILLIAM BOLITHO

---

## I

In what he liked to imagine were sweeter times, in the days before the action was monopolized by Las Vegas, gambling was as common a part of American life as jazz or Prohibition. Particularly in the South. During the Twenties and early Thirties there had been instant action in the most upright Southern towns. Before Las Vegas most gamblers were road gamblers, traveling from town to town with the confidence of men who knew there would always be another game a little farther down the line. The times, he remembered, were not so treacherous, so unreliable as now. Gambling was illegal of course; but most Southern country towns had their clandestine back rooms, often concealed in the best hotel, in which games of craps and cards were run as regularly and efficiently as the trains that brought the boys to town. Rare dependable wells, they were, in otherwise dry and inauspicious country.

Those had been his dream decades, his fine high-rolling days, when, as a matter of course, he had risen late and read the morning line, practiced his propositions, backed a horse or bought a car, killing time till that day's play began. There were

197

few games he would not play; and because he was one of the
few really big high rollers, the sort of man who bet twenty
thousand on the turn of a card, he was courted constantly by
his fellow travelers—by those who hoped to get a piece of his
play or, in a moment of folly, to break him altogether. Therefore, long before the action died in whatever town he happened
to be, he had received the news of other games in other places:
in Hot Springs the hustlers were anxious to play some pool; a
millionaire in Lubbock had offered a lucrative golfing proposition; a high-stake poker game had started in Tulsa the day
before and, should he have cared to travel north, there were
rumors of really serious action in Joplin and St. Jo.

Thus, in the late spring of 1932, Titanic Thompson, as he was
known, motored down from Dallas to the boom town of Tyler
in East Texas. Titanic had nothing particular in mind, that is
no definite wager had drawn him there, but he had a friend or
two in town and Tyler had always been good for ready action.
In 1932 Tyler was in the midst of a big oil boom. Between Tyler
and the little towns of Longview and Gladewater and Kilgore,
the derricks stretched across the open prairies as far as the eye
could see. There was a lot of money around—Texas money—
and the town had attracted the usual assortment of prospectors,
speculators, oilmen and gamblers. Everyone, it seemed, was
rich or just about to be. It was the kind of town Titanic knew
well and felt most at home in. Where there was oil there was
loose money and loose money meant action.

In the early part of the century the professional gambler was
still a romantic figure—a fallen man, perhaps, and evil, if the
melodramas of the period are to be believed. He was a free-
booter, a man who took the long chance at a time when the
country still believed in dark horses. Titanic Thompson was at
the heart of that belief. In 1932 he was forty years old and had
achieved a kind of mythical status in his profession. Reverent
tales of his gambling prowess are still told along the Vegas
Strip. He was a master of the cunning proposition, a crack shot,
a scratch golfer, a champion bowler, a good pool player and an

expert at craps and all forms of cards, particularly poker. He had won more than a million dollars in places as far afield as San Francisco, Chicago and New York. In the early Thirties Titanic and Nick the Greek Dandolos were reputed to be the shrewdest gamblers in the country.

In a photograph of Titanic taken about that time, he is standing next to one of his favorite cars—a 1930 Pierce-Arrow. Posed languidly beside a robust girl, a rifle under his arm, he appears insouciant and boyish. They look as though they have just committed a particularly amusing crime. The girl wears a cardigan and long skirt, Titanic wears a double-breasted suit and hat; there is a more than passing resemblance to Bonnie and Clyde.

He must have looked much the same when he drove into Tyler in 1932 with his third wife, Yvonne, and her sister Joanne, who would ultimately become his fourth. They put up at the main hotel and Ty went out to scout the action. He did not have far to look. At the local golf course the club professional, Jimmy Haines, wagered Ty that he could not shoot the front nine in less than 35 strokes. The bet was agreed at five hundred dollars and the stakes were held by the young caddymaster. Ty had been playing golf for only ten years. He had become an extraordinary golfer, though he liked to belittle the fact, claiming it was an impertinent rumor put about by his enemies. That afternoon in Tyler, he shot the front nine in 34.

Ty had driven down to Tyler in a Lincoln Continental. It was a new car and as was his custom he had fitted it with a special horn, a kind of early burglar alarm. Ty favored such precautions. That evening, while he was sitting in his hotel room with his wife and her sister, the alarm suddenly sounded. Pulling back the curtain Ty peered out of the window, but it was dusk and difficult to see. Only that afternoon he had heard rumors that out-of-state hijackers had come to town. Someone in a car had tried to hijack him two days before, but had driven away when he pulled out his gun. Ty was an expert shot with both pistol and rifle and had killed five men in his time. Looking out of the hotel window he shrugged. He was used to these little interruptions. Ty carried a .45, the butt taped with adhesive to ensure a firmer grip. He had always favored a big gun. "Shoot a man with a .32," he said, "and he might get up and shoot back." Ty did not believe in second chances.

That evening, therefore, when he heard the alarm he picked up his .45 and slid it inside his belt. He checked with his wife to see if she had touched the gun. He did not want any accidents. He was wearing wide flannel golf trousers; slipping on a sports jacket to cover the gun, he went outside to investigate.

Ty walked cautiously down the path to his car. There was no one about. Except for the horn it was quiet and everything seemed in order. But as he approached the car a man jumped out from behind a tree to his left. Despite the semi-darkness Ty could see that he wore a mask pulled down over his face. The man brandished a gun and shouted, "Throw up your hands, mister, or I'll shoot you down!" Ty did not hesitate. Dropping swiftly to his knees and pulling the .45 from his belt, he shot the man an inch or two above the heart. At twenty feet he was an easy target. As a boy Ty had hit washers thrown in the air at twenty feet. The masked man was thrown back against the tree. Taking no chances Ty shot him again through the mouth. The figure crumpled to the ground. Ty walked slowly up to him and kicked away his gun. Shouting to his wife to telephone the police, he knelt down over the fallen man. He was still alive. His face twitched behind the mask. "Help me up. Help me up, Mr. Thompson," the man mumbled, "I think you've killed me." The voice was familiar and Ty pulled off the mask. In the darkness the face was very white. The jaw was slack and pulsed with broken teeth and blood. Ty recognized the young caddymaster who had held the stakes that afternoon. "Boy, I hope you'll be able to tell the police this was your idea," said Ty. The boy nodded. When the police arrived, he mumbled that he had tried to rob the older man. He was taken away. That night, in hospital, he died.

"I was surprised he lived as long as he did," said Ty. "I really felt bad about that kid. If I'd've known it was a young boy like that I'd've given him the money. I hated to shoot a kid, but how could I know who it was with that mask on? Could've been anybody. It was just one of those things, I guess."

Next day it was agreed that he had shot the boy in self-defense. Nonetheless a young police lieutenant suggested that Ty might be happier in another town—in Hot Springs, perhaps, or Oklahoma City, in any town that was not in Texas. The young lieutenant looked smug. Ty smiled and said nothing. He had seen that look before. By nightfall he had disappeared.

## II

To the end of his life Titanic remained a backwoods Southern boy. Even in what he liked to regard as his sophisticated days, when he favored yellow polo coats and drove nickel-plated limousines, he seemed somehow out of context, inconvenienced, like a farm boy made to slick his hair and wear his Sunday suit. Fashion was not Ty's métier. Gambling had taken him off the farm and into some of the country's largest cities, but he rarely dallied in them. He disliked cities; he thought them stiff, uncomfortable and cold. He preferred the slow country towns of the South—towns such as Grapevine, Texas, Lafayette, Louisiana, Marked Tree, Arkansas, or Monett, Missouri, where he was born in the winter of 1892.

He was christened Alvin Clarence Thomas, though he rarely used the name once he left home. His people were itinerants and soon after he was born they drifted south into Arkansas, taking up farming in the foothills of the Ozarks midway between the hayseed towns of Eureka Springs and Rogers. But his father was not a farmer; he would rather gamble. Ty's mother often told him his father had been gambling up in the hills the night that he was born. He had come home for a time, apparently, but disappeared when Ty was five or six months old.

During his boyhood the family moved constantly from one

rented farm to another. It was a kind of flight, this constant moving, a long retreat. The farm he remembered most clearly was one of about forty acres, crisscrossed with creeks and springs, in the woods above the White River. There, in a three-room log cabin, Ty lived with his mother, his stepfather, two half-sisters and two half-brothers. His stepfather, one Willie Hendricks, was a hard-working silent man with none of Ty's father's vices. They did not get on.

The farm was self-sufficient. They raised corn and peas, potatoes and beans, the vegetables used as fodder for the pigs and cattle. While the rest of the family farmed, Ty cut railway ties from the white oak trees growing in the nearby woods. He could cut up to twenty ties a day, which he carried by mule and wagon into Rogers, eight miles away, selling them to the railroad for thirty-five cents apiece. His people were poor. Two of Ty's more vivid memories were of the old tin tub in which the family bathed and of the windy outdoor privy at the edge of the yard.

Rogers was a town of seven hundred people, but it seemed a metropolis to Ty. Out in the hill country his only friends were his family. Their nearest neighbors were four or five miles away. They were thrifty people and they tended to keep to the farm. Baptists, they rarely went to church and Ty attended school infrequently. He was needed at home and besides the clapboard school was a four-mile walk. As a result Ty never learned to read and could barely write. Much later he liked to brag, and would bet accordingly, that he could spell any number of complicated words such as "Mississippi" or "rhinoceros," but he had merely memorized them for profit. His last wife, Jeanette, said that Ty would not have been able to spell "there."

As a boy Ty spent most of his free time alone and, despite his poverty, led a relatively carefree life. A loner, he developed a talent for solitary pursuits. He fished the White River for bass and catfish and trout and perch. His grandfather gave him a shotgun before he was ten and Ty became an expert marksman. With Carlo, his pet water spaniel, he hunted squirrel and rabbit and possum and coon. He claimed an ability to hit quail on the wing with rocks and often hunted them that way. He was good with animals; he had not only taught Carlo to retrieve game, but had trained him to dive to the bottom of the river to retrieve small rocks. Thus his boyhood passed—splitting railway ties when necessary, hunting and fishing when he could slip away. And so it might have remained; but he had also learned the more seductive arts of gambling.

Excepting his stepfather, most of the men in Ty's family gambled, particularly his grandfather and uncles who worked a farm on the other side of the river. They gambled at mountain games—shooting at targets with a .22, rock-throwing, pitching to the crack, penny-ante poker, coon-can, checkers and dominoes. Ty was always good with his hands; he had an excellent memory and, curiously, was clever with numbers. Before he was fifteen he could beat his older relatives at their own games easily. He liked to practice tricks such as pitching coins into a small box at a distance of twenty feet and learned to get ten to fifteen in the box in a row. Tricks of this kind, his propositions, were to earn him a great deal of money when he was older. "All I ever wanted to do was gamble," he said, and that longing was intensified by what he came to see as the romantic flight of his gambling father.

Fortified with thoughts of his father, Ty began to look on gambling as a way out, as a means of exit to the world that lay beyond the river. He wanted to gamble. He was good at gambling—too good; his own people refused to gamble with him anymore, though it never deterred him from asking. He had become an opportunist, though he had few opportunities. Disgruntled, Ty continued to work at home, but he spent more and more of his time alone with his dog in the woods.

On summer weekends, during his fifteenth year, Ty began to encounter strangers, or what he called "city folk," in the woods. That summer, he remembered, they often drove up from Fayetteville, the only city in the area, to that part of the White River noted for its fishing. They favored one fishing hole especially; it was fifteen feet deep with a sandy bottom. Ty often saw them there. Accustomed to a wooden fishing pole, he admired their expensive casting rods and had set his heart on getting one when he was older. He had not anticipated an opportunity would come so soon.

One Saturday, having spent the morning with Carlo hunting in the woods, Ty encountered a stranger at the fishing hole. They began to talk and the stranger said how much he admired Ty's spaniel. They talked some more and the stranger offered to buy the dog. Ty refused, explaining he could never part with Carlo for money. Then, with shrewd timidity, he suggested the gentleman might make a bet instead. Since the gentleman, he said, seemed taken with the dog, he would be willing to bet the dumb brute could retrieve a rock from the bottom of the fishing hole, which was twenty foot deep, at least, and in order to avoid any accidents, such as bringing up the wrong rock, he would be more than willing to mark the rock with an X; the gentleman could throw it in any part of the pool he liked. Ty would bet the dog, he said, against the gentleman's fishing rod.

The stranger instantly agreed. Picking up a rock about the size of a small ball, Ty marked it with his knife and handed it over. The stranger smiled. Looking out over the pool, he lobbed the rock into what seemed to be the deepest part. At a word from Ty, Carlo sprang into the water and swam out toward the ripples, a moment later sinking from sight. The man and the boy waited silently. Nearly thirty seconds elapsed. Suddenly the dog broke the surface, its front paws flailing at the water, the rock clenched firmly in its mouth. The stranger swore. Paddling to the shore, Carlo shook himself and dropped the rock at Ty's feet. Grinning, Ty picked it up, showing the stranger the carved X.

"Well, I guess I'll just take that there rod, mister," he said.

The stranger drew back. "Now, boy, you should know I was foolin' with you. Just foolin,' that's all. But it's a damn good trick. That's some dog you got, I'll tell you that."

Ty looked at the man. He was not grinning now. His .22 was

under his arm and he slid back the bolt. "Tell you what," he said. "You hold that rock up in the air and I'll make another bet with you that I can knock it outta your hand."

The stranger looked suspiciously at Ty. Ty lifted the gun. The stranger handed over the casting rod.

"That dog of mine was good at that trick," Ty conceded later. "He was very good. But I ain't one for taking chances. A few days before I'd covered the bottom of that hole with dozens of marked rocks. That slicker never had a prayer."

Ty's triumph over the stranger, and he thought it a triumph, was the first indication of a personal gambling credo he defined when he was older. "To be a winner," he explained, "a man has to feel good about himself and know he has some kind of advantage going in. Smart is better than lucky."

When Ty turned sixteen he weighed 180 pounds, stood 6′ 1″ and was "as strong as a wild razorback hog." The time had come, he reasoned, to leave home, as his father had before him. His mother, who disapproved, made few efforts to detain him, only extracting a promise that he would not take up with whiskey or tobacco, a promise Ty was to keep. Going out into the world required scant preparation. Ty donned his best overalls, made a bundle of his old ones and a spare shirt, kissed his mother good-bye, walked the eight miles to Rogers and, hiding until it passed the station, jumped aboard the northbound train. Riding the blinds, he traveled the fifty miles to Monett, the town of his birth.

Monett was midway between Joplin and Springfield, Missouri—a town about the size of Rogers when Ty arrived in the late spring of 1909. They were auspicious times. William H. Taft had just been inaugurated as the country's new president, Henry Ford had invented the Model T, and Admiral Peary had reached the North Pole the month before, but these were events that barely touched this remote Missouri border town. Then, as now, Monett concerned itself with the production of ship's berries.

Dropping from the train at the town depot, Ty was almost

immediately accosted by a drummer hawking maps. Five-leaf fold-out general-information maps, they were filled with such educational squibs as the history of the Panama Canal, the amount of barbed wire required to surround an acre of land and the names and dates of all the Presidents, complete with colored photographs. They were selling, the drummer explained, for only a dollar apiece. Instead of buying Ty asked the man for a job. Surprisingly the drummer agreed and for the next six months Ty wandered round southern Missouri selling maps and asking awkward questions as to the whereabouts of his wayward father.

Toward the end of the year he arrived in Springfield, the first large town he had ever seen. The streets, Ty remembered, were deep in mud, but here he encountered his first automobile, his first tall building, his first poolroom, and he began to consort with professional gamblers. He was just seventeen. In Springfield he learned more of cards and craps, how to bluff, when to raise and when to fold, how to throw and how to fade the dice; he broadened his knowledge of odds and propositions and picked up the rudiments of pool. He made a little money here and there and began to see that he would make his way. He bought a hat and a second-hand suit in sound repair; hooking his thumbs in his waistcoat pockets, he strutted up and down the main street of the town.

He gave up selling maps and joined the traveling medicine show of one Captain Adam Beaugardus. The Captain, a hawker of patent medicines, bore a close resemblance to Buffalo Bill and claimed to have ridden with Roosevelt on the charge up San Juan Hill. Ty's task was to lure the crowds with demonstrations of trick shooting; once the crowd had gathered around the wagon, the Captain, in loud prophetic declamations, flogged his magic medicines, which cured everything from old age to apoplexy. Competing for prizes in small-town turkey shoots along the way, Ty traveled through Oklahoma (which had been admitted to the Union two years before), Kansas and Missouri, circling finally toward Memphis through northern Arkansas.

In Memphis, weary of the bumptious captain, Ty took to gambling in that city's notorious saloons. One night in a card game, he listened as the other players gossiped of a riverboat pilot and gambler called Green. Green was a rounder, a man who gambled at anything, but particularly at dice, at which he claimed to be invincible. Despite warnings that he was known to be a shakedown man, Ty set off to find him.

A fat, ungainly man, Green operated a riverboat called *The Rambler* out of Marked Tree, Arkansas, hauling produce and passengers up and down the St. Francis River. In Marked Tree the two men met and agreed to a session of low-stake dice. Green, sly and affable, invited Ty to accompany him on the downriver run. On the first day out Ty saw that although Green liked to gamble, he knew very little about percentages. Ty promptly suggested they raise the stakes. Green was delighted and three trips later he was broke. Back at Marked Tree, lamenting his bad luck, Green insisted they play some more. He offered his boat as collateral, assessing its worth at twenty-five hundred dollars. It was an open-and-shut proposition, Ty recalled. Two days later he became the owner of a thirty-foot, flat-bottomed riverboat and acquired his first employee—Green.

They were fine days adrift on the open river. Ty lounged on the deck and took the sun, played cards or craps with newfound friends, while the sulky Green labored above in the pilot-house. Soon Ty became enamored of a local girl, "a little black-haired beauty" called Nellie. He invited her for an outing on his new boat. Green suggested a friend of his from Memphis, a gambler by the name of Jimmy Johnson, should come along. He couldn't play much, said Green, with a conspiratorial air, but he liked to gamble high. There would be something in it for both of them. Early one spring morning the party set off on the run downriver.

While Green piloted the boat and Nellie sat in the sun, Johnson and Ty played craps. Johnson proved a truculent companion. He had begun to drink soon after he came aboard and an hour later was aggressively drunk. To begin with, the two men seemed evenly matched and for most of the morning neither player was more than a few dollars ahead; but gradually, Ty began to win and just before lunch Johnson swore, shouted he was being cheated, pulled a knife and threatened to slit Ty's throat. For almost the first and certainly the last time in his life, Ty had failed to arm himself. Forced over the rail by the older, heavier man, Ty fell into the river. A strong swimmer, he pulled himself back aboard. Johnson and Green roared with laughter. The episode seemed to have put Johnson in a better humor for he put his knife away.

Late that afternoon, at Parkin, their first port of call, Ty went ashore to fetch supplies. When he returned he found Nellie in tears, clamoring to be taken home. Johnson, she whimpered, had tried to take off her clothes. Ty said nothing, but ordered Green to put the boat into midstream. Johnson continued to drink; slouched on the deck, he taunted the girl with loud obscenities. When Ty reprimanded him, he reached into his belt and pulled out the knife again. Stumbling to his feet, he shouted, "Boy, I'm gonna cut off your goddamned head." As he lurched up the deck, Ty picked up a hammer. Johnson swung and missed. Ty struck him on the head; he struck him again and Johnson, falling back against the low rail, careened over the side into the river. Breathing heavily, Ty watched him bob behind in the wake. He sank, rose to the surface, and sank again. It was clear that Johnson was in no condition to swim. Ty turned from the rail, and ordered Green to return to Marked Tree.

They found Johnson's body two days later. Inquiries were made and Ty was placed under arrest. Someone it seemed had seen him knock Johnson overboard and reported it to the sheriff in Marked Tree. Although the witness preferred to remain anonymous, Ty never doubted that it had been Green. The next morning a kangaroo court was held in the train depot. The sheriff consented to act both as Ty's lawyer and judge. Four townsmen dropped by to sit on the jury. No witnesses were called. The sheriff read out the evidence. The townsmen seemed sympathetic. Their decision was unanimous and Ty was found guilty. The townsmen were pleased that justice had been upheld so effectively and exchanged little looks of exultation. The sheriff rose to pronounce sentence. "Boy," he said, "now you give us all that money you got and sign a bill of sale for the boat. Then git. As your lawyer, that's what I advise you to do. And if that ain't satisfactory, your ass is gonna wind up in this here jail for a right long spell. Y'hear?" Ty did as he was told. That afternoon he took the train to the state line.

For the next year Ty worked the small towns of Missouri, going as far north as Kansas City. "In those days," he recalled, "every little town had a poker game or two. It was illegal, a course, a twenty-dollar fine if you was caught, but once you got to a town you always checked at the pool hall and chances were the game was being held in the back room or down the street at the hotel." Before Ty turned nineteen he had picked up a sound if eccentric education.

"It used to be that people would bet anything on anything," he said. "They bet pitching half dollars to the crack or put a dime down and pitched to that. They bet on pool and poker and dice and pitchin' horseshoes and on card games most people never heard of. It used to be that people really loved to bet. And so did I."

Thus, in one or another of those Southern towns, Ty learned to shoot craps, how to place the six and the ace in the middle, false shake them and roll them straight out so that he could not crap. He learned the odds on every proposition—the true odds on how many coins will come up heads or tails should you throw a handful into the air at once, how many throws of the dice it takes to obtain a specific number, the odds on securing a pair in a five-card hand, of drawing the highest spade, or the price on getting aces back to back. He learned how to scuffle, how to cheat and to connive, learned all the card cons—playing to the light, how to mark cards or use spotted edges to change the suit, the art of signals, the use of pig-joints or thumpers, dealing seconds, cold-decking, anything that gave him "the advantage going in." He practiced such dodges by the hour. "I learned to beat people at their own game," he said. "And if I couldn't beat 'em, I'd find someone who could." He was to beat the checker champion of Missouri, for example, by installing a better player in a peekhole in the ceiling, who signaled the correct moves to Ty through the use of a thumper wired to Ty's leg. And, should emergencies arise, he always carried a gun, which he kept on the floor next to his chair when playing.

"I learned to play any game you could name for any amount of money you could count. And I never made bets on even chances." To that end, he began carrying his own horseshoes, bowling ball, pool cue, throwing rock (made to order—beveled on top, flat on the bottom), his own rifle and pistol. "No sense takin' a chance on somebody else's," he said. "Might be rigged. I learned to do things pretty good or else I didn't do 'em. I aimed to do everything a little better'n the other fellow. And those were the things I bet on, that's all." At eighteen, his apprenticeship was over.

In the winter of 1910 Ty arrived in Kansas City. On his first night in town he fell in with some gamblers who steered him to a black club where he became involved in a crooked game of five-card stud. But he was used to such things now and played on. Toward dawn when the game ended he had won fifteen hundred dollars. That morning over breakfast one of the losers, in answer to Ty's now familiar question, said that he had played with a gambler by the name of Thomas a few months before in a saloon in Oil City, Louisiana. A slicker with diamond rings, the man recalled, played stud. After breakfast Ty purchased a brown-striped suit and a brown derby hat and caught the southbound train.

Oil City, a boom town on the Texas-Louisiana border, was crowded with drillers, roughnecks and roustabouts. It had the rude and heady air of any gold-rush town and those who struck it rich by day celebrated at night in the noisy saloons and poker rooms. In 1910 most of Oil City's streets were still unpaved. It was a clapboard town cluttered with banks, saloons and general stores. Inside one of the main-street saloons he found the man he had spent more than two years searching for. Sitting at a table next to the bar dealing cards was a slim, well-dressed man in his early forties with fast and graceful fingers, two of which were covered with diamond rings. Ty joined him.

"It'll cost you cash to play in this game, son," the man said. "Twenty-five dollars cash." Ty paid and the game began.

I have heard more than a few sentimental versions of that encounter, depending on to whom Ty told it over the years. The other players either dropped from the game or his father, recognizing an unusual opponent, asked them to leave the table; his father dubbed him "The Derby Kid" or one of the other players did; they played head-to-head for six or maybe fifteen hours; Ty won consistently or beat his father on the final hand; his father was an excellent player or second-rate; his father lost $5,000 or $2,500. But all accounts agree that he lost and that somewhere toward midnight, or perhaps it was dawn, the older man rose from the table and said, "You're a winner, son. That's all I care to lose today."

Smiling, Ty counted up the chips and pushed them back across the table. "You never had a chance to beat me," he said. "I'm giving you your money back." The older man looked at Ty, a derisive smile on his face. "Son, nobody ever gave me back my money," he said.

"Maybe not," said Ty, "but I have my reasons."

The two men spent the next few weeks together. "But, other than gambling, we had little in common," Ty recalled. Ty spent most of his time in the crowded saloons fleecing the resident oilmen at cards and dice. Toward Christmas he drifted back to Missouri. He never saw his father again. Thirteen years later Ty heard the old man had died in Denver or San Francisco. The rumor was never definitely confirmed.

In the spring of 1912 Ty turned up in Joplin, Missouri, shortly after the White Star liner *Titanic* hit an iceberg in the North Atlantic. In one of the downtown poolrooms he beat the boys at poker and took the local shark, a man called Snow Clark, for five hundred dollars at straight pool. Giving Clark an opportunity to get his money back, Ty offered him a double-or-nothing bet that he could jump across his five-by-ten-foot pool table without touching it. The bet was promptly taken. Taking a running start Ty dived headfirst across the table, landing safely on the other side. He retired to count his money. Across the room, one of the sweaters who had lost a bundle on side bets asked Snow Clark the stranger's name. "Don't rightly know," said Clark, "but it must be Titanic. He sinks everybody."

As Titanic Thomas then, he continued his ceaseless drift through the small towns of the South and the Midwest. Hubert Cokes, as a boy of thirteen, remembered seeing him in Hot Springs, playing poker in the Arlington Hotel. In Joplin he married a girl called Nora Trushel, who worked as a maid in one of the boardinghouses in which Ty lived. The marriage, however, did not survive his move to better lodgings and Nora, Ty claimed, went on to marry Pretty Boy Floyd. Ty himself drifted on, continuing his pursuit of what he sometimes called "the big bonanza." And he was resolute; he was reckless and lucky. By the time he was twenty-five he had acquired a large bankroll—and a reputation.

In the period between 1912 and the end of the First World War, Ty became famous in the netherworld of gamblers and confidence men for the success of his improbable propositions. Not that he sought notoriety in any way, since it was "hard to get somebody to take your proposition," he said, "if they knew your reputation." But by changing the common hustle into a pure and elegantly constructed con, Ty earned an envious respect among his fellow gamblers. Tales of his feats were recounted so often they acquired the legitimacy of legend.

During the 1920s in New York, Damon Runyon, who had met Ty on many occasions, must have heard those tales in one or another of their fanciful forms, since he based one of his most famous characters on him—Sky Masterson, the gambler in

"The Idyll of Miss Sarah Brown." "Of all the high players this country ever sees," wrote Runyon, "there is no doubt that the guy they call The Sky is the highest. He will bet all he has, and nobody can bet more than this. The Sky is a great hand for propositions, such as are always coming up among citizens who follow games of chance for a living. And no one ever sees The Sky when he does not have some proposition of his own."

A proposition, it should be explained, is a neat and often preposterous ploy used to lure the innocent into parting with their cash. Thus the example given Sky Masterson by his father, prior to leaving home, that he should not bet a man who offers to make the jack of spades jump from a brand-new deck of cards and squirt cider in his ear is a proposition. Does the jack of spades have hydraulic talents or not? Therein lies the wager. In "The Idyll of Miss Sarah Brown," Runyon related several of Ty's cannier propositions. The reality, however, had a seductive and more complicated charm.

In the summer of 1917, for example, Ty was sitting on the porch of the Arlington Hotel in Hot Springs, Arkansas, eating a bag of Danish walnuts. He still had that fresh, uplifted look that often passes for innocence. A local merchant walked onto the porch, said hello, and the two men fell into conversation. Ty continued to eat the walnuts, occasionally offering the merchant one. The merchant seemed to like the walnuts, since he asked for another and referred in passing to their light, piquant qualities. Ty offered him the bag and then, almost absentmindedly, he said, "I'll tell you what. I've got an interesting proposition for you, since I know how much you like them. What odds will you give that I can't throw one of these Danish walnuts over that hotel cross the street?"

The merchant smiled, looking across the street at the hotel. It was five stories high. "Ty," he said, "you're some thrower, I know that, but not even Ty Cobb could throw a nut over that hotel. Not on a good day with the wind behind him."

"Maybe not," said Ty, "but I'm willin' to bet I can. Shucks, I'm willin' to bet a hundred dollars if you could see your way to givin' me odds of, uh, say, three-to-one."

"One of *these* walnuts, Ty?" said the merchant pointing to the bag.

"Yep. You can pick any walnut in this here bag." Ty cracked another, eating it noisily.

The merchant agreed to the odds and selected a walnut from the bottom of the bag. Balancing the walnut in the palm of his hand, Ty stepped off the porch and into the street. Cocking his arm and throwing effortlessly, he lofted the walnut over the hotel. He turned round and grinned. The merchant scratched his head, began to remonstrate, then reluctantly reached for his wallet. And he never discovered, as many others were not to do, that Ty had palmed the walnut for one of his own special nuts, which he carried with him everywhere—a Danish walnut filled with lead.

Another of Ty's propositions, which Runyon reworked in "Sarah Brown," occurred in Toledo, Ohio, in a club owned by Johnny ("Get Rich Quick") Ryan. The club was in an old building in the center of the city. To reach the men's room, one descended a broken flight of stairs and crossed a darkened storeroom. One night, returning from the men's room to the poker game, Ty nearly stepped on a large rat scuttling between the packing cases and he instinctively knocked one of the heavy cases over, pinning the creature to the floor. Assuring himself the rat was secure, Ty hurried upstairs to the card room.

A few minutes later, in the middle of a hand, Ty turned to the player at his left, a mobster from Cicero, and said: "Say, why are there so many rats in this place? There are so many rats runnin' loose in that room down there, a man could shoot one of 'em between the eyes inside a minute."

The mobster continued to look at his hand. "I saw 'em, mister," he said. "But get this. It'd take a sharpshooter to hit a rat in a cage. To hit a runnin' rat in the eyes in the dark, guy'd need a machine gun, at least."

"Hell," said Ty, "I used to pop rats when I was a kid. Ain't nothin' in that."

The mobster looked up at Ty. He took the cigar from his mouth. Turning, he looked around the table. "Boys," he said, "gotta kid here thinks he's Buffalo Bill. Kid, I'll lay you five hundred says there's more to it than you think."

"You got five hundred," said Ty. He put down his cards and picked up his gun from the floor. "But I want odds. This ain't no ordinary proposition."

"I'll give you two-to-one. Can't give a great ratkiller like you more'n that."

The game stopped and Ty covered an additional five hundred in side bets. Checking his gun, he walked to the door.

"Hey, kid, wait a minute," said the mobster. "Don't get cute with me. That rat better be warm. I ain't bettin' money on a rat you knocked off day 'fore yesterday. And I'm timin' you. You got sixty seconds, kid."

Down in the storeroom the rat was still struggling to get out from under the packing case. Ty shot it in the head, upended the case, took the rodent by the tail, walked back upstairs, and dropped it on the poker table. The mobsters, Ty recalled, treated him with a certain reverence thereafter.

Another of Ty's stratagems occurred in Joplin before the war. Ty had become friendly with two gamblers called Hickory and Beanie. They were local boys and when they were not gambling they took Ty around Joplin or to their fishing camp outside of town. Driving into town one day, Ty noticed some workmen putting up a signpost which said, JOPLIN—20 MILES. That night he returned to the site, dug up the signpost and planted it five miles nearer to Joplin, checking carefully on the way home that it was exactly fifteen miles to the city limits.

Next day, as the three men were driving back from the fishing camp, they passed the sign and Ty suggested they stop so that he could take a leak. Before getting back into the car he seemed to notice the sign for the first time and shook his head. "Hey, look at that sign," he said. "Those boys just don't know what they're talkin' about. That there sign is an outright lie. Couldn't be more than fifteen miles to Joplin from here."

"Oh, they're pretty careful about that sort of thing," said Beanie. "Check it real good. You better believe it."

"It ain't right, Beanie," said Ty. "I'd bet on it."

"How much?" said Hickory, nudging Beanie.

"Why, hell, I'd bet a hundred. That sign just couldn't be right. Only took me twenty minutes to drive into Joplin from about here yesterday. I remember that. I'd bet a hundred it's no more'n fifteen miles from here to Joplin."

"Well, I'll bet you five hundred it's at least sixteen," said Hickory.

"And I'll take five hundred on that too," said Beanie.

"Well, okay, boys," said Ty, "but I'm tellin' you. That sign is wrong."

The three men drove back to town and, of course, it was exactly fifteen miles. "Christ," said Beanie. "I'm gonna raise hell with the road department. They don't have no right foolin' the public that way."

In 1917 Ty married again—a seventeen-year-old girl called Alice, whom he had picked up in a Pittsburgh movie house. Alice was pretty and had a certain crafty charm. Hubert Cokes, who admired her, remembered her to be "a good driver, loyal as could be and one of the best shoplifters in the country."

In April of 1918 Ty was unexpectedly drafted into the Army and spent seven months and twenty days at Camp Taylor in Anniston, Alabama. The time, however, was not entirely wasted. The war was remote, too remote to interfere with Ty's more immediate concerns. He passed the time playing craps and cards and making propositions. He remembered earning about fifty thousand dollars in the Army. He had worked hard and was disappointed that the Armistice was signed so soon.

Discharged from the Army, Ty returned to Missouri—to St. Louis and the tenderloin. He had money now and in keeping with his station he hired an erstwhile hoodlum as a chauffeur-bodyguard. In those days it was customary for protection men to take ten percent of their employers' winnings and Ty believed, when gambling in dangerous neighborhoods, they more than justified the additional expense.

In St. Louis, Ty had taken to gambling in the back room of a tailor shop owned by a shakedown man. An intimate of bootleggers and bondsmen, he was a morose and truculent man, who drank too much and liked to play in his own game. He was a consistent loser. In three months of shooting craps, Ty won forty thousand dollars from him. He paid, reluctantly, but when he lost two thousand more he drunkenly refused payment. Ty shrugged and gave him twenty-four hours to change his mind. The next night, bringing his gun and his bodyguard, Ty returned. Now sober and repentant, the tailor paid up and as a show, perhaps, of further faith offered to steer Ty into a high-stake, payday crap game; in return, they agreed that he would cash the paychecks himself for twenty percent of Ty's winnings. That Friday Ty was taken to a warehouse on the Mississippi. Playing craps with river toughs and dockers he won twelve thousand dollars. He turned the checks over to the tailor, who promised payment the following night. At the appointed time Ty and his bodyguard drove round to the tailor's shop.

As usual the back room was crowded with players, with bondsmen and bootleggers, one or two reformed heisters and a few of the owner's chorus girls. Drinks were poured and he gave Ty his money. As Ty said good night and turned to leave, he noticed one of the tailor's flunkies at the back door flicking the light switch on and off. The switch, Ty knew, operated a light just outside the tailor shop. Talking loudly, Ty approached the door; he turned the handle, beginning to open it, then said to one of the chorus girls: "Darlin', I'll tell you one last story for the road." Closing the door, he began some old and favorite tale. As the girl began to giggle, Ty pulled out his .45. Yanking open the door, he looked down the stairs. There, motionless and waiting, were two men with handkerchiefs covering their faces. Surprised, they hurriedly raised their guns, but it was too late. Ty shot them both. They catapulted backward down the steep, dark stairs. Pushing the flunky aside, Ty turned on the back light. The men, like lovers, lay one upon the other. They were both dead.

Ty turned back into the room. "I oughta kill you for that," he said. The tailor cringed against the wall, but Ty's bodyguard persuaded Ty to leave. The two men decided to go to the police station, where Ty described the incident. He was detained. Later that night he was awakened by one of the chief detectives. "You're a lucky man," he said. "I'm going to let you go. Those two guys you killed were wanted for murder, kidnapping, and armed robbery. We've been after them for five years."

Not long afterwards, a similar incident took place in St. Joseph, Missouri. Ty and his bodyguard were playing five-card stud in a room above a closed saloon. It was a regular game and carefully guarded, since it had been hijacked before. The men who operated the game had wired the outside stairs with a bell-alarm—a crude, but effective early warning system. Late one night the alarm sounded. Ty ducked quickly under the table, pulling out his gun. Two hijackers rushed into the room, shooting. One of their shots missed Ty by inches. He and his bodyguard shot the two men down. The police were not involved on this occasion. Checking their wallets, Ty found the names and addresses of the gunmen. Before leaving town he sent telegrams to their wives, telling them their men were dead and where their bodies were.

It is difficult to know just what these deaths would have meant to Ty, even had he stopped to think of them. Presumably he would have told the usual tale that a man must protect himself, that the country was crammed with head-hunters, that he was only guarding what was rightfully his own. He would have felt no sense of wrongdoing or remorse, no complicated guilts. He had a simple give–take relationship with the world. "If a man comes at me with a gun," he had said, "he had better expect something. He ain't gettin' something for nothing. He's a fool to think otherwise. I ain't gonna lie down for no man. Now how can you call that murder? Heisters are enemies. You can't murder enemies. It's impossible." The idea of murder appalled him. He liked to imply that he had killed no one, that his victims had merely committed suicide.

In 1921 Ty went to Chicago. "Everybody was talkin' about a guy called Nick the Greek," he said, "and I decided it was time we met." At that time Nick the Greek Dandolos was considered the highest gambler in America. No gambler since the days of Richard Canfield had achieved his reputation. Nick claimed to have won and lost some $500 million in his lifetime. He once dropped $797,000 to Arnold Rothstein in the biggest stud-poker pot ever recorded, Nick's kings losing to Rothstein's diamond flush. "The exhilaration of this form of economic existence is beyond my power to describe," he liked to say. He died broke in 1966.

In 1921, however, Nick approached the zenith of his fame. Although he claimed to have been broke some seventy-three separate times in his life, he never seemed to want for money. "He used to go broke two or three times a year," said Ty, "and the next time you'd see him, he'd have a couple of hundred thousand in his pocket. Nobody ever knew where he got his money from."

The two gamblers met in Chicago and left almost immediately for San Francisco. They had heard rumors of high-stake poker games at the Kingston Club. Ty and the Greek were to spend more than a year playing poker there. It was a running game and big—three-hundred-twenty-dollar-limit poker. The players included many of the city's politicians, lawyers, bankers, bootleggers and a couple of local gamblers called Joe Bernstein and Nigger Nate Raymond, both cardsharps of talent.

Nick had the stamina to play for days at a time without sleep, whereas Ty, as he had always done, played for fifteen or sixteen consecutive hours, then slept for twelve. They played as partners, or, as it was called, "did a little business together." They had practiced signals and by arranging their cards or nodding their heads in surreptitious ways they let one another know who had the best hand, when to raise or when to fold, and at the end of the day they split the take. Not that this chicanery was essential to their game: Ty was an excellent player and according to Hubert Cokes, "Anytime it got down to four or five in a poker hand, Nick was eight-to-five to win, he was that good." But it gave them the extra "advantage going in." With that advantage, at the end of eighteen months Ty had won two automobiles and just under a million dollars.

"Some folks," Ty recalled, "thought I bet too fast. They'd take me on because they reckoned I was bettin' without stoppin' to think. But I can't help thinkin' fast. These fellows who stroke their chins and say, 'Now, what was that proposition again?' are marks for me. I figured so far ahead of 'em that their money was gone before they knew they'd been bettin'.

"In poker," he said, "money is power. And I always made sure I had it. I not only played my own hand, I played everybody else's. I watched every card, every draw, every bet, every expression. I don't trust on luck. I am bettin' all around the table, on every card drawn by every player. I often have more on side bets than I have in the pot. I have to think fast and figure my percentages. I can't relax for a second. I treat everything like playin' roulette. And the only way to win at roulette is to own the wheel. I tell you, gambling is hard work."

During his San Francisco days Ty learned a new game—golf. He had just turned twenty-nine. Golf was to become his best game and his favorite, when he learned there were more ways to bet on golf than on cards or craps. It came naturally to him. The first time he ever hit a ball, he remembered, he drove it nearly three hundred yards. When the nightly poker sessions at the Kingston Club ended, Ty spent his mornings on a local course practicing golf. He told no one; he always practiced behind the bushes on the back nine, taking care to keep out of the sun. Since driving came easily to him, he concentrated on chipping and putting. In a matter of weeks he found he could almost always hole in two strokes and never in more than three from distances up to one hundred fifty yards. "It was the easiest thing you ever saw," he said. "I played golf almost as well as

I breathed." However, he had never actually played a round.

One of those who came to watch the late-night poker games at the Kingston Club was a local golf professional called Buddy Brent. One night he and Ty fell into conversation and Ty, who liked to brag that he would bet on anything, told Brent that he could probably beat him at golf. "I hear golf is a child's game," said Ty, "pick it up in a morning." Brent knew that Ty had never played the game, but condescended to compete with him for ten dollars a hole.

The following day Brent beat Ty on every hole and collected ninety dollars for the nine-hole wager. Driving back into San Francisco, Ty sulked. He complained that nothing had gone right for him, that his luck had been atrocious, that his clubs were borrowed, that his back ached from all-night poker games, and that had he been fit he would have given a better account of himself. Brent smiled and sympathized; he could see, he said, that Ty was a natural golfer, that all he required was a little practice, but for the moment he should concentrate on playing poker. He said that Ty was a terrific poker player.

That night at the Kingston Club a few of the poker players, having heard the story, heckled Ty unmercifully. Ty glowered, insisting Brent had merely been lucky. Later that evening, when Brent dropped into the club, Ty challenged him to a match the next day; he would play, he said, for one thousand dollars a hole, but he had to have three shots a hole. Everyone laughed. The incredulous Brent agreed to the wager, but would only concede one shot a hole. Ty insisted the cash be put up front. As always happened, a group of enthusiastic gamblers wanted as much side action as possible and when the betting was concluded nearly sixty thousand dollars lay on the table. Ty covered the bets and went back to playing poker.

The next morning a little crowd of joyful gamblers gathered around the first tee. When Ty arrived there was much sympathetic applause. Ty, driving first, hit his ball about 275 yards down the middle of the fairway. Brent blanched. The gamblers looked uneasily at one another. Ty never remembered what he shot that day, only that it was a stroke or two better than Brent. He won $56,000. "I never, ever shot more than a stroke or two better'n the opposition," he said. "If a man shoots eighty-nine, I shoot eighty-eight. If a man shoots sixty-eight, I shoot sixty-seven. I never liked to add insult to injury."

It is inaccurate, of course, to give the impression that hustlers, even the best of them, never lose a bet. Ty himself lost dozens of wagers, but like most gamblers became wonderfully absentminded when one referred to them. One bet, however, which rankled him for years was made in San Francisco in 1922. He was playing golf with Nick the Greek and coming down to the last hole had beaten him for twenty thousand dollars. On the last green Nick was lying some twenty feet from the hole. Ty offered to bet him double-or-nothing on the twenty thousand if he could sink the putt and Nick agreed. "It was four-to-one Nick couldn't make that putt," Ty recalled. "Hell, it was two-to-one against *me* making it and I was a great putter. Nick had five hundred grand in his pocket that day and I could have got it all if he'd missed. But the son of a bitch put it in."

Toward the end of 1922 Ty and Nick the Greek set out for New York City. Nick wanted to gamble with Arnold Rothstein in one of that gambler's famous "floating crap games" and Ty assured the boys in the Kingston Club that he would take the Eastern tracks for millions. But Ty had never had much luck with the horses; he claimed to have lost over two million dollars at the track over the years. Even Nick, who gambled at anything, warned Ty that "only madmen and drunks bet seriously on the horses." Referring to the intensity with which such gamblers threw away their money, Nick claimed that "a woman could walk naked at Aqueduct ten minutes before post time and she'd be safer than riding in a Brink's truck with two eunuchs." But Ty was not so easily deterred.

Ty lost most of his Western winnings at the Eastern tracks. But he was never broke for long, nor long disheartened, and during the next few years, whenever he won at golf or cards or craps, he continued to hustle the horses. In 1925 at a racetrack in Tijuana he knew he was finally onto a sure thing.

On this occasion, Ty reckoned, nothing would be left to chance. He had carefully checked the morning line; he had watched the early morning practice runs; he had held lengthy discussions with the local trainers and been chummy with the jockeys. Toward race time Ty concluded that a horse in the sixth race called Nellie A could not possibly fail to win. Even so he took additional precautions. He paid off most of the jockeys and, taking the favorite aside, informed him that should he decide to put his horse's nose so much as an inch in front, a sharpshooter, employing a telescopic sight, was installed in the stands and would not fail to do his duty.

"That morning," Ty recalled, "I put calls through all over the country. I bet a thousand here, a thousand there, on all the other horses in the race to get their prices down. Now, Nellie A was going off at five-to-one, but when I'd finished with them other nags, she'd dropped to twelve-to-one. In bits and pieces, here and there, I laid a hundred and twenty grand on her sweet head. It was a cinch. I had the nuts.

"That old horse started out just fine, held the lead, increased it, and when she hit the stretch she was a hundred yards ahead of the field. Things were going real good. I was excited, and almost nothing excites me. I yelled and slapped my sister on the back. I started to walk up to the window to get my winnings, when I heard this awful moan come outta the crowd. I turned around and that goddamned horse, less'n thirty yards from the wire, had fallen down. Collapsed and broke her leg. They had to shoot the bastard later. I was plain disgusted. Nobody in the whole history of gambling ever lost a bet like that."

During the mid-Twenties Ty lived mainly in California in a large home in Beverly Hills. Hubert Cokes was also in California at the time and the two friends saw a lot of one another. "We gambled night and day," said Cokes. "Gambled high at pool and golf and cards. Ty was a better golfer than me, but at pool he had no more chance than a Chow. Ty went to bed every night trying to figure out ways to fuck me and I did the same thing to him. Ty was extraordinary. He had a remarkable memory. You could give him a proposition he hadn't heard of in twenty years and he could give you the right odds on it. And great eyesight. He could see around corners."

On one occasion the two men were driving outside of Los Angeles when the car hit a rock on the side of the road. Hubert stopped the car and got out to see what had happened.

"My God," he said, "where did this enormous rock come from?"

"Don't rightly know," said Ty.

"Well, as long as we're here, I'll bet you five hundred I can guess the weight of this rock within two pounds."

Ty got out of the car to look at the rock. "Why hell, Hubert," he said, "that rock's not from this part of the country. Where'd you find it? That's a different class of rock altogether."

Hubert smiled. "You smart son of a bitch," he said. "They broke the mold when they made you."

The two men played a great deal of golf. "I was a low eighties shooter," said Hubert, "and Ty normally shot around seventy, when nobody was looking. I remember once at the El Rancho Country Club we were practicing, when up comes George Von Elm, who had just beaten Bobby Jones at the National Amateurs. 'Ty,' he said, 'why don't you throw away them clubs and let me get you some decent ones?' He didn't like Ty too much. He had just come home and the members had chipped in to buy him an automobile. Ty and I had chipped in more than anyone else. Well, a bet started up. Von Elm said he'd give Ty nine strokes in eighteen holes and would bet anything. He had a big head. He'd just beaten Bobby Jones. Now, I had a lot of money then and I told Ty to just go in and get as much money as he could find and I'd cover it. I've forgotten how much money was on that match, but it was a lot.

"Well, the short of it was that when they got to the ninth green they were dead even. Ty was about three feet away from the hole and Von Elm was about thirty. The only way he could win was to win that hole and all the last nine. He just threw down his club and walked off to the clubhouse. He got Ty barred from the club for cheating, called him a golf shark. Hell, Ty could have beat him even. Couldn't anybody give Ty much, but if he matched up and got the money down it was three-to-one Ty was going to win."

In the early summer of 1928 the two friends traveled to New York. In those high years just before the Crash, New York was a gambler's paradise. The center of the action was on or around Broadway. Most of the city's popular pool halls and poker rooms were here. Along that brief strip of the boulevard near Broadway and Fiftieth Street, which Runyon called Jacob's Beach, were to be found the more glamorous members of the fight mob, hustlers, gamblers and grifters, the racetrack touts, bookies, mobsters, their bodyguards, and journalists such as Walter Winchell and Runyon himself. Nightly this colorful crowd would gather outside Lindy's. It was here the "floating crap games" originated, since outside Lindy's there was always a steerer who knew every player in town and passed the venue of that night's action on to them.

The high rollers might also be found at any of the fashionable gin mills in the area—the 50 Club, the Parody Club, the Yacht Club, the Club Madrid, the Silver Slipper, the Rendezvous or the El Fay, run by the infamous Texas Guinan, who greeted her customers with the words, "Hello, suckers." When the Square Club, the most popular card room on Broadway, closed for the night, the players drifted down to the Democratic Club in St. Mark's Place to a game run by "The Count," to a West Side warehouse for craps, or up to the Cotton Club in Harlem for music and pool. There was, Ty recalled, a whole gang of action.

On the night of September 8, 1928, George McManus, a New York bookmaker, arranged a high-stake poker game in the apartment of Jimmy Meehan in the Congress Apartment Building on the corner of Fifty-fourth Street and Seventh Avenue. Meehan, a florid-faced gambler and ex-convict, was an old friend of Arnold Rothstein—the game's main draw. The other players were Ty, McManus himself, some local high rollers called Sol Fusik, Oscar Donnelly and Abe Silverman, and two of Ty's old San Francisco cronies—Joe Bernstein and Nigger Nate Raymond, who, though he was on his honeymoon, had left his bride in California.

Arnold Rothstein was the most notorious gambler among them and the wealthiest. He had won $500,000 on the first Dempsey-Tunney fight and in 1921 had won $800,000 on a colt called Sidereal at Aqueduct. His high-stake crap games with Nick the Greek were legendary. He was the man who had fixed the 1919 World Series and was known in the underworld as "The Big Bankroll" or "The Man Uptown." Damon Runyon called him "The Brain" and Scott Fitzgerald based Wolfsheim, his gambler in *The Great Gatsby,* on Rothstein. The police referred to him as "The J. P. Morgan of the Underworld," since his business interests included protection rackets, gambling, nightclubs, bootlegging, and the running of drugs. At one time or another in his career, he employed such men as Legs Diamond and his brother Eddie, Dutch Schultz, Waxey Gordon and Lucky Luciano. He bankrolled or had business associations with Nicky Arnstein, Dapper Dan Collins, Dandy Phil Kastel, Ownie Madden, Frank Costello and Albert Anastasia.

Before the game of five-card stud began that night Rothstein took Ty aside and suggested they play partners and Ty agreed. But later in the evening when Nigger Nate Raymond entered the game, Ty decided to end the partnership in order to work with Nate. "We knew each other real well," Ty recalled. "I mean we knew all the angles, how to fix the cards and how to build 'em so they would come out like you wanted 'em to. Nate was one of the really great fixers and connivers and I thought we might do a little business together that night."

The game, beginning with antes of hundreds, soon rose to thousands. Rothstein then suggested that they play high card, that is, betting to see who obtained the highest spade on the first card of the stud hand. Ty let the other players know that he would take half their action if they would bet with Nate. The signals flashed around the table. The high-spade betting began

at five hundred dollars a card, but rose rapidly to five and ten
thousand a card. Not surprisingly, Rothstein began to lose; and
the more he lost the higher he bet. There was never any of
Rothstein's cash on the table, since, whenever he lost, he threw
markers in the pot. On the last hand of the evening, Rothstein
offered to cut the deck for high card with Nate for forty thousand dollars. They cut, and Rothstein lost again. "Don't appear
to be your night, Mr. Rothstein," said Nate. Rothstein stood
up from the table; reaching into the pot, he tallied his markers
and tore them up, promising to pay them in a day or two.

The game had lasted for thirty hours. When it ended on
the morning of September 10, Rothstein owed Nigger Nate
$319,000, Joe Bernstein $69,000, Sol Fusik $29,000, Oscar
Donnelly $20,000, Abe Silverman $8,000, and Ty $30,000—or
a total of $475,000. Only George McManus had lost to Roth-
stein and paid his debt, $51,000, in cash that night.

"Christ," said Nate, when Rothstein left the room, "not even
a scratch. All we got is his word."

"Is this the way he always does business?" said Ty.

"That's A.R.," said McManus. "Hell, he's good for it. He'll
call you in a couple of days, don't worry."

But weeks passed and Rothstein remained elusive and silent.
Round Broadway rumor had it that Rothstein claimed the
game had been rigged and refused to pay. He told Nicky Arnstein the game was rigged and Arnstein had laughed and said,
"Rigged or not, you have to pay off. No point advertising you
were a sucker." Rothstein told Damon Runyon, however, that
he never welched, that he was "just making them sweat a little."
He stalled them with tales that he had "over-invested." He had
bet heavily on the New York gubernatorial and Presidential
elections that year, backing Franklin Roosevelt and Herbert
Hoover. His creditors, however, were apprehensive. One night
outside of Lindy's, Abe Silverman screamed at Rothstein for his
money and was told to come to his office the morning after the
election, November 7. Nigger Nate, eager to return to California and his bride, encountered Rothstein on Broadway and

was ignored. Ty never saw him. And no one was paid.

Shortly after ten o'clock on the evening of November 4, Rothstein walked into Lindy's, as he habitually did, and sat down at his table. Although Lindy himself disliked it, Rothstein used the restaurant as a kind of second office. He was given his telephone messages by the night cashier, nodded to acquaintances and talked briefly to those who approached his table. About 10:30, he received a telephone call; he listened for a moment, hung up, and told Jimmy Meehan to follow him outside. Rothstein told Meehan that George McManus had asked him to come to the Park Central Hotel. As the operator of the game, McManus felt responsible for any debts incurred and presumably for this reason had asked Rothstein to meet him. Giving Meehan his gun, Rothstein sauntered up Broadway.

When Arnold Rothstein was seen again, it was just after eleven o'clock; he was discovered by a young elevator operator staggering through the service area of the hotel with a bullet in his groin. Taken immediately to a hospital, he refused to name his assailant, though still conscious. Two days later on November 6, election day, he died. He was forty-six years old. Had Rothstein lived, he would have won just over half a million dollars on the election.

It was later proved that the telephone call had come from Room 349 in the Park Central Hotel; the hotel register showed the room had been booked in the name of one George Richards. When police arrived, the Chesterfield overcoat of George McManus was found in the room. Though McManus disappeared—hiding in a Bronx apartment rented by Dutch Schultz—he gave himself up three weeks later and was indicted for murder. Ty and Nigger Nate were also arrested as material witnesses. Ty was dumbfounded. "Why should I have killed him?" he said. "You can't collect from a corpse." But he and Nate had ironclad alibis for the night in question and ten days later they were each released on ten thousand dollars bail.

It was not until November of 1929, a year after the Rothstein killing, that McManus was brought to trial. During that time

Ty had gambled desultorily in the Midwest and when the trial took place he was running a gambling joint in Milwaukee. During the trial, in which Ty appeared as a witness, the New York press continually misprinted his name as Thompson, an error he made no effort to correct. But it was the first time a photograph of him had ever been published; it was not to his liking. In court, Ty admitted that he was a gambler who gambled high at everything. He told the judge that the high-card game had been entirely on the level and that, in his opinion, George McManus was "a square and honest guy." The judge seemed satisfied.

The prosecution's case was pathetically weak. There was little evidence, no eyewitnesses, and the defense asked for a directed verdict of acquittal, which was granted by the judge. There were too many people, it seemed, both in politics and the police department, who would not have benefited from an investigation into Rothstein's murder. Wearing the Chesterfield which had so recently been the prosecution's main exhibit, McManus left court a free man. Today the case is still marked "open" in the records of the New York City Police Department. George McManus died a natural death in 1940.

Most of the players in that high-spade game knew who had killed Arnold Rothstein. For months afterwards it was the main gossip along Broadway. Ty knew; Nigger Nate Raymond knew; and so did Joe Bernstein. Today, Bernstein, who in his younger, more flamboyant days was known as "The Silver Fox," is seventy-four and lives in a small apartment in Las Vegas. Deeply tanned, with slick white hair, he dresses as he always did, in the manner of a Palm Beach dandy.

"The night of the game," said Bernstein, "McManus was the house. He was responsible for collecting the debts of the losers. But when Rothstein hadn't paid he became worried and he drank. He drank a lot. He telephoned Lindy's that night, hoping he could talk A.R. into paying off. It was his last chance. The boys were getting plenty nervous. When A.R. arrived George was drunk and he had a gun, which I guess he hoped would frighten Rothstein into paying at least some of the money. He pointed it at A.R. who was sitting down. A.R. pushed the gun away, and accidentally it went off. George just panicked and, throwing the gun out the window, he ran from the room. It was an accident. George did a lot of people a real big favor, though. But it screwed me out of seventy grand."

When the trial ended Ty left New York, never to return. For the next few years he drifted around the Southwest. The trial had done him little good. "It got so everybody was afraid to bet with me," he said. "It used to be I could go around and make bets and nobody knew who I was. But after my picture and stories about what a smart gambler I was were in all the papers I couldn't make any money. Why, I was out in Tulsa after that, playing golf, and such a big gallery got to following me around because of the stories in the papers that I couldn't play. Another time a man came up to me and said he wanted to bet with me just so he could say he had bet with Titanic Thompson. So I fixed up a little proposition just to oblige him, but he quit after losin' a couple of thousand."

Whenever he had an audience Ty tended to speak in mournful tones and liked to pretend that he inhabited blind alleys. But in 1930 he was still only thirty-seven years old and had more than a few propositions left to perform. The Depression years were to coincide with some of his most extravagant hustles and the period of his greatest fame. "After all that publicity I couldn't make any money," he would say when anyone was listening; and when they weren't: "A good gambler can get money out of a lamp post."

During the Thirties Ty defeated the world champion horseshoe thrower by luring him into what he assumed was a regulation length court, not knowing that Ty had extended it by a foot. The champion could not understand why his throws kept falling short. Ty beat Nick the Greek in a shooting contest —the bet being that Ty could not hit a stationary silver dollar eight out of ten times at ten feet. Nick, of course, did not know that Ty could hit a dime ten out of ten times at greater distances. Ty beat countless innocents at countless propositions. But throughout the Thirties his favorite hustling game was golf.

Ty spent thirty years barely breaking 100 in public and he always ignored the official handicaps. Johnny Moss remembered seeing him take a thousand dollars from Byron Nelson over nine holes by shooting a 29. Ty often played with the young Ben Hogan. "I had to teach the kid how to play," said Ty. "We played a lot together and I took him to Shreveport to play some matches." In a Fort Worth newspaper, Lee Trevino acknowledged his debt to Ty's teaching skills.

In the Thirties there was little point in turning professional as there was no money in the game. And hustling, of course, was forbidden. In those days Ty contrived dozens of ingenious hustles. He would bet standers-by that a man in a wheelchair could beat them—previously having trained the man to play brilliantly from the chair. He challenged a Texas pro, who demanded a handicap. "All right," said Ty, "I'll let you hit three drives off each tee and you can play the best drive. Is that enough of a handicap?" The pro assented, for stakes of one thousand a hole. Playing the best of three drives, the pro won the first seven holes, but on the eighth tee, he sliced all three drives into the rough; on the ninth, obviously fatigued, he missed one ball altogether. Ty swept the last eleven holes and won four thousand dollars. "Course, he was tired," said Ty. "Hit three drives a hole and on a tough course you'll be lucky to break a hundred."

On another occasion, in the dead of winter, he was bragging in the clubhouse about how far he could drive the ball. The other golfers were becoming exasperated. "On some days I'm so good," said Ty, "that I can drive a ball four hundred yards." Anxious to teach the braggart a lesson one of the golfers took the bet. Selecting a tee on the downward side of a hill overlooking a lake, which given the season was frozen, Ty drove his ball. It was still rolling as he pocketed his winnings.

But Ty's most devious hustle, which he employed again and again throughout his career, first occurred in the little town of

Ruidoso, New Mexico. Ty had arranged a match with the town millionaire. The millionaire, who believed himself to be the best golfer in the state, was left-handed and liked to gamble high. After protracted negotiations, Ty agreed to give him three strokes a side for a twenty-five-thousand-dollar wager. A little crowd of enthusiasts, including Johnny Moss, followed them around the course.

"Ty," Moss remembered, "always cut these things pretty close, but he hadn't meant to cut it as fine as this." Approaching the eighteenth green the two men were even. The millionaire two-putted; but he was not particularly worried since Ty had hit a poor iron shot to the far side of the green, leaving himself a difficult, downhill twenty-foot putt to win the match. Ty lined it up carefully, stroked the ball and it curved round the downward slope of the green and dropped into the hole. Ty looked up, his face expressionless. The millionaire was livid.

"Goddamn, boy, that's the luckiest shot I ever saw. You're lucky, goddamned lucky. I got a good mind not to pay just because of some freak shot. That ball must have had a magnet in it. Goddamn."

Ty looked blankly at the man. "You're lucky to have lost by one shot," he said. "I shoulda beat you by three or four. You're the worst golfer I've ever seen in my life. I know children that can beat you. Why, you're so bad I could beat your ass with your own clubs, those left-handed doodads you carry around with you. I could beat you using them."

The millionaire looked suddenly calm. "For double-or-nothing?" he said.

"Sure," said Ty, "double-or-nothing." He turned away.

"Okay, you're on," said the millionaire.

Ty looked surprised. He shrugged his shoulders. "A bet's a bet," he said.

The millionaire laughed. They walked to the first tee. Three hours later, Ty had beaten him by four strokes. He pocketed the millionaire's check and walked back to the clubhouse. The millionaire was in anguish. "I don't understand it," he mumbled, "I just don't understand it."

"You would, sir," said one of the attendant caddies, "if you knew Titanic was a natural-born left-hander."

In 1938 Ty turned up in Evansville, Indiana, where his old friend Hubert Cokes had settled. Outside of town the oil boom had just erupted and word was out that the boys were playing higher in Evansville than anywhere else in the country. Ty remained there during the early war years, living with Joanne, his fourth wife.

"He didn't have a whole lot of cash when he first came," Cokes remembered. "He put up at the McCurdy Hotel. There were more oil wells drilled in the lobby of the McCurdy Hotel than in the oilfields outside of town. I remember once, after Ty came, I heard about a big card game down in Charlotte and I staked Ty to twenty-five hundred and told him to go down and check the game out. And if there was no action to come back and tell me. The money was also supposed to cover his expenses. Ty came back after about a week and gave me a thousand. I said to him, 'Christ, Ty, what did you spend the money on? I could've taken three girls and spent a week at the Waldorf-Astoria and not spent that much.' Little did I know, that's just what he'd done. He was the limit, Ty. It wouldn't make no difference if Ty was married to the Queen of England, he'd still have two or three tramps around.

"Ty said there hadn't been no action, so the next week I send him down again. He comes back and says he won about fifty thousand. I ask him how much he thinks he owes me and he says about twenty grand. Well, I then sent one of my boys down to Charlotte to check out that game, run by a fellow called Slim. He hangs around down there and finds out they won ninety thousand and are owed twenty-six thousand more. When it came to cuttin' up money Ty always took care of Ty. He was stopping at the McCurdy Hotel and that night I went up to his room. He was in bed and I stormed into his room and said, 'Ty, do you have a pistol? Because if you don't, I have two and you can use one of mine.' He said, all nice and meek, 'Hubert, would you kill your best friend while he's lyin' asleep in his bed?' He was always wily, Ty, but I confronted him and he finally paid me my money."

Ty spent much of his time in Evansville buying and selling oil leases, trading and promoting. "I made seven hundred and forty thousand dollars out of oil wells on five acres out in Salem," he said. But he still found time to gamble at cards and at pool. Minnesota Fats was in Evansville at the time and he and Ty and Hubert played a lot of cards. "Fats was only good at knock rummy," said Ty. "He was a terrible clabbiasch player. He'd play clabb, win two games and quit."

The Fat Man, however, did beat Ty at pool. "He killed me at pool," Ty remembered. "At Adolf's Bowling Alley and Pool Hall. I'd been pitchin' to the crack for fifty dollars a throw the night before the match and my arm just went dead when I came to play, but I didn't know it till too late. He beat me outta thirty thousand before I knew what was wrong. But, of course, the Fat Man says it was seventy-five thousand and claims he was playin' one-handed. That Fat Man. He was always windy."

In his autobiography the Fat Man describes one of Ty's favorite cons. "Ty was driving in from the oilfields outside of Evansville when he sees this farmer hauling a whole truckload of watermelons to market. So Ty stops the farmer and right away he buys the whole batch of watermelons for a very inflated sum. Then he pays the farmer to count each watermelon and pays him another tremendous price to drive past the old McCurdy Hotel in downtown Evansville at an appointed hour.

"Now Ty hustles to the McCurdy, and all the high rollers are standing in the lobby and out on the sidewalk in front, and after a while here comes the farmer driving out First Street with the load of watermelons. So Ty gets the show on the road by allowing he will wager any amount that he can estimate exactly how many watermelons the farmer has on the truck. It looked like such a Hungarian lock that the high rollers all got down real heavy, and when they stopped the farmer to inquire about his inventory, Titanic just happened to have hit the precise number. He won a fabulous bundle on the watermelon con, but I obligingly relieved him of most of it on pool."

Toward the end of the war Ty moved to Virginia, where, again according to Fats, he was one of the leading luminaries around Norfolk in the middle Forties. "He had hit the gold roll in oil out around southern Indiana and when he came to Norfolk, he moved in like a real Sultan. He was on a brand-new wife, a gorgeous doll named Maxine. But he also brought along Maxine's sisters, Betty and Bonnie, who were even more fabulous-looking than Maxine.

"Ty was always very particular about his wives. He insisted on being surrounded by raving young beauties at all times and when his wives got a little old, like maybe twenty-six or twenty-eight, he divorced 'em real quick. That's on the square.

"When Ty first came to Norfolk he couldn't find suitable housing for his ladies so he moved out to Virginia Beach and took over one of those mansions the generals built right out on the ocean front. It was a fabulous joint and Ty entertained the way Perle Mesta wished she could. All the high rollers would call a recess on the weekends and drive to Virginia Beach just to be on hand for Ty's soirees.

"Even though Ty was already in his fifties, he never looked a day over twenty-five, and when he entertained he loved to have young people around him, especially young tomatoes. He had a real tall, trim build and a full head of brown hair and dark, deep-set eyes that were always dancing.

"But the most fantastic thing about Titanic was his hands. He had the hands of an artist, which is as good a word to describe Ty as you can find. He could do almost anything with his hands, everything except play pool. . . . He could do all sorts of amazing card tricks and sleight-of-hand gimmicks on account of his fingers were long and agile. Just watching him perform was fascinating. The way he moved his eyes and his fingers at one and the same time was liable to hypnotize you on the spot. He was a regular Houdini."

And like Houdini, Ty seemed locked in a box from which, for once, he could not escape. His postwar activities became secretive and more and more obscure. Sometime in 1946 or 1947 he left Norfolk for Tucson, Arizona, where he remained until 1955. He seems not to have gambled a great deal. His only public activities were winning three consecutive Arizona State trapshooting contests and a party he gave in early 1954.

The party was held in his large home on the outskirts of Tucson. That night Ty may or may not have noticed a teenage girl roaming drunkenly from room to room. If so, he thought nothing of it. He had many other guests to attend; he was good at giving parties. The next day Ty was arrested by the local constabulary. The girl claimed that she had been assaulted by one of Titanic's guests. Ty was charged with contributing to the delinquency of a minor. In efforts to circumvent any possible sentence Ty contributed $35,000 to various police charities, but during the trial, when his background was recounted to the suburban jury, he was pronounced guilty and sentenced to two years in the state penitentiary at Florence. Eight months later he was paroled. He was sixty-two years old.

Ty drifted round the Southwest—from Arizona to California and New Mexico and thence to smaller and smaller towns in Texas—Dallas, San Antonio, Corpus Christi, Colleyville, and finally to Hurst, an obscure suburb midway between Dallas and Fort Worth. For nearly twenty years there was only silence. In the summer of 1972, when I set out to find Titanic, I was told by an elderly gambler in Las Vegas, a man who concerned himself with such things: "Him? Old Ty? Why, hell, son, Ty's dead. Ain't no tellin' how long he's been gone. A long time. Years and years."

## III

The little town of Hurst, divided by the main Dallas-Fort Worth highway, has all the stiff and stilted charm of a suburban shopping center. One of those instant modern towns, it might have been built yesterday and could well be gone tomorrow. It contains the usual array of supermarkets and gas stations, bars and bowling alleys, parking lots and five-and-ten-cent stores. Out beyond the drab main plazas are the curled rows of suburban dwellings, as neat and normalized as soldiers on parade. It was to this remote and inconspicuous place that Titanic Thompson had come to die.

Ty had come to Hurst the year before from another suburb twenty miles away. Here he lived in a rented house with his sixth wife, Jeanette, their thirteen-year-old son and his in-laws. He did not foresee further moves. Hurst was as good a place as any to while away what little time remained.

In the kitchen at the rear of the house, Titanic sat at the breakfast table playing blackjack with his son. He wore pajamas and a robe. His white hair fell in disarray about his head; it had not been cut for months, apparently, and lay thick at the back of his neck. He was unshaven. He was tall, though bent, and hard of hearing. He was plagued with arthritis in his left hand. His new set of teeth did not quite fit, causing crankiness and complaint. His eyes were dulled with resignation. He looked like a patient in a nursing home waiting for visitors who would never come. He would soon be eighty.

Ty rarely left the house anymore. He missed the action, but was not prepared to make the journey. Until the year before he played golf every day, pitching and putting on the local course, but arthritis had intervened. Jeanette tried to take him to the bowling alley each afternoon when she came home from work. Occasionally, when the weather was good, he pitched horseshoes in the backyard. He led an uneventful life. He had arrived, as Casanova said, at that age which chance despises. His wife went out to work, the little house was rented, the car was on the never-never. He had no possessions, no bank account, no insurance, none of the humdrum securities. All he had ever owned was his bankroll and now, old and out of favor, even that had gone. The game was over and only now and then did Ty pretend that he would play again.

During the long afternoons, waiting apprehensively for Jeanette to return, Ty talked of his life and showed me tricks and propositions. "One proposition's as good as another," he said in his clipped Southern monotone. "Depends on your advantage. I'd just as soon deal blackjack as play it." Ty always talked as though talent were an ability to get away with things. He showed me endless coin and match conundrums, betting small sums that I could not unravel them. And it was not the money (which I invariably lost) that excited him. It was the slow flush of amazement, the startled cry of comprehension, that brought a light to those sad eyes. Once cash had been enough; he now required applause.

Ty talked eventually of promises of money, of fame, of films of his life story. He had been, he said, the most colorful gambler of his time. He could do more things than any man he had known. Nick the Greek? Hah! Could only play cards and shoot craps. Nothin'. "The smartest gambler I ever knew was old Hubert Cokes. The best cheater and conniver was Bill Douglas till he was shot down in a poker game in Memphis two year ago. And Little Man from Alabama was the highest gambler I ever saw. Real high. Would bet everything on anything, that Little Man. But I could outsmart, outcheat, outconnive, and roll higher than 'em all in my day. And that's no lie."

He clicked his teeth. Looking out into the backyard he fell silent, conjuring up the old high-rolling days again. Gambling was all he had ever known; it had been everything. Because he did not read, because he had not taken part in any of the events of his time—elections, wars, depressions—he seemed curiously remote, not merely outdated, but outcast, detached from life. He had spent a lifetime casting lots in back rooms and the world, for what it was worth, had passed him by.

"My teeth. They still don't set right," he said to no one in particular. Jeanette said she would take him to the dentist after work the next day. He seemed not to hear, that odd vacant look coming into his eyes again. Standing up from the table and drawing his robe around him, he shuffled out of the room to bed.

The next day Titanic came into the kitchen just before noon. He had tried to shave the stubble from his face but most of it remained. He wore his best trousers, a plaid shirt, and a baggy jacket. He looked frail and vulnerable. Putting a little water in his hand from the kitchen tap, he smoothed down his rumpled hair. He took me into the backyard, betting he could ring seven out of ten horseshoes. His son's bicycle lay across the pitch. I moved it. Picking up the rusted horseshoes he pitched them easily, but without enthusiasm. Only two of them curled round the stake. He could not seem to get his eye in, he said. It began to rain. We went inside.

In the kitchen Ty said that he would wager anything he could hit a target eight out of ten times with his .45. At twenty feet. With either hand. "I'll get my gun," he said. He shuffled from the room. Almost immediately he returned. "Can't find my gun," he said, scratching his head. "They're always movin' my things around." Just out of his sight in the next room, Jeanette's mother, the gun in her hand, shook her head at me and put a finger to her lips. Titanic sat down on the worn sofa and ground his teeth.

Outside the rain continued to fall, a thin enveloping rain, wrapping itself round the trees in the backyard, the bicycle, the rusty horseshoes, wrapping itself round the house like a winding sheet. A little later when Jeannette came home, she straightened Ty's collar and reminded him to bring his glasses. Looking into the distance Ty ground his teeth. He placed a cheap fedora on his head. Taking his hand Jeanette led him out of the house to the waiting car.

# HIGH STAKES PUBLISHING
# NEW TITLES & STOCK LIST

| Title | Author | Pub Date | Price |
| --- | --- | --- | --- |
| Forecasting Methods for Horseracing | Peter May | Available | £14.99 |
| The Education of a Poker Player | Herbert O Yardley | Available | £9.99 |
| Greyhound Racing to Win | Victor Knight | Available | £9.99 |
| Total Poker | David Spanier | Available | £9.99 |
| Win at Greyhound Racing | H Edwards Clarke | Available | £9.99 |
| The Science of Winning | Burton P Fabricand | Available | £14.99 |
| Profitable Football Betting | P N Steele | Available | £29.95 |
| Placepot Annual: National Hunt 2002 | Malcolm Boyle | Available | £9.99 |
| The Science of Poker | Mahmood N Mahmood | May '03 | £14.95 |
| Phantoms of the Card Table | David Britland | Available | £25.00 |
| Sports Spread Betting | Dan Townend | June '03 | £12.99 |
| Betting to Win | Prof L V Williams | Available | £25.00 |

High Stakes Publishing, 21 Great Ormond St, London,
WC1N 3JB, ENGLAND
T: 020 7430 1021 F: 020 7430 0021 orders@highstakes.co.uk

Please add 10% P&P for UK orders, 15% elsewhere.

We accept cheques in £Sterling, drawn on UK bank and payable to **High Stakes**. Switch, Delta, Mastercard and Visa. Please enclose expiry date with Mastercard and Visa and issue number with Switch/Delta cards plus card number and full name on card.

For a full range of books on all aspects of gambling go to:

www.highstakes.co.uk

...or contact High Stakes Bookshop at the above address for a FREE catalogue.